Pastora
An Independent-Study Textbook
by Richard Exley

Third Edition

**Berean School of the Bible,
a Global University School**

1211 South Glenstone Avenue
Springfield, MO 65804 USA

1-800-443-1083
Fax: (417) 862-0863
E-mail: berean@globaluniversity.edu
Web: www.globaluniversity.edu

GLOBAL
UNIVERSITY

Richard Exley's rich variety of ministry spans about forty years. He completed the course of study prescribed by the South Texas District Council of the Assemblies of God and studied at Gulf Coast Bible College in Houston, Texas. Richard and his wife, Brenda, served as evangelists for almost a year and a half before accepting their first pastorate in Holly, Colorado, in 1967. The Exleys also served congregations in Florence, Colorado; Houston, Texas; and Craig, Colorado. Following this ministry, they served for twelve years in the senior pastorate of Christian Chapel in Tulsa, Oklahoma. During Richard's tenure as pastor, Christian Chapel established The Lay Ministers Training Institute for equipping the laity, the Straight from the Heart Counseling Center, and a Crisis Pregnancy Outreach ministry. Pastor Exley also founded and hosted a live, nationwide call-in radio program called *Straight from the Heart* as well as a daily teaching broadcast called *God's Word for You.*

Since 1992, Richard Exley has served as a "pastor at large," devoting his time to writing and speaking. He often ministers at retreats and conferences for ministers and missionaries, both in the U.S. and abroad. With his wife, he has developed three marriage seminars: *Forever in Love, Predictable Crises in Marriage,* and *Blended Families: Making the Most of Remarriage.*

His writing ministry includes hundreds of articles in numerous magazines such as *Leadership Journal, Charisma, Ministries Today, Today's Pentecostal Evangel, Advance, Enrichment,* and *New Man.* He has authored thirty books. Among his best-known books are *Witness the Passion, Strength for the Storm, Deliver Me, The Making of a Man, Perils of Power, When You Lose Someone You Love, The Rhythm of Life, Man of Valor, and Encounters with Christ.* His first novel, *The Alabaster Cross,* was released in 2006.

In 2003, he was awarded the Doctor of Divinity *honoris causae* by the Joint Academic Commission of the Methodist Episcopal Church USA and the National Clergy Council Board of Scholars. The degree was awarded after a review of his outstanding ministry of pastoring, speaking, and writing.

Global University
Springfield, Missouri, USA

PN 03.12

ISBN 978-0-7617-1481-1

Printed in the United States of America by Gospel Publishing House, Springfield, Missouri

Table of Contents

Digital Course Options

This printed independent-study textbook (IST) represents only one of the ways you can study through Global University's Berean School of the Bible (BSB). Global University offers electronic delivery formats that allow you to complete courses without using printed material.

You may choose one or more of these course delivery options with or without the printed IST.

Digital Courses

- Online Courses. Complete your entire ministry training program online with fully interactive learning options.

  You can complete your chapter reviews, unit progress evaluations, and final exam online and receive instant results, even if you use print or other digital study versions.

- Logos Bible Software. Purchase an entire digital library of Bibles and Bible reference titles and the Berean courses specifically created to function inside these digital library environments.

- Electronic courses. Check Global University's Web site for additional electronic course versions (for e-readers and other devices) and their availability.

Enrollment Policies and Procedures

Enrollment policies and procedures are provided in the most current Berean School of the Bible Academic Catalog. An electronic version of the catalog is available at the Global University Web site.

Contact Global University for Enrollment Information

Phone: 1-800-443-1083 (9 a.m. to 6 p.m., CST, Monday–Friday)

> **Spanish language representatives are available to discuss enrollment in Spanish courses.**

E-mail: berean@globaluniversity.edu

Web: www.globaluniversity.edu

Fax: 417-862-0863

Mail: 1211 S. Glenstone Ave., Springfield, MO 65804

How to Use Berean Courses

Independent study is one of the most dynamic and rapidly growing educational methods. Although different from traditional classroom study, the goal is the same—to guide you, the student, through a systematic program of study and help you gain new knowledge and skills. Berean courses are independent-study courses. Some students may participate in a Berean study center, where a facilitator enhances the learning experience for a group of Berean students. Berean courses are also offered online or on CD, additional learning options for today's independent-study student.

All Berean courses are printed in a comprehensive independent-study textbook (IST). The IST is your teacher, textbook, and study guide in one package. Once you have familiarized yourself with the course components, explained below, you are ready to begin studying. Whether you are studying for personal growth or working toward a diploma, the Berean faculty, advisers, and student service representatives are available to help you get the most out of your Berean program.

General Course Design

- Each course is based on course objectives.
- Each course is composed of several units.
- Each unit is composed of several chapters.
- Each chapter is composed of two or more lessons.
- Each lesson contains one or more lesson objectives.
- Each lesson objective corresponds to specific lesson content.

Course Objectives

Course objectives represent the concepts—or knowledge areas—and perspectives the course will teach you. Review these objectives before you begin studying to have an idea of what to focus on as you study. The course objectives are listed on the course introduction page.

Unit Overview

A unit overview previews each unit's content and outlines the unit development.

Chapter, Lesson Content, Lesson Objectives, and Numbering System

Each *chapter* begins with an introduction and outline. The outline presents the chapter's lesson titles and objectives. Chapters consist of short lessons to allow you to complete one lesson at a time (at one sitting), instead of the entire chapter at one time.

The *lesson content* is based on lesson objectives.

Lesson objectives present the important concepts and perspectives to be studied in the course.

Each chapter, lesson, and objective is uniquely numbered. This numbering system is designed to help you relate the lesson objective to its corresponding lesson content. Chapters are numbered consecutively throughout the course. Lessons are numbered within each chapter with a two-digit decimal number. For example, Lesson 2 in Chapter 3 is numbered 3.2. The first number is the chapter (3), the second number is the lesson (2) within the chapter.

Lesson objectives are tagged with a three-digit decimal number. For example, Chapter 1, Lesson 1, Objective 1 is identified as Objective 1.1.1. Chapter 1, Lesson 2, Objective 3 is Objective 1.2.3. The first number is the chapter, the second is the lesson, and the third is the objective. The numbering system is to assist you in identifying, locating, and organizing each chapter, lesson, and objective.

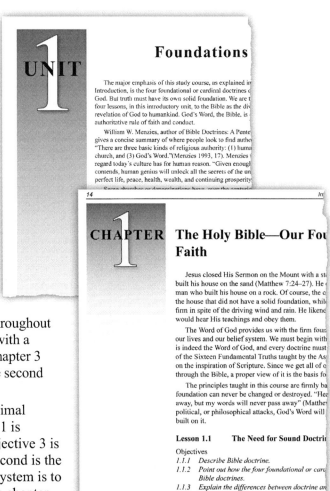

UNIT 1

Foundations

The major emphasis of this study course, as explained in Introduction, is the four foundational or cardinal doctrines of God. But truth must have its own solid foundation. We are t four lessons, in this introductory unit, to the Bible as the div revelation of God to humankind. God's Word, the Bible, is authoritative rule of faith and conduct.

William W. Menzies, author of Bible Doctrines: A Pente gives a concise summary of where people look to find autho "There are three basic kinds of religious authority: (1) huma church, and (3) God's Word."(Menzies 1993, 17). Menzies regard today's culture has for human reason. "Given enough contends, human genius will unlock all the secrets of the un perfect life, peace, health, wealth, and continuing prosperity

14

CHAPTER 1

The Holy Bible—Our Fou Faith

Jesus closed His Sermon on the Mount with a st built his house on the sand (Matthew 7:24–27). He man who built his house on a rock. Of course, the c the house that did not have a solid foundation, whil firm in spite of the driving wind and rain. He likene would hear His teachings and obey them.

The Word of God provides us with the firm foun our lives and our belief system. We must begin with is indeed the Word of God, and every doctrine must of the Sixteen Fundamental Truths taught by the Ass on the inspiration of Scripture. Since we get all of o through the Bible, a proper view of it is the basis fo

The principles taught in this course are firmly ba foundation can never be changed or destroyed. "Hea away, but my words will never pass away" (Matthew political, or philosophical attacks, God's Word will built on it.

Lesson 1.1   The Need for Sound Doctri

Objectives
1.1.1   *Describe Bible doctrine.*
1.1.2   *Point out how the four foundational or car Bible doctrines.*
1.1.3   *Explain the differences between doctrine an*

took the place of Hebrew as the langua

Pharisees, Sadducees, and **Scribes—**
(small places of worship, study, and so
Jews were ruled by the powerful and l
years under the cultural influence of th
completely (Scroggins 2003, 328).

The Greek Period

The Persian Empire was in power a
and Nehemiah rebuilt Jerusalem's wal

 Test Yourself

Circle the letter of the *best* answer.

1. Why are only two chapters of the entire Bibl
devoted to the never-ending eternity?
a) Eternity will be a constant repeat of regular
activity, so no more space is needed.
b) The eternal fate of the wicked should not be
given any more attention
c) Greater details of New Jerusalem would be
meaningless.
d) The purpose of Scripture is to encourage ho
living now

2. What happens to the present heaven and eart
make way for new heaven and earth?
a) They are gradually cleansed and changed in

What to Look for in the Margins

Left margins contain numbers for units, chapters, and lessons. In addition, margins contain two learning tools—*lesson objectives with their respective numbers* and *interactive questions* that focus on key principles. Read, understand, and use these two learning tools to study the lesson text.

Interactive questions relate to specific lesson content and specific lesson objectives. Interactive questions, along with lesson objectives, will help you learn the concepts and perspectives that are tested in exam questions. Interactive questions are numbered consecutively within each chapter. Once you understand what the interactive question is asking, search for the answer as you study the lesson's related content section. You can compare your responses to our suggested ones at the back of each chapter.

Lesson objectives present the key concepts. These tips on using lesson objectives will help you master the course content and be prepared for exams:

- Identify the key concept(s) and concept perspectives in the objective.
- Identify and understand what the objective is asking you to do with the key concept(s).
- Think of the objective as an essay test question.
- Read and study the lesson content related to the objective and search for the answer to the "essay test question"—the objective.

Lesson Titles and Subheads

Lesson titles and subheads identify and organize specific lesson content.

Key Words

Key words are presented in **boldface** print and defined in the glossary of this IST; they are words that are used with a specific meaning in the lesson.

Reference Citations

Outside sources are documented using in-text citations in parentheses. These sources are compiled in more detail in the Reference List at the end of the IST.

Test Yourself

The Test Yourself section concludes the chapter with multiple-choice questions based on the lesson objectives, interactive questions, and their supporting lesson content. Test Yourself answer keys are in the Essential Course Materials at the back of this IST.

Glossary and Reference List

A *glossary* (which defines key words) and *reference list* (works cited in each chapter) follow the last chapter of the IST.

Recommended Reading Textbook

An optional textbook is recommended for use with each course. The textbook recommended to accompany this course is listed on the course introduction page. Some courses may provide additional suggested reading lists following the *reference list*.

Essential Course Materials in the back of this IST contain the following:

- Service Learning Requirement (SLR) Assignment and SLR Report Form
- Unit Progress Evaluation (UPE) Instructions and UPEs
- Answer Keys for Test Yourself quizzes and UPEs
- Forms: Round-Tripper (as needed) and Request for a Printed Final Examination (if needed)

Two Requirements to Receive a Course Grade:
To receive a grade for this course, you must:

1. Submit your SLR Report Form. The instructions for the SLR assignment are in the Essential Course Materials at the back of this IST. The report is required, but not graded.
2. You must also take a closed-book final examination. Your course grade is based on the final exam. The Berean School of the Bible grading scale is 90–100 percent, A; 80–89 percent, B; 70–79 percent, C; and 0–69 percent, F.

Checklist of Study Methods

STUDY METHODS	√
1. Read the introduction in the Independent-Study Textbook (IST) to learn how to use the IST.	
2. Study the Table of Contents to familiarize yourself with the course structure and content.	

If you carefully follow the study methods listed below, you should be able to complete this course successfully. As you complete each chapter, mark a √ in the column for that chapter beside each instruction you followed. Then continue to study the remaining chapters in the same way.

CHAPTERS	1	2	3	4	5	6	7	8	9	10	11	12	13	14	15	16	17	18
3. Pace yourself so you will study at least two or three times each week. Plan carefully so you can complete the course within the allowed enrollment period. Complete at least one lesson each study session.																		
4. Read Scripture references in more than one translation of the Bible for better understanding.																		
5. Underline, mark, and write notes in your IST.																		
6. Use a notebook to write additional notes and comments.																		
7. As you work through each chapter, make good use of reference tools, such as a study Bible, a comprehensive concordance, a Bible dictionary, and an English dictionary.																		
8. Complete all interactive questions and learning activities as you go.																		
9. In preparation for the Test Yourself, review the objectives for each lesson in the chapter and your notes and highlights to reinforce the key principles learned in the chapter.																		
10. Discuss with others what you are learning.																		
11. Apply what you have learned in your spiritual life and ministry.																		
UNIT EVALUATIONS																		
Review for each Unit Progress Evaluation by rereading the																		
a. lesson objectives to be sure you can achieve what they state.																		
b. questions you answered incorrectly in Test Yourself.																		
c. lesson material for topics you need to review.																		

Student Planner and Record

*This chart is for you to record your personal progress in this course. Be sure to keep it **up to date** for quick reference.*

In the boxes below, record the unit number, the date you expect to complete each chapter, the date you do complete the chapter, and the date of review.

Unit Number	Chapter Number	Expected Completion Date	Actual Completion Date	Date Reviewed
	1			
	2			
	3			
	4			
	5			
	6			
	7			
	8			
	9			
	10			
	11			
	12			
	13			
	14			
	15			
	16			
	17			
	18			

UNIT EVALUATIONS	Date Completed
Unit Evaluation 1	
Unit Evaluation 2	
Unit Evaluation 3	
Unit Evaluation 4	
Unit Evaluation 5	
Unit Evaluation 6	

WRITTEN ASSIGNMENTS & FINAL EXAM	Date Completed
Service Learning Requirement (SLR) Report	
Final Examination	
SLR report & closed-book final exam materials submitted (The SLR report does not apply to the internship courses.)	

Pastoral Ministry Overview

Welcome to the study of pastoral ministry. This course provides the tools for developing a fruitful ministry.

Jesus taught that for a house to stand, it must be built on a solid foundation (Matthew 7:24–25). In the same way, for a ministry to endure, it must rest on a firm foundation. The first unit will consider (1) the call, character, and gifts of the pastor; (2) the devotional life, study, and fasting of the pastor; and (3) a pastor's life as a spouse, parent, and friend.

Unit 2 builds on the first unit. Chapter 4 emphasizes pastors' public ministries as reflections of their private lives. Pastors can feed others only with the spiritual food they have received *from* God, because they can lead others only into places they have been *with* God. As one wise pastor said, the exact amount people have to share with others is what they receive from God—no less and no more. Thus, pastors must walk daily with God, spending time in His Word and presence. Pastors who do this will never lack spiritual food for God's sheep.

Chapter 5 considers the pastor's role in leading worship. The importance of a pastor's relationship with God is again emphasized. From beginning to end, pastors must depend on the Spirit to minister through them to others. As this happens, believers will be fruitful and grow in grace.

Skills for ministry are taught in Chapter 6. The insights of this chapter can shape and equip pastors for a lifetime of caring for the flock of God.

Unit 3 continues with the duties and work of the ministry. Chapters 7–9 include a growing emphasis on equipping the saints for ministry. Blessed are the pastors who do not try to do everything themselves, for they shall guide each member of the body to do his or her part. As the whole body builds itself up, the needs of each member will be met.

No course on pastoral ministry would be complete without a chapter on special services. This chapter is not just theory; rather, a step-by-step guide of services related to the special events of life is explained.

The fourth unit explains relationships like a final exam. Pastors must make a passing grade in their relations with workers; otherwise, they will fail in ministry. Chapters 11 and 12 give insights about working with lay leaders and staff. Chapters 13–15 discuss the relationship of a pastor's work and calling. Many of those who begin well in pastoral ministry quit after a few years. Some fail because they love their neighbor more than themselves; others develop a root of bitterness that grows into a tree with deadly fruit; and some stumble over their own pride or selfish desires. These final chapters explain the keys to a long, fruitful pastoral ministry.

Course Description   MIN381 Pastoral Ministry (5 CEUs)

This course examines the ministry of the pastor in three areas: preparation, responsibilities, and relationships. In the unit on preparation, we study a pastor's qualifications, devotional life, and personal life. A unit on responsibilities analyzes a pastor's role in preaching and teaching, worship, pastoral care, leading, training, forming cell groups, and special services. The final unit examines a pastor's relationships with lay leaders, staff, work, and calling. This is a principle-centered study to lay a lifelong foundation for pastoral ministry.

In addition to using your Bible, we also recommend that you use *The Pentecostal Pastor*, compiled and edited by Thomas E. Trask, Wayde I. Goodall, and Zenas J. Bicket, to enhance your learning experience.

Course Objectives

Upon completion of this course, you should be able to

1. Explain how pastors' calls, characters, and gifts prepare them for ministry.

2. Analyze the relationship of pastors' devotional and personal lives to ministry.

3. Summarize principles to guide pastors in preaching and teaching.

4. Describe the pastoral role of worship in the church.

5. Examine the issues and principles related to pastoral care.

6. Explain the balance between the pastoral roles of leading and training.

7. Understand and appreciate the dynamics and effectiveness of cell group formation.

8. Acquire the basic steps and recognize the purpose of special services in the church.

9. Summarize principles for relating to lay leaders and staff.

10. Identify keys for maintaining rhythm and passion in ministry.

BEFORE YOU BEGIN

Successfully completing this course requires that you apply content you study in a ministry activity. The instructions for this Service Learning Requirement (SLR) are found in the Essential Course Materials in the back of this IST. Please take time now to become familiar with these instructions so that you can be planning your SLR activity throughout your study of this course.

UNIT 1

The Pastor's Preparation

Jesus taught that for a house to stand, it must be built on a solid foundation (Matthew 7:24–25); likewise, for a ministry to endure, it must rest on a firm foundation. The first unit will consider (1) the call, character, and gifts of the pastor; (2) the devotional life, study, and fasting of the pastor; and (3) a pastor's life as a spouse, parent, and friend. *God will draw you to that.*

Pray and meditate as you study this first unit. In fact, the beginning of this course is so important that only those who obey God in the areas of Unit 1 should continue studying it.

Chapter 1   **The Considerations of a Pastor**

Lessons
1.1   The Call
1.2   Character
1.3   Gifts

Chapter 2   **The Devotional Life of a Pastor**

Lessons
2.1   Prayer
2.2   Study
2.3   Fasting

Chapter 3   **The Personal Life of a Pastor**

Lessons
3.1   The Married Pastor's Perspective
3.2   The Single Pastor's Perspective
3.3   The Female Pastor's Perspective
3.4   The Pastor as Parent
3.5   The Pastor as Friend

The Considerations of a Pastor

The ministry is not a career that you choose but a divine call to which you surrender. The call to ministry may come in any number of ways: through a vision or dream, a sermon, or the inner witness of the Holy Spirit. It may come instantaneously, or it may be a conviction that develops over a period of months or even years. No one should enter the ministry unless he or she is absolutely convinced that God has called him or her. If you have not been called, nothing else matters—not talent, commitment, or even the expectations of others. "No one takes this honor upon himself; he must be called by God" (Hebrews 5:4).

The call to ministry must be distinguished from both the call to salvation (Titus 2:11) and the call to service (Romans 12:6–8; Ephesians 4:12). While God calls everyone to salvation (2 Peter 3:9) and every believer to Christian service, only those chosen for special service receive the call to be apostles, prophets, evangelists, pastors, or teachers (Ephesians 4:11). God sets those who receive this call apart to prepare "God's people for works of service, so that the body of Christ may be built up until we all reach unity in the faith and in the knowledge of the Son of God and become mature, attaining to the whole measure of the fullness of Christ" (4:12–13).

Lesson 1.1   The Call

Objectives
1.1.1   Explain how the call of God is like an anchor.
1.1.2   Describe two ways to test a call to ministry.

Lesson 1.2   Character

Objective
1.2.1   Identify and illustrate four principles that reflect character.

Lesson 1.3   Gifts

Objective
1.3.1   Identify two principles that apply to recognizing ministry skills.

LESSON
1.1

The Call

Even the most cursory review of Scripture shows the preeminence the call to ministry played in the lives and ministry of both the prophets and the apostles. Although the form of the call varied from person to person, it was always a prerequisite for entering the ministry. Moses heard a voice speaking to him from a burning bush (Exodus 3). Isaiah saw a vision in which the Lord asked, "Whom shall I send? And who will go for us?" (Isaiah 6:8). Jeremiah was called even before he was born: "Before I formed you in the womb I knew you, before you were born I set you apart; I appointed you as a prophet to the nations" (Jeremiah 1:5). The word of the Lord came to Ezekiel, saying, "Son of man, I am sending you to the Israelites . . . . You must speak my words to them . . . . I have made you a watchman for the house of Israel" (Ezekiel 2:3, 7; 3:17).

The Call of God Is an Anchor

1.1.1
OBJECTIVE
Explain how the call of God is like an anchor.

1   Explain how the minister's call is in many respects like an anchor

God's call to ministry is the minister's anchor. An anchor keeps ships in place despite storms or high winds. When despair tempts them to doubt their worth, ministers fall back on the hope and promise of God's call to steady them and to strengthen their faith.

As we read Paul's epistles, we see how often Paul anchors his soul in the call of God. In fact, Paul defined himself by God's call. In Romans 1:1, he refers to himself as "a servant of Christ Jesus, called to be an apostle and set apart for the gospel of God." In 1 Corinthians 1:1, he says he is "called to be an apostle of Christ Jesus by the will of God." This call is also Paul's driving force: "I press on toward the goal to win the prize for which God has called me" (Philippians 3:14).

I well remember my own call to the ministry at the age of thirteen. It was and is the defining experience of my life. I was praying alone, kneeling between the first and second pews at the South Houston Assembly of God Church. In the background, I could hear soft organ music and people praying. Although I did not see a vision or hear a voice, I knew—and have never doubted since—that God called me. That Sunday evening in 1960, I surrendered my life unconditionally to God's call.

Later, at home, I told my father what had happened. After affirming the validity of my experience, he gave me some of the wisest counsel I have ever received: "Let's keep this between the two of us," he said. "There's really no reason to make a public announcement until you are ready to begin preaching." I accepted my father's advice that evening without question, but only now, many years later, do I fully appreciate his wisdom. Keeping my call to myself gave me the freedom to confirm it. Time proved that the call was real, that it was not just an emotional experience. God's will, not others' expectations, was the sole criterion in determining the course for my life.

By the age of sixteen, I began to preach regularly in youth services, nursing homes, jails, and even a few revival meetings. When I was twenty, I became the pastor of a small, rural congregation. For the past thirty-seven years, I have been privileged to serve in ministry, further validating God's call to me many years ago on a Sunday evening.

The Call of God Must Be Tested

The call will be tested

1.1.2
OBJECTIVE
Describe two ways to test a call to ministry.

While working with Bible college students and seminarians, I am often asked how I knew God called me to the ministry. How could I be sure I did not just imagine the whole thing? I recognize their underlying question: How can I determine whether I am truly called? How can I know for sure? Although we

These tests will apply regardless.

may never be completely sure of anything so subjective, we can apply some tests to help us determine the validity of our call. Specifically, we can put our call of God to the time test and the open door test.

The Time Test

2   How does time test what people think may be the call of God?

An emotional experience will fade with time. When the intensity of the moment wanes, so will the person's sense of call. On the other hand, a genuine call to ministry will deepen and strengthen. Author and preacher David Wilkerson writes:

> That which is of God will fasten itself on you and overpower and possess your entire being. That which is not of God will die—you will lose interest. But the plan of God will never die. The thing God wants you to do will become stronger each day in your thoughts, in your prayers, in your planning. It grows and grows! (1967, 34)

The Door Test

3   What is the door test of a call to ministry?

If God has truly called you to the ministry, He will make a way. That is, He will open a door of opportunity. The first door may be a chance to serve as a volunteer in your local church. If you are faithful in serving in small ways, God will open a bigger door (Matthew 25:21). Next, God may open the door for you to attend Bible college or seminary to train for the ministry. Finally, He will open a door into full-time ministry.

If all the doors are closed to you, it may be wise to reevaluate your call. Of course, a closed door does not necessarily mean that you are not called, but it clearly indicates that some prayer and soul-searching is in order. You may need to resolve some spiritual issues in your life before you are ready for ministry. Or it may simply be a matter of timing. "Not now" does not necessarily mean "not ever."

Waiting for God to open a door can be extremely difficult, especially if it appears that others are moving forward in ministry while you are going nowhere. However, forcing a door open is unwise and likely a decision you will regret. Getting ahead of God's plan for your life is fraught with enormous risks, both for yourself and for those you are called to serve. Walking *with* God means walking at His pace, not too slowly or too quickly; it means staying beside Him.

4   Contrast God's first call to Moses with the call at the burning bush.

Consider Moses. Contrary to popular belief, Moses' initial call did not occur when he was an eighty-year-old shepherd in the desert. His first call came while he was a prince in Pharaoh's palace. Although Scripture gives no direct account of his original call, both Stephen (Acts 7) and the writer of Hebrews (Hebrews 11) allude to it. Moses had an inner awareness that his destiny was with the people of God. That inner assurance, that sense of destiny, became his call.

5   Explain whether your call is more like the first or second call of Moses.

For most people, the call to ministry is similar to Moses' first call, not to his burning bush experience. Few ever hear an audible voice or see a vision. God speaks to most of us in more "ordinary" ways: an inner witness of the Holy Spirit or a growing desire to be a minister. Yet these ordinary ways are just as valid as their more dramatic counterparts.

Choosing to renounce his royal privileges to identify with the Hebrew slaves could not have been easy for Moses. "[He] was educated in all the wisdom of the Egyptians and was powerful in speech and action" (Acts 7:22). We can only wonder how many nights he lay awake wrestling with his conscience. What right did he have to enjoy wealth, power, and learning while his people languished as slaves? On the other hand, he may have reasoned that one man could not do much by himself. The struggle and tension must have been excruciating. Yet, little by little, he realized that the purpose of his training was not to benefit him personally but to equip him as the emancipator of his people. His call likely began as a sense of unrest but, in time, grew into an all-consuming passion that demanded action. Stephen describes what happened next:

> When Moses was forty years old, he decided to visit his fellow Israelites. He saw one of them being mistreated by an Egyptian, so he went to his defense and avenged him by killing the Egyptian. Moses thought that his own people would realize that God was using him to rescue them, but they did not. The next day Moses came upon two Israelites who were fighting. He tried to reconcile them by saying, "Men, you are brothers; why do you want to hurt each other?" But the man who was mistreating the other pushed Moses aside and said, "Who made you ruler and judge over us? Do you want to kill me as you killed the Egyptian yesterday?" When Moses heard this, he fled to Midian, where he settled as a foreigner and had two sons. (Acts 7:23–29)

What Moses did was violent and senseless, but it did not just happen. That is, while he did not plan to kill the Egyptian, his visit to the slaves was premeditated: "He decided to visit his fellow Israelites" (Acts 7:23). According to Hebrews 11, he "refused to be known as the son of Pharaoh's daughter. He chose to be mistreated . . . . He regarded disgrace . . . as of greater value than the treasures of Egypt" (Hebrews 11:24–26). Did you notice all the action words? Moses *decided*, *refused*, *chose*, and *regarded*. In his mind and heart, Moses had already accepted the call of God. He was ready to deliver his people, but his zeal outran his judgment. His terrible mistake had far-reaching ramifications, not just for himself, but for all of the Hebrews. He was right about his call but wrong in his timing and methods.

6 Summarize three truths from Moses' life in reference to his call.

We can learn a number of things from Moses' experience. First, God not only uses diverse methods to call different people, but He also speaks to each individual in a variety of ways. Apparently, God's first call to Moses in Egypt was not dramatic like the burning bush experience. But in the palace, Moses was not living as an exile or fugitive. On the other hand, Exodus 3–4 must be interpreted in light of Moses' failure forty years earlier, which affected his self-concept. As a prince in Pharaoh's palace, he was "powerful in speech" (Acts 7:22). Yet, as a shepherd in the desert, he had stopped believing in himself. He saw himself as "slow of speech and tongue" (Exodus 4:10). As a result, God had to go to extraordinary lengths—through a supernatural, burning bush phenomenon—to convince Moses that he was the right man for the job.

Second, Moses' experience teaches us to wait for God's timing. Although his call was valid, Moses got ahead of God. His zeal and passion were not rooted in the knowledge of God's plans and purposes (Romans 10:2). Remember, in the work of the Lord, it is just as wrong to run ahead of God as it is to draw back.

Third, from Moses we learn not to take matters into our own hands. Under no circumstances should we revert to immoral, unethical, or illegal means to accomplish God's purposes. We simply cannot achieve spiritual goals in the strength of the flesh. God's work must be done in God's way and in God's timing.

Finally, Moses' experience teaches us that even serious errors do not nullify the call of God. Although Moses seemed to give up on himself, God never gave up on him. Forty years later, God renewed His call to Moses. Moses' mistake was terribly costly to himself and to God's people, but it did not disqualify him from ministry. Romans 11:29 declares, "God's gifts and his call are irrevocable."

1.2.1
OBJECTIVE
Identify and illustrate four principles that reflect character.

Character

The call to ministry is according to the sole providence of God. He calls whomever He chooses independent of any effort on our part. We cannot influence Him, either to persuade or dissuade Him. However, once we receive the call to ministry, we become partners with Him in developing the kind of personal character and professional competence that validates our call.

Character Is about Being

Ralph Waldo Emerson is attributed with saying, "What lies before us and what lies behind us are tiny matters compared to what lies within us." That which "lies within us" involves our character and competence.

Character and competence are two sides of the same coin. Character focuses on who we are, whereas competence focuses on what we do (our skills). That is, competence is about *doing* the work of the ministry. But character is about *being*—being God's person in every situation. Character is what God is doing in us: conforming us to the likeness of His Son (Romans 8:29). Competence relates to what God is doing through us: the daily tasks of ministry.

This balance between being and doing is reflected in Jesus' appointment of the twelve disciples "that they might be with him and that he might send them out to preach" (Mark 3:14). Much like the Twelve, our character grows as we spend time being *with* the Lord, and our competence is enhanced as we *do* ministry for the Lord.

7 In 1 Timothy 3:2–7, how many requirements relate to character, skill, or talent?

In 1 Timothy 3:2–7, Paul states several things that a minister should be:

- Above reproach
- The husband of one wife
- Self-controlled
- Respected
- Hospitable
- Not given to drunkenness
- Not violent, but gentle
- Peaceful
- Not a lover of money
- One who manages his family
- Not a recent convert
- A man of good reputation

8 Read Matthew 7:22–23, and explain whether you believe the people in this passage had good character.

When I think of a man with this kind of good character, my thoughts always turn to my uncle Ernie, known to his peers as the Reverend E. C. Phillips. You have probably never heard of him, because he was not a great man by the world's standards. Uncle Ernie never pastored a large church, nor did he write a book. He did not make a name for himself. Still, he was a special man who lived at a time when a minister was measured by his character and not his charisma (style). The longer you knew him, the more you appreciated him.

During most of his adult life, he pastored small country churches. While his congregations loved him dearly, they simply did not have the means to support a pastor. However, Uncle Ernie was energetic and something of an entrepreneur, so he managed to make ends meet. At one time or another, he operated a full-service gas station, performed custom swathing, bred Appaloosa horses, or painted houses. But Uncle Ernie's first love was the ministry—no one who knew him could doubt that. For him, the other jobs were like Paul's tent making, just a way to provide for his needs (Acts 18:3; 20:34).

On the surface, my uncle's life appears rather insignificant, but on a deeper level, it has great eternal value. Only God knows how many people received Jesus as their Savior as a result of Uncle Ernie's witness, and who can measure the value of a single soul? Although he has been deceased for several years, his ministry lives on in others. For instance, he deeply influenced my brother Don's decision to become a missionary. Another nephew, Orville Stewart, is now a pastor. Uncle Ernie's ministry lives on in me as well. He helped give me my start in the ministry, inviting me to preach in every church where he served as pastor. He was a special friend and my first spiritual mentor.

Uncle Ernie's character set him apart. Not once in nearly fifty years of ministry did anyone have reason to question his integrity. When some poor business decisions pushed him to the point of financial ruin, he temporarily left the ministry to pay off his creditors rather than file bankruptcy and bring reproach on the church. How different he was from ministers who value image above all else! Some pastors worry about appearances, such as wearing the right clothes, driving the right car, knowing the right people, and even pastoring the right church. Do not misunderstand me: Dressing impressively, being in leadership, and building large churches can be good things—as long as they come from a ministry based on integrity.

Integrity and congruity were important to Uncle Ernie. What he appeared to be and what he truly was had to be one and the same. To him, character was more important than image. This should be true for all ministers. Former UCLA basketball coach John Wooden said it this way: "Be more concerned with your character than with your reputation. Your character is what you really are while your reputation is merely what others think you are."

Character Is Easily Understood

9   Describe a minister you know who has good character.

Godly character of this nature is not complicated. It simply requires a person to value others above himself/herself. Such a perspective includes the following attributes:

- Choosing to live modestly and avoiding debts
- Forgiving others as Christ has forgiven
- Being honest
- Loving neighbors as oneself
- Providing for, loving, and honoring family
- Training one's children in the way of the Lord
- Bringing God honor in all things

10   According to Paul, what results if a pastor has good character, spiritual ministry, and sound doctrine?

The apostle Paul knew the importance of character. He instructed Timothy, a young minister, to "set an example for the believers in speech, in life, in love, in faith and in purity. Be diligent in these matters; give yourself wholly to them, so that everyone may see your progress. Watch your life and doctrine closely. Persevere in them, because if you do, you will save both yourself and your hearers" (1 Timothy 4:12, 15–16).   1 Cor 15:33

Bad character ruins a believer's witness and ministry. Should believers fail to work with the Holy Spirit to develop godly character, in only a matter of time, they will betray themselves and the trust others have in them. For instance, a ministerial staff member of a Colorado church went to jail in May 1986 for embezzling almost $42,000 from the church over a six-year period. When I first learned of his crime,

I remember thinking, "How could a minister do such a thing?" I was tempted to conclude that he was an aberration, an imposter, an evil man masquerading as a minister. While such a conclusion made his dishonesty easier to explain, it unfortunately did not seem to fit the facts. More likely, he was a sincere man, no better and no worse than any of the rest of us. Somewhere along the way, he took a wrong turn that probably seemed insignificant at the time. Perhaps he padded his expense account or hedged on his income tax return. Or maybe he "borrowed" cash from church funds, fully intending but never bothering to pay it back. As time passed, his nagging conscience may have become easier to ignore.

If Satan had tempted him to steal $42,000 in one lump sum, he probably would not have succumbed. The minister undoubtedly considered himself an honest man and could not reconcile a theft of that magnitude with such an image. Therefore, Satan tempted him with "insignificant" amounts—twenty dollars here, fifty dollars there. And most likely, the man convinced himself that it was just a loan. In other words, I am certain that this minister did not plan to embezzle money. After all, if a man plans to misappropriate funds, plenty of places are more lucrative than a small country church. It seems likely that he walked into this sin one small compromise at a time. Somewhere along the line, he opened his heart to the enemy, and before he knew it, he was in over his head. When he confessed before the church, the minister stated that "the depth of the deception was so ingrained, he did not even know how much he had stolen" (Bergstrom 1987). The sin of stealing had become a habit.

11 How does Satan usually tempt people?

Virtually all spiritual failures start with small steps of disobedience. Although it may not seem significant at the time, each disobedience, no matter how small, is like a fissure in the soul's wall. The acid of evil seeps in through each tiny crack and begins to destroy the foundations of character. Gradually, the spiritual will of such a person is compromised, and when temptation comes, he or she does not have the will to resist. The undiscerning may believe that the final crisis brought the person down, but in reality, the dry rot of disobedience destroyed his or her spiritual character from the inside out.

12 Summarize the principle of Luke 16:10.

On the other hand, each act of obedience, no matter how small, reinforces the foundations of spiritual character. As believers persevere in obedience, their character builds (Romans 5:4). Then, when a potentially overwhelming temptation comes, they are prepared to resist it because of their faithfulness in smaller crises. Beauty, youth, fame, and wealth will fade; but character endures forever. Dallas Willard writes, "A successful performance at a moment of crisis rests largely and essentially upon the depths of a self wisely and rigorously prepared in the totality of its being—mind and body" (1988, ix). And character development is at the heart of that preparation.

LESSON 1.3

1.3.1
OBJECTIVE

Identify two principles that apply to recognizing ministry skills.

Gifts

Godly character prepares us spiritually and emotionally to minister, but it does not give us the skills required to minister effectively. The Bible refers to these ministry skills as gifts: "We have different gifts according to the grace given us" (Romans 12:6). Paul lists some of these gifts as follows:

- Prophesying
- Serving
- Teaching

- Encouraging
- Giving
- Leading
- Showing mercy (12:6–8)

Because God is the one who gives these gifts, we cannot take pride in them. However, we are responsible for what we do with them. For example, people who are gifted in music or art must discipline themselves to fully develop their God-given gifts. God equips those whom He calls, giving us the inherent abilities needed for effective ministry. But it is up to us to fully develop and improve those gifts. If we do not, our ministry may stagnate in mediocrity.

The multiple and emotionally exhausting demands of full-time ministry might include counseling spouses in a rocky marriage, comforting family members who are coping with a terminal disease or a death, meeting with a colleague who has become disillusioned and has left the faith, encouraging a couple discouraged by their infertility, and many, many more. Thus, pastors must be men and women of prayer, guarding their own hearts and watching over the souls of those whom the Lord has entrusted to them. Their weeks are jammed with staff and board meetings, administrative details, civic demands, hospital calls, counseling, petty problems, weddings, funerals, and a continuing series of emergencies. Somewhere, somehow, in the midst of it all, they must find time to prepare themselves and their message for each church service. As the spiritual leaders of their congregations, pastors are responsible for receiving and sharing the God-given vision for the body. And those are only the church-related responsibilities. Pastors must also make time to nurture and support their families.

13 What is the greatest challenge of ministry?

While the weight of the ministry (the actual workload) is enormous, it is the breadth of the ministry (the multiplicity of tasks and the skills required to do them) that most ministers find more challenging and even intimidating. They fully expect to work, but they encounter so many different tasks that require so many different skills. Today, a pastor must be a good administrator, manager, counselor, shepherd, spiritual leader, preacher, teacher, and a person of prayer. Few of us have gifts in all of these areas, so what can we do?

Recognize Strengths

Recognizing our strengths (that is, our God-given abilities) and building on them is the first step in coping with the demands of pastoral ministry. Many of us are tempted to focus on our weaknesses to improve the areas in which we are less gifted. As a result, we fail to maximize our areas of giftedness, and we limit our effectiveness in ministry. A second and perhaps more devastating consequence of this is a growing frustration with ministry. In other words, we not only find ourselves working harder to be effective in the areas where we are less gifted, but we also experience a diminishing return. When this occurs, ministry does not renew us; it exhausts us.

Bill Hybels is a multitalented, internationally known minister with a highly effective ministry. He is not only the founding pastor of the 15,000-member Willow Creek Community Church but also a much sought after speaker for retreats and conferences worldwide. Yet he experienced an increasing frustration that neither talent nor success could alleviate and, at one point, even contemplated leaving the ministry. How did he arrive at this state of extreme exhaustion? While a staggeringly heavy workload contributed to his burnout, the real issue involved his ministry gifts:

Bill's top three gifts, in order of strength, are leadership, evangelism, and teaching. But he had allowed his ministry to become structured in such a way that he poured far more time and energy into teaching, which drains him, then into leadership or evangelism, both of which energize him. . . . It was becoming clear that if he didn't learn to minister in a manner more consistent with who God created him to be, he was going to self-destruct. Somehow he had to reorder his ministry so he could teach less. (Hybels and Hybels, 1995, 107–108)

After months of painful agonizing, he concluded that his only hope of surviving in the ministry was to share the primary teaching responsibility with another minister whose primary gift was teaching. Of course, the idea ran contrary to everything he had been taught about pastoral ministry, and Christian leaders across the country advised him against it in the strongest possible terms. "But Bill felt he had no choice. As he put it, the way he was doing the work of God was destroying the work of God in him. He had to find a different way to do it" (1995, 108). That different method of ministry meant refocusing his energies in the areas of his giftedness, his strengths, while teaming with a minister or ministers whose strengths differed from his own.

Recognize Weaknesses

Bill Hybels's concept leads us to the second step in building pastoral competence: recognizing our weaknesses and building a pastoral staff and/or team of lay ministers to compensate for them. No one person can do everything, and the sooner we realize this, the better off the whole church will be. It is not weakness but wisdom that leads pastors to surround themselves with highly capable teams. Being a competent pastor does not mean mastering the multiplicity of tasks the ministry requires. It means being wise enough to build a well-balanced team to effectively meet the many and varied needs of the body.

The need to develop a ministry team is not new, nor is it unique to today's busy pastors. Moses faced a strikingly similar situation, although on a much grander scale. Day after day, while camped in the wilderness at the foot of Mount Horeb, lines of Israelites waited from morning to night to speak to Moses. Each day it grew worse, until all Moses could see was a sea of faces, needy and impatient. The pressure and frustration became unbearable.

Then Jethro, Moses' father-in-law, visited and immediately recognized the problem. When Moses returned at the close of another exhausting day, Jethro confronted him: "What is this you are doing for the people? Why do you alone sit as judge, while all these people stand around you from morning till evening?" (Exodus 18:14). Moses had a ready answer: "Because the people come to me to seek God's will . . . [and I] inform them of God's decrees and laws" (18:15–16). His response implied that he felt no one else was qualified to help solve the people's problems. While that may have been true, it did not excuse continuing the obviously unworkable arrangement. Things needed to change. With candor, Jethro replied, "What you are doing is not good. You and these people who come to you will only wear yourselves out. The work is too heavy for you; you cannot handle it alone" (18:17–18).

This principle is still God's word for today's pastors. Do not try to do it all. It is too much for one person, and God does not want you to burn out. God never intended that the ministry be solo in nature. He designed it as a team effort, a shared ministry.

Sharing ministry is both a practical necessity and a biblical imperative. Circumstances demand it, and the Scriptures teach it for at least three reasons:

1. It is the only way for a church to minister to everyone's needs.

2. It is the only strategy that allows a pastor to develop the right quality of ministry.

3. It enables various people to discover and develop their ministry gifts and abilities.

In Exodus 18, thousands of people were standing for hours during the day, returning drained and discouraged to their tents at night. Moses was at his wits' end, and the people were frustrated and discontented. By appointing "capable" men to help him (18:25), Moses successfully avoided a potentially explosive situation.

14 How did the apostles use a team approach to ministry in Acts 6?

According to Acts 6, the New Testament church faced much the same problem. As the number of converts multiplied, it became impossible for the apostles to effectively minister to all of the needs. Soon complaints threatened to divide the community. Under God's direction, just as Moses did, the early disciples instituted a shared, team ministry. They appointed seven men, "full of the Spirit and wisdom" to shoulder the increasing responsibilities (6:3–6). As a result, the people's needs were met, and the work of the Lord went forward. Acts 6:7 declares, "So the word of God spread. The number of disciples in Jerusalem increased rapidly and a large number of priests became obedient to the faith."

Pause for a moment and consider what might have happened if Moses had not listened to Jethro's advice. Imagine the loss. Had Moses experienced premature burnout, he might not have written the book of Genesis, not to mention the entire Pentateuch. The story of creation, Abraham's faith, Joseph's dreams, the burning bush, or the Ten Commandments may not have been told through him. In fact, the whole history of Israel might have been decidedly different!

What of today's pastors? Do they have too much to do? Do they feel overwhelmed? How much time do they spend taking care of details, ministering to needs that trained laypersons could meet? How long has it been since they spent quality time in God's presence? Do they have a regular day off? Do they set time aside for themselves and for their family? When did they last read a book for the sheer pleasure of reading? Are the pastors making a lasting contribution to the Kingdom, or are they simply engaging in continuous busywork? While I do not want to belabor the point, the scriptural principles of shared ministry are clear and demand answers.

Herman Melville's *Moby Dick* contains a violent, turbulent scene in which a whaleboat scuds across a frothing ocean in pursuit of the great white whale, Moby Dick. The sailors labor fiercely, every muscle taut and all attention and energy concentrated on the task. The cosmic conflict between good and evil is joined: chaotic sea and demonic sea monster versus the morally outraged Captain Ahab. Yet in this boat is one man who does nothing. He doesn't hold an oar; he doesn't perspire; and he doesn't shout. He is languid in the uproar. This man is the harpooner, quiet and poised, waiting. "To insure the greatest efficiency in the dart, the harpooners of this world must start to their feet from out of idleness, and not from out of toil" (1998, 281).

As Melville's narrative illustrates, a shared, team approach is vital to organizational success. A shared ministry enables a pastor to enter the pulpit refreshed in mind and spirit. It allows the pastor to spend time alone with God and enhances the effectiveness and longevity of his or her ministry. Meanwhile, it gives the church body an opportunity to develop its ministry gifts. Shared ministry "will make your load lighter, because they will share it with you. If you do this and God so commands, you will be able to stand the strain" (Exodus 18:22–23).

Ministry is built on the foundations of a call, character, and gifts. A minister's call is his or her anchor, the center point and defining truth on which he or she orders all of life. The pastor's character is the heart and soul of the ministry. It keeps the pastor on course regardless of what others do, for what pastors *are* speaks louder than what they *do*. Finally, the exercise of ministers' gifts reflects their commitment to excellence, to do what they can to the best of their ability, in light of their strengths and weaknesses. Those who attend to these three principles of a call, godly character, and gifts will most likely have a long, effective ministry.

Test Yourself

Circle the letter of the *best* answer.

1. The call of God is like a minister's anchor in that it
a) shows the minister which direction to go.
b) shows who God wants the minister to be.
c) helps the minister stand firm during hard times.
d) keeps the minister from teaching false doctrine.

2. According to our study, a ministerial call is tested by time and
a) persecution.
b) education.
c) popularity.
d) open doors.

3. The time test usually proves that a minister's
a) call is genuine.
b) education is adequate.
c) age is sufficient.
d) life is sanctified.

4. If a person is called into the ministry, he or she should
a) get married and go to Bible school.
b) start preaching at large churches.
c) choose twelve disciples.
d) start serving in small ways.

5. What is the most important element of being a minister?
a) Skills
b) Character
c) Talents
d) Knowledge

6. What you do is not as important as
a) who you are.
b) who you know.
c) what you feel.
d) what others do.

7. Good character is best built by
a) studying theology.
b) listening to sermons.
c) thinking and acting right.
d) praying for a person.

8. Pastors should primarily focus on
a) developing their strengths.
b) teaching their staff members.
c) improving their weaknesses.
d) managing church business.

9. Pastors best make up for personal weaknesses by
a) hiring assistants like themselves.
b) mastering all ministry skills.
c) building effective teams.
d) acquiring more training.

10. Ministry is built on a call,
a) skills, and abilities.
b) talent, and choices.
c) character, and gifts.
d) gifts, and talent.

Responses to Interactive Questions
Chapter 1

Some of these responses may include information that is supplemental to the IST. These questions are intended to produce reflective thinking beyond the course content and your responses may vary from these examples.

1 Explain how the minister's call is in many respects like an anchor.

The call to ministry encourages, gives direction, and holds the minister on course when doubtful and discouraging times come. This is much like the anchor holds a boat steady during normal and especially stormy weather.

2 How does time test what we think may be the call of God?

It allows more opportunity for God, circumstances, and others to confirm the call.

3 What is the door test of a call to ministry?

To test whether a call to ministry is genuine, one can step through the doors of opportunity to serve, even in small ways, following through on each one faithfully. At the same time, the person recognizes that closed doors are notices to seek the Lord for further direction.

4 Contrast God's first call to Moses with the call at the burning bush.

Accounts in Acts and Hebrews teach us that Moses' first call (at forty) was an "inner sense" of purpose and direction, while his second call (at eighty) was an overt, unmistakable encounter with God that is specific and detailed.

5 Explain whether your call is more like the first or second call of Moses.

Answers will vary. Most ministers identify with the first call.

6 Summarize three truths from Moses' life in reference to his call.

God calls His servants in different ways. We must not run ahead of God, in His timing or His method, nor try to do in the flesh what must be accomplished by the Spirit.

7 In 1 Timothy 3:2–7, how many requirements relate to character, skill, or talent?

All in some way relate to character. Several can be either.

8 Read Matthew 7:22–23, and explain whether you believe the people in this passage had good character.

Answers will vary. Though they did the "right things," it was evident that God had no part in their activity.

9 Describe a minister you know who has good character.

Answers will vary but should include some aspect of the qualities listed in the course.

10 According to Paul, what results if a pastor has good character, spiritual ministry, and sound doctrine?

The foundation of truth relative to each becomes evident to others and preserves the minister and those under his or her ministry.

11 How does Satan usually tempt people?

Through small steps of disobedience; step by step

12 Summarize the principle of Luke 16:10.

Those who handle small responsibilities poorly or dishonestly are vulnerable to mishandling greater ones. Faithfulness in little things prepares a person for faithfulness in the big moments.

13 What is the greatest challenge of ministry?

The greatest challenge is handling, in God's grace, the breadth of ministry.

14 How did the apostles use a team approach to ministry in Acts 6?

They recommended that the people choose a team (seven men) with capable skills, hearts, and spirits to attend to the daily administration of the peoples' needs. The apostles were then freed to seek and prepare the teaching of God's Word.

The Devotional Life of a Pastor

Effective ministry flows from a living relationship with the Lord. For that reason, it is absolutely critical that every pastor maintain a regular devotional life. A pastor's devotional life differs from his or her prayer and study in the normal course of pastoral duties in one key way: Pastoral prayer and study are primarily vocational, focusing on ministry issues. A pastor's devotional life, on the other hand, focuses on matters of the heart, addressing the pastor's personal walk with God. Both of these are vital to effective ministry. Minimizing either one disserves the pastor and those he or she serves.

The first step in developing a meaningful devotional life is finding a good model. Any number of godly individuals could fill this role, but none is more qualified than the Lord Jesus himself. Both the purity of His personal life and the power of His ministry flowed from His relationship with the Father. The quality of that relationship with God the Father resulted from Jesus' **spiritual disciplines**—what we refer to as our devotional life. When Jesus lived on earth, He voluntarily laid aside the advantages of His divine nature (Philippians 2:6–8). He limited himself to the resources available to us, making Him just as dependent on God as we are. Peter confirmed this in his sermon at Cornelius's home when he said, "God anointed Jesus of Nazareth with the Holy Spirit and power, and . . . he went around doing good and healing all who were under the power of the devil, because God was with him" (Acts 10:38). Although the devotional life has many dimensions, in this chapter we will limit our study to the three most important **spiritual disciplines** for believers: prayer, study, and fasting.

Lesson 2.1   Prayer

Objective
2.1.1   Explain principles related to prayer.

Lesson 2.2   Study

Objectives
2.2.1   Identify questions that should be asked when studying the Holy Scriptures.
2.2.2   Discuss the value of studying books by wise authors.

Lesson 2.3   Fasting

Objective
2.3.1   Summarize the times, types, and benefits of fasting.

2.1.1
OBJECTIVE

Explain principles related to prayer.

1 Read and summarize Mark 1:35; 6:46; and Luke 22:39.

2 Identify four times when Jesus prayed before key events.

3 What can you receive from devotional prayer?

4 Define devotional prayer.

Prayer

Prayer is to the soul what breath is to the body. It restores our spiritual vitality, reshaping us into God's image. It aligns our thoughts and feelings with the Father's desires. It enlarges our vision and helps us to think God's thoughts. Prayer puts all of life into focus and brings eternity into focus.

In this section, we will focus only on devotional prayer. By its very nature, devotional prayer focuses on the inner issues of our own spiritual development. Spiritual warfare and intercessory prayer focus on the concerns of others. While these are important dimensions of our prayer life, they are beyond the scope of devotional praying in general and this study in particular.

Because Jesus is our model, we will begin by examining what the Scriptures reveal about His prayer life. Even a casual look at the Gospels shows that prayer permeated the whole of Jesus' life. He prayed in public and in private. Long after most had retired for the night, Jesus prayed. While others slept, He arose in the predawn darkness to seek the Father's face (Mark 1:35). He often slipped away to pray in the mountains (Mark 6:47) or in other quiet places (Luke 22:39).

Prayer marked every significant event in His life, from His baptism (Luke 3:21) to His death (23:34). Before choosing the twelve disciples, Jesus prayed all night (6:12). Luke reports that Jesus was praying when He was transfigured (9:29). And in Gethsemane, He prayed so earnestly that His "sweat was like drops of blood falling to the ground" (22:44).

For Jesus, prayer was a way of life. It was not a duty but an opportunity. In prayer, He experienced fellowship with the Father that nourished His soul. He received guidance for His life's work and anointing for His ministry. Prayer was the most important discipline of His earthly existence and the source of His strength. If prayer was so critical to the life and ministry of our Lord, how much more essential is it for pastors today?

Communion with the Lord

First and foremost, prayer is fellowship or communion with the Lord. Its only agenda is being with Him. Adam enjoyed this type of fellowship with God before the Fall, as they walked together in the Garden at the close of the day and talked as friend to friend. Enoch also experienced an intimate relationship with God: He "walked with God; then he was no more, because God took him away" (Genesis 5:24).

Sometimes when I pray, it seems as though God is nearer than the breath I breathe. Once, this happened to me early on a Sunday morning as I sat in my study preparing my heart to minister. Suddenly, I sensed the Lord's presence. His nearness was as real as if He had assumed a physical form and was sitting in the room with me. He was comfortably close but not intrusive. Although neither of us spoke a word, we were not separated by the silence. We were communicating without words, like familiar friends, or a couple in love for whom words are unnecessary. After a few minutes, the press of time called me back to the task of ministry, and I could almost see Jesus smile as I gave myself to the work we both loved. Yet I realized anew that the work—the ministry—would be meaningless without the relationship.

Of course, not every time of prayer will be like that, nor should we expect it to be. The rarer an experience, the more special it is. If all our prayer times were "special," they would become commonplace to us; they would lose their "specialness." More often than not, our prayer times will be ordinary—no less real than the "special" experiences, only more routine.

5 Using a New Testament Bible figure, illustrate how work for God can begin to replace a relationship with God.

It is easy, and not uncommon, to become so consumed with the work of the ministry that we allow it to replace our personal relationship with the Lord. Like the prodigal son's older brother (Luke 15:25–32), we may have a "working" relationship with the Father without really knowing Him. Devotional prayer provides the perfect counterbalance, reminding us that we are not only God's co-laborers (1 Corinthians 3:9) but also His children, "heirs of God and co-heirs with Christ" (Romans 8:17).

The work we do for God is eternally important, but it is never more important than our relationship with Him. This principle is taught throughout the Scriptures, but especially so in the account of Mary and Martha:

> As Jesus and his disciples were on their way, he came to a village where a woman named Martha opened her home to him. She had a sister called Mary, who sat at the Lord's feet listening to what he said. But Martha was distracted by all the preparations that had to be made. She came to him and asked, "Lord, don't you care that my sister has left me to do the work by myself? Tell her to help me!"

> "Martha, Martha," the Lord answered, "you are worried and upset about many things, but only one thing is needed. Mary has chosen what is better, and it will not be taken away from her." (Luke 10:38–42)

Martha's preparations and work were important, but not as essential as being with Jesus. Jesus said that Mary chose what was better by sitting at His feet and listening to Him (10:42). In other words, Jesus emphasized that *being* is more important than *doing* and that relationship always comes before ministry. You can do God's work without being God's person, but you cannot be God's person without doing God's work.

Insight from the Lord

Devotional prayer helps us become the persons God has called us to be. It focuses on matters of the heart. It causes us to examine ourselves and our relationships in light of God's Word. This introspection and evaluation is based not on our own merits but on the sanctifying work of the Holy Spirit.

Although we can be tempted in any way at any time, as we mature in the Lord, the nature of our temptations tends to change. New believers often struggle with the more obvious temptations of the human nature, such as greed, lust, and materialism. However, as we grow in the Lord, our struggles frequently involve the more subtle temptations of the heart. Since the heart is deceitful by nature (Jeremiah 17:9), people of faith must depend on the Lord to help them overcome these issues.

We learn much about ourselves by prayerfully contemplating the way we interact with people. These interactions reflect the character of our inner being, just as light and heat are manifestations of fire. The crucible of interpersonal relationships reveals the true nature of our hearts. In moments of pressure or confrontation, our true self is revealed. We often excuse fleshly displays without examining their roots, or we blame them on others. Yet Jesus said, "Out of the overflow of the heart the mouth speaks. The good man brings good things out of the good stored up in him, and the evil man brings evil things out of the evil stored up in him" (Matthew 12:34–35).

Developing the kind of spiritual understanding that prayer gives means first making a commitment to it. That is, if you want the spiritual insights of prayer, you must commit to praying. It must not be an option. You must see prayer as a spiritual discipline necessary to your personal growth and wholeness.

Then, you must set aside time on a regular basis to wait before the Lord. Present the circumstances and relationships of your life to Him for examination (Psalm 139:23–24). Be sensitive to the thoughts and impressions you receive, as these are often insights from the Lord.

6 Why should each pastor write daily in a prayer journal or notebook?

In this regard, it may be effective to use a prayer journal or notebook. By writing out my thoughts and feelings, I am better able to understand them. For instance, some years ago I was having difficulty with a staff member and found myself dealing with a lot of anger. In an attempt to get things into perspective, I wrote in my prayer journal:

Lord,
I've had to deal with anger a lot over the years.
And I've used a variety of strategies—
  I've suffered in silence and grown bitter.
  I've lashed out in revenge and lived to regret it.
  I've tried to give in and ended up feeling used and trapped.
  I've confronted in love, tough love,
    and grieved as I was misunderstood and feared.
Is there a good way of dealing with anger?
  Quickly before it gets dug in,
    before it becomes a part of my psyche?
  Confession to God . . . forgiveness of the perpetrator?
Still, Lord, there must be a better way.
An attitude, a way of looking at things, that nips it in the bud.
For me it means knowing when to give in . . . graciously . . .
  and knowing what things are mine to give.
For me it means standing firm . . . up front . . .
  when the issue is non-negotiable.
I cannot hope it will "work itself out."
I cannot need the approval of my colleagues so much
  that I am unable to take a stand.
When I postpone dealing with an issue, I hurt everyone involved.
  Anger hangs thick and heavy between us
    and by the time we deal with it
  it has become a monster raging out of control.
Sanctify me, Lord.
Let me freely yield that which is mine to yield.
Show me, help me to know,
  what is Yours to guard
  and what is mine to give.
In Jesus' name I pray. Amen.

Through that experience and others, I learned about the kind of person I was at the time. Some of it was painful and unflattering. I discovered that some of my anger stemmed from hurts, carefully tended for years, which suddenly exploded in carnal ways. The issue that finally triggered my temper was usually a legitimate concern that was lost in the outpouring of my wrath. Thankfully, the Lord is continuing to perform a sanctifying work in me, and I am no longer the angry man I was. Still, I do not believe I could have overcome my anger without the insights provided by the discipline of journaling. Madeleine L'Engle writes:

If I can write things out I can see them, and they are not trapped within . . . . Not long ago someone I love said something that wounded me grievously, and I was desolate that this person could have made such a comment to me. So, in great pain, I crawled to my journal and wrote it all out in a great burst of self-pity. And when I had set it down, when I had it before me, I saw that something I myself had said had called forth the words that had hurt me so. It had, in fact, been my own fault. But I would never have seen it if I had not written it out. (1980, 5)

Like L'Engle, we often have only a dim understanding of an experience or situation until we write it down. When we do express it in writing, our thoughts and feelings seem to crystallize, enabling us to present our true situation to God for healing and growth. Elizabeth O'Connor states:

7 Writing in a prayer journal forces a person to use what three tools?

> Among our primary tools for growth are to reflect on self, examine self, and question self. The journal is one of the most helpful ways we have to cultivate these . . . . We need structures that encourage us to use and practice them. Journal writing forces a person to reflect. When we commit what we see to writing, we are taking what is inside us and placing it outside us. We are holding a piece of our life in our hands where we can look at it, and meditate on it, and deepen our understanding of it. (1982, 100)

Robert Wood also encourages people to write in a prayer journal, saying,

> Keeping a journal is the process of digesting the spiritual meaning of the events of each day. These events have come quickly; they have come with feeling, some with thinking, some with just doing. Sometime during your hurried day you must take time out to reflect on the deeper significance of these events and to digest them into your own 'life-sustaining milk.' As you make sense of them, you will put them in perspective of their importance and lasting value to your own life. (1978, 9)

Personal journals have played a vital role throughout church history. From St. Augustine to Pascal to the Society of Friends, many believers and church leaders have used some form of journal for spiritual discipline and growth. A wise pastor will follow in the steps of these leaders of faith.

Prayer as a Privilege

Talking to God is a delight

8 What are three principles concerning prayer?

One final thought to consider is this: *Prayer is a privilege*. When I was a young man preparing for the ministry, prayer was greatly emphasized. In fact, I was left with the distinct impression that it was an obligation. But as I matured in the Lord, I began to see it as a discipline more than a duty—a discipline that, in my life, would eventually turn into a delight. Now, after nearly forty years in active ministry, I understand more clearly that prayer is, first and foremost, a privilege. If I tried to schedule a meeting with the President, I would probably have a slim chance of seeing him. Even if I were to gain an audience with the President or some other earthly dignitary, it would likely be for only a few minutes. Yet God has promised to listen, to meet with me, every time I whisper a prayer. Think of it: The infinite, all-powerful, sovereign God wants to meet with us! He has given His word that He will be there. He invites us to "approach the throne of grace with confidence, so that we may receive mercy and find grace to help us in our time of need" (Hebrews 4:16). Now that is a privilege!

Study

Whereas prayer is generally subjective, the discipline of study, specifically the study of God's Word, is more objective. As we study the Word, we realize that the Bible is not just another book for literary pleasure and admiration; it is food for the soul. It is living and active (Hebrews 4:12). If we continually put it into practice, it will change our lives.

While studying the Bible as our absolute authority of faith and conduct is essential, reading and studying other works about the inner life is also beneficial. These sources, however, must never contradict the Holy Scriptures. Still, we can learn much from the knowledge and experience of those who have walked this way before us.

Studying God's Word

In the area of Scripture study, once again Jesus is our model. The Gospels include some details about Jesus' prayer life but are silent about His study habits. However, we can clearly infer that He did study God's Word. As a member of a devout Jewish family, Jesus undoubtedly memorized the Scriptures from earliest childhood, a discipline He would have continued throughout His life. Also, in those times, Jewish boys attended classes on the Scriptures in local synagogues, and we know that Nazareth had a synagogue (Matthew 13:53). By the age of twelve, Jesus was so versed in the Scriptures that He astounded the teachers in the temple with His knowledge for three days. Luke says, "Everyone who heard him was amazed at his understanding and his answers" (2:47).

When He was tempted in the desert, Jesus resisted Satan three times by quoting from Scripture: "It is written . . ." (Matthew 4:1–11). God's Word is the sword of the Spirit (Ephesians 6:17). "Humanity, however strong or good, is never a match for evil. Only the Word of God has the authority to resist the power of Satan" (McKenna 1977, 89–90). Like Jesus, we resist the devil by using the sword of the Word.

Jesus' ability to expound the Scriptures was legendary. Again and again, He amazed the crowds with His knowledge of the Law and His wisdom: "All spoke well of him and were amazed at the gracious words that came from his lips" (Luke 4:22). He often quoted from the Psalms and the Prophets, including Isaiah (Matthew 15:7–9), and laced His teaching with references from the Law and the Prophets. He referred to the judgment of Sodom and Gomorrah (10:15), the days of Noah (Luke 17:26), the sign of Jonah (Matthew 12:39–41), and the example of David and the showbread (12:1–8). No one could teach from the Scriptures like He did. "They were amazed at his teaching, because his message had authority" (Luke 4:32).

Later, after His resurrection, Jesus used His scriptural knowledge to teach two disciples on the road to Emmaus. He answered their doubt, despair, and fear by spending hours explaining the Scriptures to them. Luke says, "And beginning at Moses and all the Prophets, he explained to them what was said in all the Scriptures concerning himself" (Luke 24:27).

We read the Bible devotionally on at least three levels. That is, we read Scripture with three questions in mind.

What Is the Context of the Passage?

This question involves several aspects: What did a particular Scripture passage mean to the author? What did it mean to the original readers? What does it mean it light of the surrounding passages? Reading on this level preserves Scripture's objectivity, its historical perspective. It also clarifies the passage's meaning for us as twenty-first-century readers.

2.2.1
OBJECTIVE
Identify questions that should be asked when studying the Holy Scriptures.

9 Give three examples that show Jesus knew the Scriptures.

10 Explain *context*, and identify its two types.

The word *context* comes from two Latin words: *con*, meaning "together," and *textus*, meaning "weave." That is, the meaning of every Scripture verse is woven into its context. Two types of contexts are (1) the historical and (2) the literary (written).

Historical context (setting)

11 Identify three aspects of historical context.

Knowing the **historical context** helps us understand the meaning of a text (Menzies and Menzies 2000, 64). To find the historical context, we must ask questions concerning the speaker, listener, and the problem and solution.

- *Speaker:* Who is writing or speaking, and when did this person write?
- *Listener:* Who was the reader or listener, what was the relationship between the author and speaker, and what were the listener's surroundings?
- *Problem and solution:* What problems and solutions did the author write about, and what principles for living are in the passage?

For example, read 1 Corinthians 13 for context.

1. *The speaker:* Paul wrote 1 Corinthians about AD 55–56, at the end of his three-year stay in Ephesus (Acts 20:31; 1 Corinthians 16:5–8).
2. *The listener:* The readers of 1 Corinthians lived in Corinth, located on a narrow strip of land between the Aegean and Adriatic Seas. It was a large, pagan city known for immorality and idolatry. The Corinthians were mostly Gentiles (1 Corinthians 6:9–11; 8:10; 12:13) who loved wisdom and knowledge (1:18–2:5; 4:10; 8:1–13), and they were proud (4:18; 5:2, 6). Paul started the church at Corinth on his second missionary journey (Acts 18:1–18).
3. *The problem and solution:* Paul wrote 1 Corinthians 13 to show that love is the path to walk on when using spiritual gifts. When believers gather, love guides them to encourage others with their spiritual gifts rather than just encouraging themselves.

In 1 Corinthians, Paul wrote to answer questions and solve problems on these topics:

- Division (1:10–4:21)
- Incest (5:1–13)
- Lawsuits (6:1–11)
- Fornication (6:12–20)
- Marriage (7:1–40)
- Food (8:1–11:1)
- Dress (11:2–16)
- Holy communion (11:17–34)
- Spiritual gifts (12:1–14:40)
- The Resurrection (15:1–58)
- The poor (16:1–11)

Literary context

12 Define *literary context.*

The word *literary* is related to the word *literature*. The **literary context** refers to the written words, paragraphs, and pages that surround a text. Words make up a verse or text; a text is part of a paragraph; a paragraph is part of a chapter; a chapter is part of a book; and a book is part of the Bible. Thus, the *literary context* of a text includes the ideas that come before and after it. For instance, in studying the literary context of 1 Corinthians 13, we must pay careful attention to the chapters immediately before and after, because chapters 12–14 all concern the same topic: spiritual gifts. The biblical authors did not write just one verse for their readers but full accounts or epistles. In fact, the chapter and verse divisions in the Holy Scriptures were added later for easier referencing; they are not from the original authors. Ernest Pettry writes, "Threads are woven into a garment, but it is possible to pull them out. This would damage both the garment and the threads. Likewise, you can pull a text out of its context. But if you do this, you will spoil both the text and the context" (1984, 66–67). The Bible is like a garment—all of it is needed, not just a few threads or a sleeve!

13 How did Satan misuse the literary context of Psalm 91:11–12?

A verse or passage taken out of its literary context is a dangerous weapon of Satan. He has twisted Scripture verses to deceive many Christians, even attempting to use this tactic with the Son of God:

> Then the devil took him to the holy city and had him stand on the highest point of the temple. "If you are the Son of God," he said, "throw yourself down. For it is written: 'He will command his angels concerning you, and they will lift you up in their hands, so that you will not strike your foot against a stone.'" (Matthew 4:5–6)

Satan quoted only part of Psalm 91:11–12. Notice that he left out the key words *in all your ways.* In this way, Satan used the verse out of its literary context. Jumping off the temple is not "in all your ways." This is something not from the heart of God but from the devil. Also, notice the way Jesus rebuked Satan: "It is also written: 'Do not put the Lord your God to the test'" (Matthew 4:7). Jesus referred to the larger literary context of the Bible, balancing one verse with another.

14 Read Matthew 10:9; 10:34; and Luke 2:14. Do you see the importance of understanding each passage in view of its literary context?

Every verse must be interpreted within the literary context of the whole Word of God. The Bible is the sharp, two-edged sword of the Spirit (Ephesians 6:17; Hebrews 4:12). However, a text can become the sword of Satan if it is removed from its context. Peter warned of those who (like Satan) twist and distort the Scriptures to their own destruction (2 Peter 3:16).

Clearly, determining the historical setting and literary context of a passage is an imperative first step when studying the Scriptures.

How Does This Passage Make God Known?

The second question to ask when studying the Bible is, "What does the passage teach about God?" Or, "how is God made known in this passage?" I am told that, when viewed at a certain angle, a copy of the United States Constitution at the Library of Congress seems to portray the image of George Washington, the father of this country. Likewise, when we read the Scriptures in faith, we see them as more than a collection of ancient poetry or proverbs; they become a revelation of God himself, a portrait of our heavenly Father.

Not long ago, my devotional reading of the Bible led me to several days' worth of lengthy genealogies. One morning in exasperation, I prayed, "What is the meaning of all these names?" I did not expect an answer, but suddenly a thought sprang full-blown into my mind. It seemed God was saying, "I am a personal God, and every individual is important to Me. Every time you read a genealogy, I am reminding you that I know your name, as well as the names of your parents and grandparents." Then I remembered Psalm 139:13–17:

> For you created my inmost being;
> > you knit me together in my mother's womb.
> I praise you because I am fearfully and wonderfully made;
> > your works are wonderful,

I know that full well.
My frame was not hidden from you
    when I was made in the secret place.
When I was woven together in the depths of the earth,
    your eyes saw my unformed body.
All the days ordained for me
    were written in your book
    before one of them came to be.
How precious to me are your thoughts, O God!
    How vast is the sum of them!

Needless to say, I will never read the biblical genealogies the same way again. Each time I read them, I will be reminded that God knows who I am and is involved in every aspect of my life.

Thus, by asking the question, "What does this passage say about God?" I come to a fuller understanding and appreciation of His character.

How Can I Personally Apply This Passage?

15   What questions should we ask when studying the Bible?

The third question is more personal: What does this passage say about my own spiritual condition, about my life and standing with God? The Bible is a living book that transcends time and place. God uses His Word to speak directly into our individual situations. We read it to receive a word from Him.

Several years ago, I underwent a difficult time. I appeared to have reached a stalemate in my life and ministry. After several years of remarkable growth, the church I was serving seemed to have reached a plateau; no matter what I tried, we seemed stuck. I felt pressured from many sides, including a small but vocal group in the church who criticized my leadership. To make things worse, my new book was not selling nearly as well as anticipated. As a result of all the stress, I began to doubt the effectiveness of my ministry.

One morning during my devotional time, I came across Psalm 138:7–8. I had read these verses many times before, but that morning the words seemed to leap off the page: "Though I walk in the midst of trouble, you preserve my life; you stretch out your hand against the anger of my foes, with your right hand you save me. The Lord will fulfill his purpose for me; your love, O Lord, endures forever—do not abandon the works of your hands."

Although my situation did not immediately change, I had peace. God had spoken to me through His Word. No matter what others did, He would fulfill His purpose in my life! He might not fulfill my dreams and goals, but He would fulfill His purpose—and that was enough.

When you read the Scriptures, act on what you learn. Apply it! Put it into practice, and let it change your life. We come to the Word of God to be changed, not just to learn facts (Foster 1978, 60).

Studying Additional Writings

2.2.2
OBJECTIVE
Discuss the value of studying books by wise authors.

While the Holy Scriptures are the only infallible, inspired Word of God, pastors should not limit their study or devotional reading to the Bible. Reading a book or article by an author whose heart and mind is steeped in God's truth is like sitting at the feet of a truly wise person. These writings can be a fountain of life (Proverbs 13:14).

Early in my ministry, I served churches in remote rural areas. My opportunities for continuing education and/or meaningful fellowship with my peers were extremely limited, so I devoted myself to reading. In this way, many different authors shaped my thoughts and enriched my life, and I will always be in their debt. Without their influence, I would not be the person or the minister I now am.

16 What is the value of reading other books in addition to the Bible?

Today, I do not have the same limitations I once had. I no longer serve in a remote area, and in recent years I have been enormously blessed to interact with some of the church's brightest leaders and anointed servants. However, my appreciation of good books is unabated. A good book renews me in a way nothing else can. And I am not necessarily talking about weighty books that tax my mind; rather, I treasure insightful books that touch my soul. Such writings give me a glimpse of both the tenderness and tragedy of life and put me in touch with God and my own life experiences. In my opinion, any book that can do these things is worth whatever it costs and more.

The books and authors that appeal to you will vary according to the particular situations you face. More than once, I have started reading a highly recommended book only to lay it aside in frustration after a chapter or two. Usually, the problem was timing. That is, I may not have been spiritually or emotionally ready for that particular book at that point in time. Sometimes when I return to the same book a year or two later, I find I cannot put it down because I am in a new and different season of my life and it speaks to my soul.

17 What do the books that pastors own tell about them?

A final thought to consider is that an individual's library or choice of reading material reveals a great deal about him or her. Ministers focused on building large churches may have many books on leadership and church growth. Ministers primarily concerned about their own personal spiritual growth may have books mostly about prayer and the inner life. However, balanced ministers will have both, since they realize the value of personal spiritual development as well as professional competence.

LESSON
2.3

2.3.1
OBJECTIVE
Summarize the times, types, and benefits of fasting.

Fasting

Fasting is an often misunderstood and ignored discipline. Although believers do not normally give fasting the same attention they give prayer and Bible study, the Scriptures put it in the same category. And fasting is for all believers—not just leaders. Arthur Wallis (1971) writes,

> Neither did Jesus say if you fast (see Matthew 6:16), as though fasting were something the disciples might or might not be led to do or as though it only applied to a select few, apostles or prophets, preachers or leaders. He stated unambiguously, categorically and without qualification to the mass of his disciples, "When you fast . . ." He left us no doubt that he took it for granted that his disciples would be obeying the leading of the Spirit in this matter of fasting.

When Should I Fast?

18 When does Jesus expect believers to fast?

Jesus simply assumed that believers would fast. Matthew 9:14–15 states, "Then John's disciples came and asked him, 'How is it that we and the Pharisees fast, but your disciples do not fast?' Jesus answered, 'How can the guests of the bridegroom mourn while he is with them? The time will come when the bridegroom will be taken from them; then they will fast.'"

Unfortunately, many pastors presume that God mandated only occasional special fasting. That is, they believe there is no need to fast unless they receive specific direction from the Lord to do so or a major crisis arises. It is true that certain circumstances or the need for distinctive spiritual direction should call us to periods of special fasting. However, Jesus seems to expect more. The inference of His teaching in Matthew 6:16–18 and 9:14–15 is clear: Our lives should include regular times of fasting, just as we engage in regular times of prayer.

How Should I Fast?

19 Summarize four different kinds of fasts.

The Bible describes several types of fasts, including (1) a normal fast, (2) an absolute fast, (3) a partial or "Daniel" fast, and (4) a supernatural fast.

- **Normal fast:** In a normal fast, a person abstains from all foods—solid or liquid—except water. Jesus may have engaged in a normal fast in the wilderness after His baptism. Luke 4:2 says, "He ate nothing during those [forty] days, and at the end of them he was hungry."

- **Absolute fast:** In an absolute (or complete) fast, a person does not eat or drink anything, even water. In the Bible, this type of fast, generally lasting three days, seems to have been an exceptional measure for an exceptional situation (see Esther 4:16). The Scriptures also indicate that a person should fast this way only because of a clear command from God and never for more than three days.

- **Partial fast:** A partial fast is sometimes called a "Daniel" fast because of Daniel's example: "At that time I, Daniel, . . . ate no choice food; no meat or wine touched my lips; and I used no lotions at all until the three weeks were over" (Daniel 10:2–3). Thus, in a partial fast, a person does not totally abstain from food but limits the *kinds* of food he or she eats.

20 Identify the type of fasting you do most, and describe your routine.

- **Supernatural fast:** Like an absolute fast, a supernatural fast calls for a person to abstain from any food or drink, including water, but for an extended period of time. Normally, a person cannot survive without water for more than a few days, but God may supernaturally enable people to fast like this for a longer period. The Bible records only two instances of a supernatural fast, the first involving Moses. He writes, "When I went up on the mountain to receive the tablets of stone, the tablets of the covenant that the Lord had made with you, I stayed on the mountain forty days and forty nights; I ate no bread and drank no water" (Deuteronomy 9:9). The second instance involved Elijah, when he traveled forty days and forty nights from the God-given strength of heavenly food (1 Kings 19:8).

What Does Fasting Accomplish?

In one church where I served as senior pastor, fasting became an important part of the spiritual disciplines our congregation practiced. For many years, we set aside Tuesday as a church-wide day of prayer and fasting. We also designated the thirteenth week of every quarter as a week of extraordinary fasting and prayer. During these times, we kept the sanctuary open for prayer all day and held special congregational prayer both morning and evening.

Initially, I expected those days to be times of intense spiritual anointing; but as a rule, they were not, at least for me personally. For example, I entered my first ten-day fast with high expectations. I not only abstained from all food but also turned the television off. I did not read anything other than the Bible and a few devotional classics. Determining to focus all my attention on God during those ten days, I anticipated hearing clearly from the Lord. I expected to receive special insight and direction. I expected to feel vibrantly alive and aware of God's nearness, but I did not.

21 What are some benefits of fasting?

It is the blood of Jesus that Cleares the "landscape"

Through my experiences, I have discovered that the benefits of fasting almost always come after it is over. While a person may have moments of spiritual insight during an extended fast, for the most part, fasting is simply hard work. It is not a time of spiritual harvest or even planting—it is more like clearing the land. That is, the spiritual landscape is covered with rocks, stumps, and underbrush. When you fast, you work with the Spirit to clear the field so it can be prepared for seed. But preparing the land is hard work! Figuratively speaking, you may get blisters on your hands, your back may hurt, and you may get sunburned and thirsty. Yet it is worth it, because you are clearing new spiritual territory for God.

Some years ago, after months of intense fasting, I finally began to reap the benefits. Ego and ambition had long formed a stronghold in my life, but I was mostly blind to it. What was so obvious to others was invisible to me. Although I realized something was limiting my spiritual growth and effectiveness for God, I had no idea what it was. Little by little, through fasting, God prepared me for the painful truth.

The first critical moment occurred while I conducted a conference with an evangelist with a prophetic ministry. One night, God gave him a vision for me in which a large green serpent rose from a river and fastened itself on my leg, pulling me into the water. Eventually, the evangelist found a lion to kill the serpent and rescue me. The moment the evangelist began sharing the vision, it seemed as though a sword pierced my heart. The conviction of the Spirit was so great that I was in physical pain. I realized that the green serpent represented the lust for power, and it had fastened itself on me. It was attempting to destroy me.

Every time I went to prayer for the next six or seven weeks, God revealed another area where I had abused power—where my ego and ambition had caused me to act in un-Christlike, hurtful ways. One day, God reminded me of something terrible I had said in anger to my wife, Brenda, years before. Although I had already apologized, until that moment, I did not realize how deeply I had wounded her. There, in God's presence, it seemed as though her pain became my own, and I became very ashamed. Another day, God brought a young man named Terry to my mind. He was part of a congregation I pastored in my early years of ministry, and I had crushed his spirit. On another occasion, the Lord revealed the hidden depths of my critical spirit, especially toward other ministers. Day after day, week after week, this soul-searching went on, this awesome battle between the Lion of Judah and the serpent of power. With each memory, I gasped with pain and wept in sorrow and repentance before the Lord. I begged Him to change me, to create in me a new heart of humility and service.

The final breakthrough came during a conference for ministers our church hosted. As I stepped to the pulpit to lead in prayer, God's presence came upon me suddenly, overwhelmingly. Wave after wave of His glorious love washed over me, and as it did, I was overcome with weeping. I could not stand. I fell to my knees and pressed my forehead against the floor. God's overwhelming holiness surrounded me, and I have never felt so unclean. Every shortcoming, every failure, was shamefully obvious, yet I did not feel condemned. I felt absolutely unworthy yet totally accepted, completely loved. Somehow I knew this was the beginning of the end. The enemy's stronghold had been broken, and victory was mine!

22 Has God revealed anything to you through fasting? Explain.

Perhaps this stronghold of power and ambition could have been broken without the discipline of fasting, but I doubt it. I am not saying that ego or ambition never tempts me, because I will probably have to contend with them all of my life. But through fasting, God has broken their grip on me. Jesus taught that some spiritual battles are won only through prayer and fasting (Matthew 17:21).

The benefits of fasting are many: increased effectiveness in ministry, anointing for signs and wonders, power in intercessory prayer, spiritual discernment, special guidance, and financial provision, among others. In short, fasting is a key discipline in becoming the man or woman God has called you to be. It is little wonder, then, that John Wesley refused to ordain anyone into the ministry who did not fast at least twice a week (Foster 1978, 44–45).

To summarize, prayer renews our spirits and reshapes us into God's image. The study of God's Word helps us put Scripture into practice and allows it to change our lives. Fasting brings benefits—many of them after the fast ends. A healthy spiritual life, with these three disciplines in operation, therefore brings about effective ministry.

Test Yourself

Circle the letter of the *best* answer.

1. During times of devotional prayer, Christians
   a) fight spiritual battles.
   b) fellowship with God.
   c) plan sermon outlines.
   d) ask God to help others.

2. What must believers do to grow spiritually?
   a) Show compassion
   b) Preach
   c) Pray
   d) Acquire training

3. What does the historical context include?
   a) Author
   b) Outline
   c) Theme
   d) Grammar

4. While studying, a preacher should always ask what the text says about
   a) Israel.
   b) God.
   c) prophecy.
   d) faith.

5. The Bible is still relevant because it
   a) is a living message.
   b) changes over time.
   c) has hidden meanings.
   d) contains some truth.

6. Pastors should read books by wise authors to
   a) help them form opinions.
   b) provide insights for theological debates.
   c) provide a break from the Holy Scriptures.
   d) acquire practical advice for ministry.

7. Personal Bible study can be replaced by
   a) studying for ministry.
   b) reading spiritual books.
   c) listening to sermons.
   d) none of the above.

8. Jesus taught that Christians should fast
   a) at least once a week.
   b) on special occasions. *(Spirit led occasions)*
   c) only for healing needs.
   d) on a regular basis.

9. A "Daniel fast" is another name for a
   a) normal fast.
   b) partial fast. *abstained wine + meat*
   c) complete fast.
   d) supernatural fast.

10. A common spiritual benefit of fasting is
    a) a larger church.
    b) financial gain.
    c) loss of weight.
    d) wisdom to lead.

Responses to Interactive Questions
Chapter 2

Some of these responses may include information that is supplemental to the IST. These questions are intended to produce reflective thinking beyond the course content and your responses may vary from these examples.

1   Read and summarize Mark 1:35; 6:46; and Luke 22:39.

Jesus rose early in the morning to privately seek God in prayer (Mark 1:35). Later in the day, Jesus went aside (mountainside) to privately seek God in prayer (Mark 6:46). Jesus prayed at the Mount of Olives, sweating drops of blood in His earnestness (Luke 22:39).

2   Identify four times when Jesus prayed before key events.

He prayed (1) at His baptism, (2) before choosing the Twelve, (3) before He was transfigured, and (4) before He was led away for trial and crucifixion.

3   What can you receive from devotional prayer?

Prayer can give fellowship with God, guidance for personal growth and ministry, and strength to do what is needed.

4   Define devotional prayer.

Answers may vary. Personal fellowship with God

5   Using a New Testament Bible figure, illustrate how work for God can begin to replace a relationship with God.

Martha (Luke 10:38–42)

6   Why should each pastor write daily in a prayer journal or notebook?

Personal writing in a journal can release and monitor a minister's spiritual direction as the Holy Spirit sheds light on it.

7   Writing in a prayer journal forces a person to use what three tools?

(1) Self-reflection, (2) self-examination, and (3) self-questioning

8   What are three principles concerning prayer?

Prayer (1) offers communion with God, (2) opens us to insight from the Lord, and (3) is a privilege.

9   Give three examples that show Jesus knew the Scriptures.

(1) Jesus confronted Satan with Scripture (Matthew 4), (2) quoted and personally identified with Isaiah 61 (Matthew 15:7–9), and (3) clarified the meaning of many messianic Scripture verses to the two disciples on the road to Emmaus (Luke 24:27).

10 Explain context, and identify its two types.

Context is the entire passage into which a text is woven, or the entire situation within which an event occurs; (1) historical context and (2) literary context

11 Identify three aspects of historical context.

(1) Speaker (writer), (2) listeners (audience), and (3) problems and solutions (purpose of the document)

12 Define literary context.

Studying literary context means trying to understand a passage in relation to the additional information before and after it, as well as its specific part as a segment of a larger subject. The context to consider may include either the words, paragraphs, and chapters around the passage or the entire Bible.

13 How did Satan misuse the literary context of Psalm 91:11–12?

Satan implied that divine protection (not being harmed) promised in the psalm was independent of total reliance on God and obedience to Him.

14 Read Matthew 10:9, 10:34, and Luke 2:14. Do you see the importance of understanding each passage in view of its literary context?

Answer may vary.

15 What questions should we ask when studying the Bible?

(1) What is the context? (2) What does the passage teach about God? (3) How can I apply the passage to my life?

16 What is the value of reading other books in addition to the Bible?

You can gain from the wisdom learned by others who have applied the truth of God's Word to their life and ministries.

17 What do the books that pastors own tell about them?

A pastor's library reveals his or her focus or particular ministry emphasis and desired area of spiritual growth.

18 When does Jesus expect believers to fast?

Jesus said when, not if, you fast (Matthew 6:16). Obedience in this area will keep all believers attuned to the Spirit's teaching and leading today, as it did the early disciples.

19 Summarize four different kinds of fasts.

(1) Normal fast: short time of prayer, denying all but water; (2) Absolute fast: limited time of prayer, denying all foods or liquid; (3) Partial fast: limited time of prayer, denying certain foods; and (4) Supernatural fast: extended prayer, denying all foods and liquids

20 Identify the type of fasting you do most, and describe your routine.

Answers will vary.

21 What are some benefits of fasting?

Increased effectiveness in ministry; anointing for miracles; power in intercessory prayer; spiritual discernment, among others

22 Has God revealed anything to you through fasting? Explain.

Answers will vary.

The Personal Life of a Pastor

Ministry is almost always public, to some degree. Still, the quality of ministry is shaped in large part by pastors' personal lives. An individual's personal life encompasses his or her core relationships, including relationships with God, family members, and friends. Paul addresses these issues in 1 Timothy 3:2–7, where he lists some qualifications for ministers:

> Now the overseer must be above reproach, the husband of but one wife, temperate, self-controlled, respectable, hospitable, able to teach, not given to drunkenness, not violent but gentle, not quarrelsome, not a lover of money. He must manage his own family well and see that his children obey him with proper respect. (If anyone does not know how to manage his own family, how can he take care of God's church?) He must not be a recent convert, or he may become conceited and fall under the same judgment as the devil. He must also have a good reputation with outsiders, so that he will not fall into disgrace and into the devil's trap.

Today, many women are answering the call to ministry. They face not only all the challenges of confronting people who are opposed to their place in the ministry but also a host of other problems unique to their gender. One of their greatest challenges is finding a place to serve. Although the Assemblies of God has a long history of ordaining women, many congregations remain skeptical toward women who serve in the role of pastor. Women who are able to find a position must often balance the demands of both ministry and family.

This chapter will address issues surrounding the personal lives of both men and women, whether married or single, in ministry.

Lesson 3.1   The Married Pastor's Perspective

Objective

3.1.1   Describe what happens to a marriage when a pastor puts ministry first.

Lesson 3.2   The Single Pastor's Perspective

Objectives

3.2.1   Identify perceptions of single ministers held by peers and superiors.

3.2.2   Explain the focus on marriage and family within the evangelical church, and list its potential problems for single ministers.

3.2.3   Identify and describe single people in the Scriptures who were used by God.

3.2.4   Identify and describe five misconceptions about single ministers.

Lesson 3.3   The Female Pastor's Perspective

Objectives

3.3.1   Examine the biblical basis for women in ministry and leadership.

3.3.2   Summarize the Assemblies of God position concerning women in ministry.

3.3.3   Describe the Christlike response of obedience to a call.

Lesson 3.4   The Pastor as a Parent

Objectives

3.4.1   Identify the parenting mistakes of Eli, Samuel, and David.

3.4.2   Explain principles concerning children's spiritual training.

Lesson 3.5   The Pastor as a Friend

Objectives

3.5.1   Explain the limitations of pastor–parishioner friendships.

3.5.2   Discuss keys to having healthy ministerial friendships.

3.1.1
OBJECTIVE

Describe what happens to a marriage when a pastor puts ministry first.

The Married Pastor's Perspective

The most important relationship for pastors is their relationship with God. Second to that is their relationship with their spouse. Pastors with good marriages can overcome virtually anything—financial adversity, chronic illness, and even failure and rejection. However, success in other areas cannot fill the void of a strained marriage.

Ministry can be hard on a marriage. For instance, spouses may be tempted to resent the church because of the time and energy a pastor gives to God's work rather than to the family. A spouse may feel guilty for considering the church as a rival for the pastor's attention. Often pastors feel divided, torn between the needs of the church and the needs of their family. They may resent their spouses' attitudes, feeling that the spouses do not value them or their work.

Is there a solution? Can a pastor have an effective ministry without compromising his or her commitment to marriage and family? Rev. Thomas Trask, who formerly served as a general superintendent of the Assemblies of God, USA, counsels pastors to establish biblical priorities. According to Trask, our first priority must be our relationship with God; the second, marriage and family; and the third, ministry. While most pastors agree with these priorities, in reality, they often invert the order, as evidenced by their schedules. Time for God and family is often all but lost in the press of busyness.

Reversed priorities may work for a while, but eventually, the strain on the pastor's marriage takes its toll. Dr. Dennis Guernsey, former associate dean of psychology at Fuller Theological Seminary, stated, "A pastor's wife is put in a terrible bind when the church becomes The Other Woman—but her husband isn't unrighteous for sleeping with her. No one considers this obsession immoral; he's 'doing God's work'" (Merrill 1985, 55). When her pleas to her husband continue to fall on deaf ears, a pastor's wife will likely go to one of two extremes: (1) she may withdraw and suffer in silence, or (2) she may throw herself headlong into becoming a supermom, hoping to win her husband's approval. Effects on male spouses can be equally damaging.

Despite their busyness and apparent success, pastors who invest all their time in ministry are likely as unfulfilled and unsatisfied as their spouses. In their minds, they have probably achieved not only more "success" than they ever dreamed possible but also more frustration. They may puzzle over why they feel this way, wondering where the fulfillment and satisfaction are. Who can they find to share their achievements? Intimacy with their spouse is almost nonexistent, and they discover that their children seem like strangers. To compensate for their inner emptiness, these pastors often work that much harder at ministry, but this only compounds the problem. No matter how much success a pastor achieves in ministry, he or she cannot fill the void left by an empty marriage.

It is not hard to imagine what happens next. In the course of pastoral duties, a minister may need to counsel an estranged spouse in another troubled marriage. This spouse's inner emptiness mirrors the pastor's. Almost without realizing it, the two form an emotional bond, and for the first time in a long while, the minister feels alive. After all, this person appreciates him or her as an individual and a minister. This person really listens and truly cares about the pastor's feelings.

Pastors involved in such a situation would probably be shocked if someone suggested it could quickly lead to a sexual affair. Although they may have never allowed the thought of infidelity to enter their minds, these ministers are now in grave danger of violating their marriage vows and compromising their ministry. They are likely not lustful but simply lonely. Thus, temptation comes disguised as a fulfilling relationship. One professor of pastoral ministry described it this way:

> We pastors really don't have a way to know whether we are successes or failures. We're trying to please a lot of people, and sometimes we don't please any. And along comes this warm, spiritual woman who affirms, affirms, affirms. This is what is so often confessed to me: "But she understood me. She was the only one who affirmed me." And that affirmation can so easily lead to closeness, then affection, then sexuality. ("Forum" 1988, 20)

Of the host of questions this discussion raises, none is more important than "How can I prevent this from happening to me?" The answer is that prevention begins with paying attention to your marriage. Since unpremeditated affairs often result from unfulfilling marriages, you can minimize the risks of infidelity by working to make your marriage all God intends it to be. Spend time with your spouse; share deeply; and forgive easily. While investing in this way may seem simple, it is not easy. To love like that requires a lifelong commitment renewed day by day. You must constantly choose to give your marriage priority time and energy.

In almost forty years of marriage, my wife and I have learned some guidelines that have served us well. We call them the "Ten Commandments for a Healthy Marriage":

1. *Protect your day off at all costs, and spend it together.* If an emergency makes it impossible for you to take your regular day off, reschedule another day immediately. Nothing is more important than the time you share as a couple or a family.
2. *Eat dinner together.* A simple meal can still be a special family time. Dinner conversation is a time for sharing and making memories. Difficult issues should be saved for another time.
3. *Go to bed at the same time.* Nothing undermines marital intimacy faster than separate bedtimes. This too is a time for sharing. It is your opportunity to really talk, to make sure hectic schedules have not caused you to drift apart. Without these set times for togetherness, you risk losing contact with each other in the busyness of life.
4. *Let nothing rob your marriage of the sexual joy God intended.* Sexual intimacy is a God-given gift to be received with thanksgiving and enjoyed within the holy bonds of marriage. It is designed not only for procreation but also for expressing love, giving pleasure, and cultivating intimacy.
5. *Do not hold a grudge.* Do not let past hurts rob you of today's joy. All of us have been hurt by those we love, though some more than others. Nevertheless, the only hope for a marriage lies in the husband and wife's ability to forgive and forget. If you insist on nursing yesterday's hurts, life will lose its flavor and you will become old and bitter.
6. *Do not take separate vacations.* Take trips together. Shared experiences bond you together, whereas separate experiences distance you from one another. Time is one of the most valuable commodities in your marriage, so use it wisely.

1   Briefly explain how a minister can invest in his or her spouse.

7. *Pray together.* Nothing is more personal than your relationship with God. When you invite your spouse to share in your communion with God, you are opening the deepest part of yourself to him or her. It can seem threatening at first, but the rewards more than justify the effort.

8. *Make memories.* Some memories just happen, but the most endearing memories result from careful planning and considerable forethought. While you cannot necessarily plan a memory, you can prepare for it. The couple who makes memories will celebrate growing old together. They will be warmed against winter's chill by the memories of a lifetime cherished and shared.

9. *Do not forget to do the little things.* Little things make the difference between a mediocre marriage and a truly good one. Things like kind words, help with the children, a listening ear, remembering special days, and the feeling that you really care determine the quality of your relationship.

10. *Pledge yourselves not only to physical faithfulness but also to emotional fidelity.* Determine that your emotional needs will be fulfilled only within your marriage. Do not allow friends, family, or work to supply these needs of belonging. Providing for each other's emotional needs will become the strength of your relationship.

Maintaining a healthy marriage does not eliminate temptation, but it does minimize its impact. When your deepest spiritual and emotional needs are met in relationship with God and your spouse, you can respond as a whole person to those who seek your counsel and support. Since your needs are being fulfilled in appropriate ways, you will not need to use ministry situations to establish your value as a person. You may still be tempted, but now you can respond out of wholeness rather than need.

2 How do pastors develop and maintain peace and joy in their families?

A pastor's healthy and fulfilling marriage can serve as a model for other couples in the church. When the congregation sees the pastor's family living out the principles in Ephesians 5:22–33 and other scriptural passages, they are encouraged to do the same. Whatever we teach in precept must be reinforced by example. This is especially true when it comes to marriage. If you are considerate and respectful to your family (1 Peter 1:7), affirming and helpful, loving and kind, your home will likely be a place of joy and peace.

Christ came not to be served but to serve others (Matthew 20:28). He taught that the greatest among us would be the servant of all (23:11), and He modeled such selfless love by washing His disciples' feet. Afterward, He said, "Now that I, your Lord and Teacher, have washed your feet, you also should wash one another's feet. I have set you an example that you should do as I have done for you" (John 13:14–15). In the same way, pastors should love their spouses selflessly. Selfless love has no goal other than to love. It has no hidden agendas and seeks no advantage. It looks for nothing in return. Selfless love simply seeks the highest good for another person. Paul teaches, "Do nothing out of selfish ambition or vain conceit, but in humility consider others better than yourselves. Each of you should look not only to your own interests, but also to the interests of others. Your attitude should be the same as that of Christ Jesus" (Philippians 2:3–5).

An outstanding example of selfless love is the story of Dr. Robertson McQuilkin. In March 1990, he resigned as the president of Columbia Bible College to care for his wife, Muriel, who suffered from the advanced stages of Alzheimer's disease. In his resignation letter, he wrote:

My dear wife, Muriel, has been in failing mental health for about eight years. So far I have been able to carry both her ever-growing needs and my leadership responsibilities at CBC. But recently it has become apparent that Muriel is contented most of the time she is with me and almost none of the time I am away from her. It is not just "discontent." She is filled with fear—even terror—that she has lost me and always goes in search of me when I leave home. Then she may be full of anger when she cannot get to me. So it is clear to me that she needs me now, full-time.

Perhaps it would help you to understand if I shared with you what I shared at the time of the announcement of my resignation in chapel. The decision was made, in a way, 42 years ago when I promised to care for Muriel "in sickness and in health . . . till death do us part." So, as I told the students and faculty, as a man of my word, integrity has something to do with it. But so does fairness. She has cared for me fully and sacrificially all these years; if I cared for her for the next 40 years I would not be out of debt. Duty, however, can be grim and stoic. But there is more; I love Muriel. She is a delight to me—her childlike dependence and confidence in me, her warm love, occasional flashes of that wit I used to relish so, her happy spirit and tough resilience in the face of her continual distressing frustration. I do not have to care for her, I get to! It is a high honor to care for so wonderful a person. (Hughes 1991, 35–36)

As a husband and a minister, I am deeply moved when I read this story. Intuitively, I realize that is the stuff real marriages are made of—commitment and integrity, for better or for worse. Yet we would be mistaken to assume that Dr. McQuilkin's choice was an isolated choice, independent of the hundreds of lesser choices that went into their forty-two years of marriage. In truth, a decision of that magnitude is almost always the culmination of a lifelong series of smaller, daily decisions.

As such, it challenges every one of us to examine the choices we make each day and the way we relate to our spouse. If we hope to have the strength to make that kind of decision when necessary, we must practice selfless love all the days of our lives.

3.2.1
OBJECTIVE
Identify perceptions of single ministers held by peers and superiors.

The Single Pastor's Perspective[1]

Little has been written concerning pastors who are unmarried. It should be stated from the start that the word *single* refers to at least three types of people: the never-married, the widowed, and the divorced.

Single pastors receive a variety of responses from colleagues and congregants concerning their service in ministry. Following are two questions and responses from six single ministers about how people perceive them:

Q: Do you sense any difference in attitude or response from your peers because you are a minister who is single rather than married?

"My peers have been very accepting and supporting of my ministry as a single adult. There hasn't been any negative response that I can recall."
—John, age 40, pastor/director of single adult ministry in an Assemblies of God church

"Having never been married, my peers who have been through divorce are concerned that I may not be able to relate to their circumstances, and rightly so! Although I empathize and am comfortable talking with them about their concerns, I do realize that those who have walked in their shoes may be able to respond more effectively to their questions and needs."
—Vickie, age 44, pastor/director of single adult ministry in a nondenominational church

---

[1] This lesson was written by Rev. Dennis Franck, National Director of the Assemblies of God Single Adults/Young Adults ministry.

"There is more of a 'social attitude' than a ministerial attitude concerning this. Your gifts make a place for you, married or single."

—Sylvia, age 58, missionary in a foreign country

Q: Do you sense any difference in attitude or response from your superiors because you are a minister who is single rather than married?

"I mostly sense different responses when it comes to my personal life. . . . Often people think that being a single person means that life is filled with partying and fun."

—Vickie, age 44, pastor/director of single adult ministry in a nondenominational church

"I can think of none."

—Paul, age 52, Assemblies of God editor/writer/administrator

"Sometimes I feel awkward as a single adult at some church functions (because of others' attitudes) . . . . As years have gone by, though, these people seem to be more comfortable around me."

—Colleen, age 44, pastor/director of single adult ministry in an Assemblies of God church

"Those in authority over me sometimes do not see the opportunity that I have as a single person to serve in ministry without the responsibilities of marriage. They may think not being married is a huge disadvantage and I do not somehow relate to married people."

—Jim, age 30, former development coordinator, national Assemblies of God Single Adult/Young Adult Ministries

The responses show that the opinions and perspectives from the ministers' peers regarding their singleness are usually positive, except in the case of a never-married single adult relating to formerly married single adults. However, the opinions and perspectives of the ministers' superiors about the same issue varied more.

In my twenty-six years of singles ministry in six churches, sermons to thousands across the country in hundreds of churches, and beginning the national single adult ministries office for the Assemblies of God, one thing has become clear: The majority of American evangelical churches focus primarily on marriage and family. That is, pastors and church leaders are usually more concerned about reaching families than about reaching single adults.

The desire and effort to reach families is certainly biblical and should not be discouraged. The dilemma, however, is that most churches put little or no emphasis on reaching single adults. Only 20 percent of the 12,300 U.S. Assemblies of God churches have a targeted ministry to single adults! This reality automatically puts the single minister at a disadvantage because of two major problems:
1. The traditional expectation is that adults should "settle down" and marry, have children, and take their places as responsible, mature families in the church.
2. The reality is that most churches and Christians do not know what to say to a divorced, widowed, or never-married person. Most people do not become involved in their lives beyond polite, expected phrases such as "How are you doing?" and "How can I pray for you?"

Many unmarried ministers are acutely aware of these issues and must work to keep them from hindering their personal and ministry life.

3.2.2
OBJECTIVE

Explain the focus on marriage and family within the evangelical church, and list its potential problems for single ministers.

3   How can ministers help today's church to more effectively reach single adults?

3.2.3
OBJECTIVE
Identify and describe single people in the Scriptures who were used by God.

Single Ministers in the Old Testament

Although marriage was the norm and singleness the exception among the people groups in Old Testament cultures, single ministers clearly existed. The Old Testament gives several significant examples of unmarried people whom God used to fulfill His purposes. Three of these were the prophets Jeremiah, Ezekiel, and Hosea.

Jeremiah

This major prophet was commanded not to marry: "Then the word of the Lord came to me: You must not marry and have sons or daughters in this place" (Jeremiah 16:1–2). Understand that God's command to Jeremiah to stay single was not a rejection of marriage; rather, it related to the particular historical situation. Although we do not know whether Jeremiah's restriction to not marry was ever removed, clearly he is an example of a great prophet who was single.

Ezekiel

Marital status did not seem to be of importance to Ezekiel's ministry either. The Lord took Ezekiel's wife suddenly. He was not even allowed to weep or mourn for her, but was to continue in the ministry God had assigned him (Ezekiel 24:15–18).

Hosea

Although the prophet Hosea experienced a broken marriage, he continued in a recognized ministry. God told him to marry Gomer, a prostitute, who He knew would later leave Hosea for other men. God used this circumstance to illustrate the one-sided love between God and Israel (Hosea 1–3).

In all three of these examples, effective ministry did not depend on marital status. God was interested only in the prophet's integrity, obedience, and ability to speak His word.

4   Choose one Old Testament single adult, and explain how God used him or her to tell His message.

The Lord certainly used a variety of Old Testament single adults to minister to and influence others. Besides Jeremiah, Ezekiel, and Hosea, God proclaimed His message through the stories and ministries of single adults such as Miriam, Hagar, Naomi, and Ruth. Daniel, Shadrach, Meshach, and Abednego may also have been single.

Single Ministers in the New Testament

Jesus addressed singleness in Matthew 19:11–12. Paul also expounded on singleness and its accompanying benefits for ministry in 1 Corinthians 7. Many single men and women in the New Testament exemplified this treatment of singleness: Paul, John the Baptist, Anna, Mary, Martha, Lydia, Mary Magdalene, and Jesus himself.

Singleness as a Gift

The New Testament brought a new emphasis on and recognition to singleness as a viable option for ministry. Both Jesus and Paul taught that not everyone will be married in this life; some will continue in the privilege, the gift, of singleness.

Teaching

From Jesus

In Matthew 19:1–12, Jesus expounded on the subject of marriage, a contemporary, relevant issue during His time. When His disciples questioned whether it was better not to marry, Jesus replied, "Not everyone can accept this word, but only those to whom it has been given. For some are eunuchs because they were born that way; . . . and others have renounced marriage because of the kingdom of heaven. The one who can accept this should accept it" (vv. 11–12). Thus, Jesus considered singleness to be a gift.

I strongly believe the "gift of singleness" is a valid, credible, and biblical gift that is alive and resident in the lives of many single ministers today. Although knowing who has this gift may be impossible, it is still an important biblical concept to teach. Sadly, few churches teach the gift of singleness along with the gift of marriage. Ministers who have the gift but are unaware of it could benefit greatly from biblical teaching on this subject.

From Paul

Paul's comments concerning singleness show unity with Christ's remarks. Yet Paul takes the subject a step further by recommending that widows and the unmarried remain single. He addresses the gift of singleness in 1 Corinthians 7:7–9:

> I wish that all men were as I am (single and self-controlled). But each man has his own gift from God; one has this gift, another has that. Now to the unmarried and the widows I say: It is good for them to stay unmarried, as I am. But if they cannot control themselves, they should marry, for it is better to marry than to burn with passion.

Later in the chapter, Paul further explains his view. He desires that all Christians have the ability to remain single, like him, so they can

- avoid the troubles in life that stem from marriage (7:28).

- be free from the concerns and anxieties that result from the demands placed on spouses to care for each other (7:32–34).

- devote themselves totally to the Lord, wisely using the extra time that results from not having to care for a spouse (7:34–35).

From the church today

Paul's admonitions certainly apply to single ministers. However, not all leaders recognize the validity of Paul's advice concerning celibacy. Consider the comments of single ministers when asked a third question:

Q: If you could help pastors and Christian leaders understand one thing about being a single minister, what would that be?

> "Validate that one can live well single, and encourage us in this journey, just as we want to encourage you to live well married and support you in your marriage."
>
> —Vickie, age 44, single, pastor/director of single adult ministry in a nondenominational church

> "Don't exclude us because of our marital status. We can make very significant contributions to the body of Christ based on the gifts God has given us."
>
> —Paul, age 52, single, Assemblies of God editor/writer/administrator

> "I believe the perceptions of leaders are changing, but not fast enough. In the Catholic Church, men and women of the cloth who give their lives for the service of the church have been highly revered and honored for thousands of years. Why is this not true in the evangelical church? Why is singleness considered by many to be dishonorable or second best?"
>
> —Jim, age 30, newlywed, former development coordinator, national Assemblies of God Single Adult/Young Adult Ministries

These ministers' experiences and reflections clearly illustrate a disparity between Paul's perspective of singleness and Christian leaders' perspective.

Examples

Jesus

Christ's singleness actually enhanced the opportunity for God, His Father, to do great things in and through His life. Could it be that Jesus had the gift of singleness as Paul describes it? Certainly, having the gift of singleness would have aided Him in accomplishing His ministry while on earth. Jesus' challenging years of travel, continuous speaking and ministry opportunities, discipleship and mentoring, and numerous stressful circumstances seem to fit single life better than married life. His singleness is not a prescription; however, it is a great example. It validates singleness for ministers as a viable and credible option.

Paul

No concrete biblical evidence exists to show Paul's marital status during his entire adult life. However, it is clear that he was not married when he wrote 1 Corinthians 7:1–40, since he states his wishes for the unmarried and widows to remain single as he was (v. 7). In verses 25–26, he concludes that it is better for a virgin (a person not yet married) to remain single, whether female or male (see v. 29).

Paul preferred singleness for himself and other Christians, especially those in the ministry, for at least three reasons:

1. Paul realized that marriage was not for everyone and that singleness was a workable option. Not all adults choose to marry.
2. Paul knew that singleness freed him to better accomplish God's will for his life. The incredibly tumultuous and time-consuming life of ministry Paul led may have been too much for a wife to bear. His wife's needs would have taken away from his ability to focus on his ministry.
3. Paul could develop more meaningful, personal relationships as a single minister. He realized that the need for close relationships could also be met outside of marriage and constantly referred to his "coworkers," "brothers," and so forth. The last chapter of Romans mentions twenty-seven friends, most with a special, individual word.

The church today

The church should give more credit to Paul's opinion of having more flexibility and less anxiety as a single adult (1 Corinthians 7:32–33). The traditional expectation and commendation of marriage—especially for pastors, missionaries, and key church leaders—seems to need scrutiny in light of the apostle's exhortation that singleness is more conducive to ministry. We should note again that Paul himself was single when he wrote this admonition (7:8).

In view of Paul's strong preference of the single life for himself and others, it is extremely intriguing that many church leaders have made him the chief authority for the "husband of one wife" test for ministers, elders, and deacons (1 Timothy 3:2, 12; Titus 1:6). Interpreting this phrase the way many do eliminates all females and all single people; in fact, such an interpretation would have barred Paul, Jeremiah, John the Baptist, Jesus, and others!

Misconceptions about Singleness

Many common misconceptions of singleness in the church today affect unmarried ministers. Such erroneous ideas seem more prominent in the church

3.2.4
OBJECTIVE
Identify and describe five misconceptions about single ministers.

5   How might common misconceptions discourage a single adult from pursuing a call to ministry? What can you do to help?

than in society at large because of the church's emphasis on marriage and family. Unfortunately, they have resulted in a lack of emphasis on single adults. These five misconceptions are some of the most obvious:

1. Single ministers may not be as complete or spiritually mature as married ministers.

Paul, a never-married editor, writer, and administrator at the Assemblies of God national office, states with conviction that he is called to a life of singleness. Yet he says, "The question 'Why aren't you married?' was asked at my ordination interview." Sylvia, a never-married missionary in the Assemblies of God, also addresses the issue: "There is often a higher level of confidence in those who are married because of maturity issues. A single adult must prove by their conduct they are a person of integrity, maturity, and are responsible (more than a married person must)." The apostle Paul addresses the issues of completeness in Colossians 2:10 by saying, "You have been given fullness in Christ." Marriage has nothing to do with being complete. Most people know many single adults who are complete and mature spiritually, emotionally, and relationally. Conversely, most people also know married adults who are not complete and mature in these ways.

2. Single ministers have more time than married ministers.

Some married adults think unmarried people have more time to spend on themselves. It is true that single adults do not have to spend time meeting a spouse's needs, however, they must perform the many domestic tasks of a household such as cleaning, washing, paying bills, shopping, and decision making without the help of a spouse. Two usually can do more than one. Vickie, a never-married minister to single adults, relates, "I find myself reminding them that the chores of life, if they are to get done, will be accomplished only by me." Married people may claim that their children are a huge responsibility and consume much of their time; yet many single people have children as well.

3. Single ministers are threats to married adults.

As I have ministered to single adults, more than a few have told me they were neglected, ostracized, or made to feel uncomfortable by married adults who perceived them as a threat. Married people can become jealous if their spouse develops a working relationship with a single person. Therefore, married ministers of the opposite sex often distance themselves from single pastors. John, a single pastor to single adults, explains, "Their wives have seemed to be very uncomfortable with me as a single adult in ministry. There has not been any direct confrontation or any allegations of wrongdoing. Yet they have treated me with greater distance than my married counterparts." All Christians should live with agape love toward one another. A married minister can be as readily guilty of sexual improprieties as a single pastor. Moral fiber is not determined by marital status.

4. Single ministers have fewer problems than married ministers.

Single pastors may, in fact, have more problems than married ministers because they have no partner to assist them with their daily responsibilities. They must make everyday decisions alone. Colleen, a single pastor to single adults, explains, "I do not have someone to talk to (as married couples do) when I get home. . . . [I have] no one to . . . share [my] burdens with."

5. Single ministers want to be married.

Well-meaning married adults usually perpetuate this attitude. They do not mean to be rude, presumptuous, or pushy, but their concern, usually only observed but sometimes voiced by a comment or question, comes across the wrong way to single ministers. Many married adults like to help unmarried people find "Miss or Mr. Right." Although most single adults do want to marry someday, they do not need to be reminded they are single, nor do they usually need "help" in finding God's person for them. God is fully able to reveal that person in His way and time.

Some single adults do not feel the need or desire to marry. Colleen illustrates this point by saying, "Some singles are not called to be married, and it is okay to be single. Many people are happy in their singleness. Do not push people to find a mate."

The Female Pastor's Perspective[2]

Women have answered God's call to ministry throughout the history of the church. They face not only all of the challenges confronting men in the ministry but also a host of others unique to their gender. One of the greatest challenges is finding a place to serve. Although the Assemblies of God has a long history of ordaining women, many congregations are reluctant to call a woman to serve as a pastor. Those women fortunate to find a place must often balance the demands of both ministry and the home. Regardless of a person's gender, when preparing for pastoral ministry, it is important to understand the biblical basis for women in ministry and to have a spirit of cooperation.

The Biblical Basis for Female Pastors

3.3.1
OBJECTIVE
Examine the biblical basis for women in ministry and leadership.

(In their book *God's Women: Then and Now*, ministers Dr. Deborah M. Gill and Dr. Barbara L. Cavaness present the biblical basis for women in ministry. The material in this section is a summary of their findings.)

It is common for people, including Christians, to differ in their views about women as leaders. Many differences are based more on people's background or training than on biblical understanding. People often look for texts that seem to agree with their culture to build a case against women's ministry and leadership.

6   Knowing that Christians derive different conclusions from the same passages, how can we study the Bible objectively?

The Bible records that both men and women are created equally in the image of God; both are equally fallen; and both can be equally redeemed. Contrary to the divine design, humanity's fall into sin has imposed false, hierarchical distinctions between the sexes.

7   How is Christ's treatment of women significant concerning their ministry callings?

Jesus' teachings and example confirm that He came to reverse the effects of the Fall—bringing forgiveness of failure and freedom from oppressing others. In the first-century Jewish and Greco-Roman world, where women were treated as less valuable than men, Christ's equal treatment of women was revolutionary. His ministry reached out equally to men and women; His teachings were directed to men and women equally; and His doctrine applies to men and women identically. Jesus' model prompted the early church's remarkable use of women in leadership.

The New Testament describes various ways in which women were involved in ministry and leadership in the first-century church. Women were commissioned to testify of Christ's resurrection (Matthew 28:9–10; Mark 16:7, 9–11; Luke 24:10–11; John 20:14–18). Dorcas was a disciple (Acts 9:36); Philip's four daughters prophesied (21:8–9); and Euodia and Syntyche were Paul's coworkers (Philippians 4:2–3). Among the ten esteemed women Paul lauded in

---

[2]   This lesson was written by Dr. Deborah Gill, Professor of New Testament Exposition at the Assemblies of God Theological Seminary.

Romans 16:1–7, 12–13, 15, Phoebe, Chloe, and Priscilla were probably pastors, and Junias was an apostle.

As seen in these passages, the apostle Paul was a great supporter of women in ministry. Only two places in his epistles, 1 Corinthians 14:34–35 and 1 Timothy 2:11–12, appear to limit women's ministry and leadership. Interpreting these passages as totally prohibiting women's ministry and leadership would make Paul self-contradictory; thus, they do not call for universal prohibition but address specific local problems that needed correction. What, then, were these local problems and how do these texts apply to today?

8 What is the meaning and application of 1 Corinthians 14:34–35 and 1 Timothy 2:11–12?

In 1 Corinthians 14:34–45, Paul was not addressing women who were ministering. Rather, he was silencing the perpetual questions of new female converts in Corinth who were interrupting the worship service. The application of this text for readers of all times is not to prohibit female leadership but to urge that "everything should be done in a fitting and orderly way" (1 Corinthians 14:40).

In 1 Timothy 2:11–12, Paul was silencing a female false teacher in Ephesus. The timeless truth of this passage is to prohibit not female teachers but false teachers. The problem in Ephesus was not a matter of gender but of deception.

The Assemblies of God's Position on Female Pastors

OBJECTIVE
Summarize the Assemblies of God position concerning women in ministry.

Since its first General Council in 1914, the Assemblies of God has recognized the role of women in ministry and granted their ordination. Its first constitutional statement included an article on the "Rights and Offices of Women" (Gill 1995, 33). At that time, although many women were pastoring Assemblies of God churches, the original statement permitted women's ordination "as missionaries and evangelists" only. By 1935, however, the General Council specifically stated that women could serve as pastors as well as evangelists (Bicket 1997, 80–82). The Bylaws have maintained that stance and even strengthened it since that time:

9 What is the Assemblies of God position on women in ministry, and where is it stated?

ARTICLE VII. MINISTRY, Section 2. Basic Qualifications, m. Eligibility of women. The Scriptures plainly teach that divinely called and qualified women may also serve the church in the ministry of the Word (Joel 2:29; Acts 21:9; 1 Corinthians 11:5). Women who meet the qualifications for ministerial credentials are eligible for whatever grade of credentials their qualifications warrant and have the right to administer the ordinances of the church and are eligible to serve in all levels of church ministry, and/or district and General Council leadership. (*Minutes* 2005)

Additionally, the Executive Presbytery assigned the Commission on Doctrinal Purity the task of preparing a position paper on women in ministry. That paper, adopted by the General Presbytery in August 1990, serves to reaffirm the historical and constitutional position of the Assemblies of God concerning women in ministry. Historical theology teaches that official ecclesiastical statements are made in response to issues being debated. Thus, the very existence of a Bylaw and position paper on women in ministry show that this has been an issue in the Assemblies of God's ranks.

10 How does the Assemblies of God's position on women in the ministry relate to Pentecostal theology?

Still, the position of the Assemblies of God is rooted in Pentecostal theology. In these last days—from Pentecost to the Second Coming—the Holy Spirit is being poured out freely on *all* people. The New Testament teaches that the Holy Spirit equips *all* people (male and female) for God's work. It describes women as full participants in church services, equal recipients of spiritual gifts, and leaders at all levels of ministry. To be a true New Testament church, Christians must welcome all of those whom God calls and all gifts for service.

Female ministers have faced many challenges. The early period of the Assemblies of God saw great numbers of women evangelists, pastors, and missionaries. Women ministers opened many fields to the gospel overseas and planted hundreds of churches in the United States. Compared to that era, however, the percentage of credentialed female ministers of total credentialed ministers is significantly lower. Though the numbers of credentialed women is on the rise again, sadly, only a minority of female ministers are ordained.

Christlike Obedience with a Spirit of Cooperation

3.3.3
OBJECTIVE
Describe the Christlike response of obedience to a call.

Everyone called into the work of the Lord will face challenges. They may be even greater at times for a woman, but if God has called her, she must be obedient.

Women pastors must get connected, for friendships are very important. Every woman minister needs to have friends who are pastors and ministers with whom she can talk "shop." She needs to have relationships with other women who are leaders. Women need the support of one another as they advance in areas such as leadership where they have not traditionally been accepted. One female pastor put together a peer-mentoring group of five female senior pastors of several different denominations in her city. These pastors developed rich and rewarding relationships. Being a minority can be lonely, but friends can really help.

Women pastors also need to connect with helpful resources. Truth is so empowering, and learning about others can be encouraging. Many websites, journals, and newsletters have a wealth of advice and encouragement for pastors.

Several districts in the U.S. Assemblies of God have become proactive in encouraging women in ministry. A number of them have established Credentialed Women's Fellowships, others offer a special session for women ministers at their Schools of Ministry for new ministerial candidates, and still others offer prayer partners and mentoring opportunities.

Christians in general can support a woman who is called by God to serve as a pastor in seven steps:
1. Establish the legitimacy of her calling from the Word.
2. Affirm the authorization of her calling from denominational statements.
3. Inspire the pursuit of her calling with models from the past.
4. Facilitate the fulfillment of her calling with mentors from the present.
5. Articulate your personal endorsement of her calling by encouragement and example.
6. Contribute to the realization of her calling with opportunities to serve.
7. Pray that the Lord will raise up workers, and be careful not to send away those God calls. (Gill 1997, 33–35)

11 How will you cooperate with those whose view of women in ministry differs from your own?

Differences of opinion regarding female pastors abound in the Christian world. All Christians, especially leaders, need to guard their hearts against discouragement or negativity. If the enemy can make believers bitter, he can render our own ministries worthless. As servants of Christ, pastors need to respect their colleagues who are fellow servants of the Lord, whether male or female.

3.4.1
OBJECTIVE

Identify the parenting mistakes of Eli, Samuel, and David.

12 Does a child's God-given free will affect the application of 1 Timothy 3:4–5? Why or why not?

3.4.2
OBJECTIVE

Explain principles concerning children's spiritual training.

The Pastor as a Parent

A pastor with children has no greater responsibility than their spiritual training. Achievement in this area reflects a minister's ability to lead the church. If pastors fail to do this, Paul questions whether they should be pastors at all. He says, "He [the pastor] must manage his own family well and see that his children obey him with proper respect. (If anyone does not know how to manage his own family, how can he take care of God's church?)" (1 Timothy 3:4–5).

Both Scripture and history detail tragic accounts of great men who failed in this critical assignment. Eli the priest, Samuel the prophet, and David the king are three examples. According to 1 Samuel 2:12, "Eli's sons were wicked men; they had no regard for the Lord." Samuel's sons were no better, for they "did not walk in his ways. They turned aside after dishonest gain and accepted bribes and perverted justice" (1 Samuel 8:3).

However, no one suffered more grief from his children than David did. His family history saddens the heart. David's son Amnon raped his half-sister, Tamar, creating scandal in the palace. Two years later, Tamar's brother Absalom took revenge by murdering Amnon. Later, Absalom led an armed rebellion against his father David, driving him from Jerusalem and breaking his heart.

Although Eli, Samuel, and David were godly men, their parental failures somehow diminish the greatness of their achievements. The Bible gives only glimpses of their relationship with their children, but it is enough to give us insight into some of their parental shortcomings. For example, Eli may have been too permissive: "For I [the Lord] told him that I would judge his family forever because of the sin he knew about; his sons made themselves contemptible, and he failed to restrain them" (1 Samuel 3:13). Samuel was simply too busy. He apparently gave himself to the work of the Lord at the expense of his relationship with his sons. David's failure, however, was more overt. He betrayed his children's trust when he committed adultery with Bathsheba and then had her husband murdered. From that moment on, his children lost all respect for him.

From examples such as these, we can draw several important truths.

Place Priority on the Family

Other than our relationship with God, nothing is more important than our relationship with our family, including our children. If we lose them, anything else we achieve is somehow tainted.

I was just twenty-three years old when our daughter Leah was born. Had I known then what I know now, I would have been terrified! I did not fully realize then that my relationship with Leah would shape her relationship with her heavenly Father, as she unconsciously attributed to God the strengths and weaknesses she saw in me, her earthly father. Nor did I comprehend that my words would forever shape her self-image, giving her confidence to follow her dreams or locking her in a prison of inferiority. I had no idea how important the gift of my presence would be or how much she would depend on my counsel and guidance. On the day Leah was born, I was too naïve to realize that I was embarking on the most important assignment of my life.

Engage in Spiritual Training

Spiritual training does not just happen; it takes patience and persistence. We have to work at it.

All spiritual training must be grounded in God's Word. To the parents of ancient Israel, God instructed: "These commandments that I give you today are to be upon your hearts. Impress them on your children. Talk about them when you sit at home and when you walk along the road, when you lie down and when you get up" (Deuteronomy 6:6–7).

The first thing we must teach our children is to love God. Jesus said, "'Love the Lord your God with all your heart and with all your soul and with all your mind.' This is the first and greatest commandment. And the second is like it: 'Love your neighbor as yourself.' All the Law and the Prophets hang on these two commandments" (Matthew 22:37–40). This is as important for our children as it is for us.

Then we must teach them not only to trust fully in the Lord (Proverbs 3:5–6) but also to obey Him. The author of Ecclesiastes admonishes, "Fear God and keep his commandments, for this is the whole duty of man" (12:13).

Children are born with a desire to learn, yet every child is unique. Encouraging children to ask questions and taking the time to answer them is important for many children. Still, the key to effective spiritual training is to know your child. As parents, we can ask for the Holy Spirit's help in discovering how our son or daughter learns best and then fit our teaching style to his or her learning style. Of course, all children learn by example, which we will discuss more in the next section.

Timing is crucial. While there is probably no wrong time to share spiritual truths, some moments are more conducive to learning than others. Wise parents know the difference and seize those special moments, recognizing them as opportunities to shape their children's understanding of God and of life. This reminds me of the saying, "Strike while the iron is hot," originating from a blacksmith's shop. It referred to the moment when a piece of metal in the fire was red-hot and ready to be shaped. However, the iron was red-hot only for a few seconds. Once it cooled, it had to be reheated before the blacksmith could finish his work. It is the same way with children's spiritual training. Parents must be aware of the times when their children are most open to learning spiritual truths.

In addition, spiritual training for our children should include times of regular family worship. This sets the spiritual tone for each family member. While such times may not have a dramatic impact, their importance cannot be overemphasized. This time of family devotions or worship prepares children's hearts, lays a firm foundation, and establishes good habits of spiritual discipline. Thus, our children's spiritual formation requires both spontaneous moments and regular instruction.

Teach by Example

13 What principles guide ministers in spiritually training their children?

Children learn the most by imitating the examples of their parents and other adults. Therefore, what we teach in precept, we must also model. For instance, children learn to pray as they watch their parents pray and as their parents pray with them; and they learn to value God's Word as they see their parents value God's Word and study it with them.

Evangeline Booth worked in ministry all of her life. When she was eighty-one years old and still leading the Salvation Army, someone asked her when she had first wanted to be a part of the ministry. "Very early," she answered. "I saw my parents [founders of the Salvation Army] working for their people, bearing their burdens. Day and night. They did not have to say a word to me about Christianity" (Hughes 1991, 36).

My experience is much like hers. I cannot recall a single time when my father sat down with me and imparted some spiritual truth or moral lesson. Yet I learned from him almost everything I know about living for God—not through what he said, but by the way he lived. On many mornings, I awoke in the predawn darkness to the sound of my father's voice lifted in prayer. I remember tiptoeing down the hallway to stand just outside the living room door so I could hear him better. Never have I felt more loved, more secure, than when I heard my father call my name to our heavenly Father in prayer.

Although the spiritual traditions that one generation passes to the next are seldom practiced in exactly the same way, the spiritual values and benefits remain intact. For example, I seldom pray alone in the living room as my father did, but I make a regular habit of driving to the church for early morning prayer. When Leah was still at home, I often knelt beside her bed after she was asleep to pray for her. Even now, when she and her husband face a challenging situation, they often call so we can pray together over the phone. My wife and I often share a prayer before we turn out the lights at the end of each day.

As I near senior adulthood, I realize there are many things I may never accomplish. I will probably never be invited to preach at a General Council meeting, and I may never write a best-selling book. I will probably never be elected to an important denominational or governmental position. But that is all right. Successes of that nature, while gratifying, pale in comparison to the true achievements of life: shaping the faith and character of our families.

Someday, when we each stand before God, He will not ask us to describe the honors and awards we won. He will not ask about degrees or wealth. Rather, I am convinced He will ask, "Where are the children I entrusted to you?" In light of this, the greatest reward ministers could hope to receive, this side of heaven, is seeing their children cherish the faith entrusted to them. What a joy to watch them make the family's spiritual values their own and teach them to their own children.

3.5.1
OBJECTIVE

Explain the limitations of pastor–parishioner friendships.

14 Why can pastors seldom be "just friends" with their parishioners?

The Pastor as a Friend

Another core relationship that impacts your ministry is your relationship with your friends. Friends influence your values, help you shape your character, and determine to a significant degree what you become. Choose them wisely, and they will prove an invaluable asset. On the other hand, the wrong friends can cause more grief than imaginable.

Pastoral Friendship with Laity

People often ask me, "Can pastors be friends with members of their congregation?" The answer is, absolutely. But there are limits to pastor–parishioner friendships. Live within these limits, and your friendship can flourish to a good degree. Violate the limits, and your friendship will have many negative consequences.

No matter how close the friendship, you can very seldom be "just friends" with congregants. Friends will always consider you as their pastor first and friend second. They will always hold you to a higher standard than that to which friends usually hold each other. No matter what situation you are facing, your friends will likely expect you to think and act like a pastor. And if they feel obligated to choose between their loyalty to you and their loyalty to the church, they often side with the church.

A pastor friend of mine learned this firsthand following the untimely death of his wife. On top of his pastoral duties, my friend suddenly found himself solely responsible for his home and his four children. He not only had to prepare three sermons each week, oversee the pastoral staff, conduct meetings, provide pastoral care, and administrate for the church; but he was now also a single parent. For the first time in his life, he was both breadwinner and homemaker. He had no one to help him with household chores or share the mundane details of managing a family. He was responsible for cooking, cleaning, laundry, and child rearing as well as servicing the cars, doing yard work, paying the bills, and balancing the checkbook. Despite the burden, he held up amazingly well, especially considering that his children had been traumatized by his wife's death. To one degree or another, each child dealt with the grief by acting out.

For a brief time after the funeral, his congregation rallied around him in support. But not long afterward, they grew critical. When his teenage children misbehaved—as is common after a parent's death—some people suggested that my friend was no longer fit to lead the church. When grief continued to dog his steps and color everything he did, some suggested that he resign his position.

What finally broke this pastor was the behavior of his close friend on the church board, a man into whom he had poured his life. This man called the district superintendent to seek help in removing the pastor. Although the district superintendent refused, informing the church board that they had absolutely no grounds on which to do this, my friend had finally suffered enough. Within a few weeks, he resigned the church and left the pastorate.

What happened? Why did the pastor's "friend" respond that way? Why was the church not more supportive and understanding? A number of factors were involved, including the congregation's unrealistic expectations. They simply assumed their pastor would recover from his wife's death as quickly as they did. They failed to understand that the grieving process after a spouse's death generally lasts up to three years. However, the most significant factor most likely centered on their inability to perceive of their pastor as a friend—a normal human being—and to respond accordingly.

While my friend's situation is an extreme case, it illustrates the limits of pastor–parishioner friendships. It also highlights the need to build relationships with our peers in ministry.

Pastoral Friendship with Other Ministers

3.5.2
OBJECTIVE
Discuss keys to having healthy ministerial friendships.

Without a doubt, there is something special about friendships between Christian brothers and sisters. We tend to think of such friends as a team rather than simply as individuals. For instance, it is difficult to think of David without Jonathan, Ruth without Naomi, D. L. Moody without Ira Sankey, or Billy Graham without Cliff Barrows or George Beverly Shea.

Learn the Difference between Ministry and Friendship

15 How is ministry different from friendship?

In my work as a pastor, I have found it not only helpful but also necessary to monitor my relationships and maintain an appropriate balance between ministry and friendship. I define *ministry* as those relationships from which I receive nothing but the satisfaction of knowing I have faithfully served my Lord and His hurting people. On the surface, these relationships may appear much like friendships. They may include shared meals, long talks, and even holidays together. But in reality, I am constantly giving of myself without receiving anything of eternal value in return.

Develop Give-and-Take Relationships

To maintain spiritual vitality, we must balance ministry relationships with nourishing friendships. These are reciprocal relationships in which each person's soul is edified and strengthened. We exchange ideas, discuss Scripture, joke, and pray together as friend with friend. Proverbs 27:17 states, "As iron sharpens iron, so one man sharpens another." Spiritual ministry does occur in these friendships, but it is a consequence rather than an objective.

True friends hear you when you speak from your heart. They support you when you struggle, correct you gently and lovingly when you are wrong, and forgive you when you fail. Such friends prod you to personal growth and stretch you to your full potential. Most amazing of all, they celebrate your successes as if the achievements were their own. This kind of friend "loves at all times" (Proverbs 17:17).

Such friendship requires reciprocity. Both participants must receive from the relationship. A relationship that consistently drains one or the other is bound to dissolve sooner or later. In a genuine friendship, both participants give and receive. Without this balance, no lasting friendship can be maintained or can even be called true friendship.

Take Your Time

With this in mind, we should develop friendships with caution. This maximizes the benefits of friendship while minimizing the risks. Proverbs 12:26 advises, "A righteous man is cautious in friendship." In other words, do not rush things when building friendships, no matter how interesting or exciting your potential friends may seem. Time has a way of revealing true character, including defects not always readily obvious. We can avoid many hurtful experiences simply by taking things more slowly. Jim Smith, of Highland Park Presbyterian Church in Dallas, Texas, recommends that people be as bold as turtles when forming friendships. He says, "To move to something more intimate requires a careful testing of the other person over a long period of time" (Robbins 1984, 27).

Proverbs provides some helpful advice concerning the kinds of people to avoid. For instance, Proverbs 20:19 notes, "A gossip betrays a confidence; so avoid a man who talks too much." Proverbs 22:24–25 says, "Do not make friends with a hot-tempered man, do not associate with one easily angered, or you may learn his ways and get yourself ensnared." Proverbs 25:19 counsels that relying on a fickle person is "like a bad tooth or a lame foot." Thus, when selecting potential friends, do not choose individuals who talk too much, are hot-tempered, or are unreliable. Instead, look for people who are wise (13:20), offer encouragement (27:9), and choose their words carefully (17:27).

Be a Good Friend

While peer friendships do provide a place for accountability, the ultimate purpose of friendship is not to be accountable but to be nurtured. Of course, true friends are committed to protecting each other. Yet if this becomes the relationship's primary function, it will not survive long. The bread that nourishes our souls is acceptance and communication, not accountability. Even as Jonathan "helped him [David] find strength in God" (1 Samuel 23:16), Christian friends should strengthen one another in the Lord.

To build such friendships with others, each of us must strive to be the good kind of friend ourselves. In loneliness, we may be tempted to pray, "Lord, give me a friend like that." Instead, we should pray, "Lord, make me a friend like that."

Test Yourself

Circle the letter of the *best* answer.

1. If pastors put ministry above their families, their
a) marriages will be blessed.
b) ministries will suffer.
c) spouses will be proud of them.
d) marriages will weaken.

2. Regarding singleness in ministry, today's church generally teaches that
a) some ministers should remain single as Jesus and Paul were.
b) single ministers are usually more mature spiritually.
c) an itinerant minister should remain single if possible.
d) the pastor of a local church should be married.

3. Our study shows that churches generally need to put more emphasis on
a) senior adults.
b) single adults.
c) teenagers.
d) families.

4. What is the best biblical justification for singleness in ministry?
a) Jesus was single.
b) Paul was single and expected singleness for others.
c) Jesus treated singleness, like marriage, as a special gift.
d) One should not take on the responsibilities of marriage if the times are especially difficult.

5. Paul's apparent limitations on women's ministry should be interpreted as
a) addressing specific local problems that needed correction.
b) not being practical or applicable in the twenty-first century.
c) pertaining only to the early church.
d) being Paul's personal opinion.

6. What is the best theological basis for ordaining women to the ministry?
a) Jesus commanded that women be ordained to the ministry.
b) Paul specifically taught that women should be ordained.
c) The Holy Spirit equips all people, male and female, for God's work.
d) Both men and women are created in God's image.

7. For help in obeying the call to ministry, women should
a) isolate themselves so they can better hear God's voice.
b) debate with those who oppose their ministry.
c) interpret challenges as closed doors.
d) connect to each other and to valuable resources.

8. Samuel's parenting struggles resulted from his
a) sin and the loss of his children's respect.
b) greater attention to ministry than to his family.
c) failure to adequately discipline his sons.
d) strict and unrelenting attitude.

9. Children should primarily learn about God from
a) pastors.
b) teachers.
c) parents.
d) friends.

10. The Bible teaches Christians to
a) slowly build friendships.
b) have few friends.
c) limit time spent with friends.
d) become friends with everyone.

Responses to Interactive Questions
Chapter 3

Some of these responses may include information that is supplemental to the IST. These questions are intended to produce reflective thinking beyond the course content and your responses may vary from these examples.

1 Briefly explain how a minister can invest in his or her spouse.

One can spend time with his or her spouse; share deeply; and forgive easily.

2 How do pastors develop and maintain peace and joy in their families?

Pastors must be kind and show respect to their family, praising, affirming, helping, and loving them.

3 How can ministers help today's church to more effectively reach single adults?

Answers will vary.

4 Choose one Old Testament single adult, and explain how God used him or her to tell His message.

Answers will vary but might include Jeremiah, Ezekiel, Hosea, Miriam, Hagar, Naomi, Ruth, and possibly Daniel, Shadrach, Meschach, or Abednego.

5 How might common misconceptions discourage a single adult from pursuing a call to ministry? What can you do to help?

Answers will vary.

6 Knowing that Christians derive different conclusions from the same passages, how can we study the Bible objectively?

The student of the Bible must consider all of Scripture, identify its timeless truths, and interpret texts within their historical and literary context.

7 How is Christ's treatment of women significant concerning their ministry calling?

In the first century, women were devalued in both the Jewish and Greco-Roman cultures. Yet Jesus treated women as equal to men, restoring God's ideals. His example was revolutionary for its time and set the standard for all who follow Him, from the first-century church to believers today.

8 What is the meaning and application of 1 Corinthians 14:34–35 and 1 Timothy 2:11–12?

Distinguish between Paul's speaking to local church problems in first-century Corinth and Ephesus and the timeless truths of the passages.

9 What is the Assemblies of God position on women in ministry, and where is it stated?

Women's call to ministry is recognized and affirmed by credentialing and placement to any level in the Fellowship. The Bylaw on "Ministry: Eligibility of Women" and the position paper on "The Role of Women in Ministry as Described in Holy Scripture" record the official position.

10 How does the Assemblies of God's position on women in the ministry relate to Pentecostal theology?

This position is rooted in Pentecostal theology. The Holy Spirit equips those whom God calls; and as He has poured out His Spirit on both "sons and daughters" to prophesy, He means both men and women to use their gifts together in His service.

11 How will you cooperate with those whose view of women in ministry differs from your own?

Answers will vary.

12 Does a child's God-given free will affect the application of 1 Timothy 3:4–5? Why or why not?

Answers will vary.

13 What principles guide ministers in spiritually training their children?

Answers may include these ideas: (1) Give priority to your family. (2) Be patient and persistent. (3) Ground all spiritual training in God's Word. (4) Be aware of appropriate times. (5) Teach by modeling (example).

14 Why can pastors seldom be "just friends" with their parishioners?

Pastors are most often considered ministers first and friends second.

15 How is ministry different from friendship?

In ministry, I give of myself without receiving anything in return. Friendships are reciprocal in that each person is edified.

UNIT PROGRESS EVALUATION 1

Now that you have finished Unit 1, review the lessons in preparation for Unit Progress Evaluation 1.
You will find it in Essential Course Materials at the back of this IST. Answer all of the questions without referring to your course materials, Bible, or notes. When you have completed the UPE, check your answers with the answer key provided in Essential Course Materials. Review any items you may have answered incorrectly. Then you may proceed with your study of Unit 2. (Although UPE scores do not count as part of your final course grade, they indicate how well you learned the material and how well you may perform on the closed-book final examination.)

The Pastor's Responsibilities Part 1

Unit 2 builds on the first unit. Chapter 4 emphasizes the pastors' public ministries as reflections of their private lives. Pastors can feed others only with the spiritual food they have received *from* God; therefore, they can lead others only into places they have been *with* God. As one wise pastor said, the exact amount people have to share with others is what they receive from God—no less and no more. For that reason, pastors must walk daily with God, spending time in His Word and presence. Pastors who do this will never lack spiritual food for God's sheep.

Chapter 5 then considers the pastor's role in leading worship. Again, as in all of the earlier chapters, the importance of a pastor's relationship with God is emphasized. From beginning to end, pastors must depend on the Spirit to minister through them to others. As this happens, believers will be fruitful and grow in grace.

Finally, Chapter 6 teaches skills for ministry. The insights of this chapter can shape and equip pastors for a lifetime of caring for the flock of God.

Chapter 4   The Ministry of Preaching and Teaching

Lessons
4.1   Prioritize
4.2   Prepare
4.3   Proclaim

Chapter 5   The Pastor as Worship Leader

Lessons
5.1   The Holy Spirit's Leading
5.2   The Holy Spirit's Gifts
5.3   The Worshipper's Decision

Chapter 6   The Ministry of Pastoral Care

Lessons
6.1   Presence
6.2   Empathy
6.3   Caregiving

The Ministry of Preaching and Teaching

The pastor has many roles:

- Administrator
- Leader
- Visionary
- Caregiver

- Counselor
- Mentor
- Teacher
- Preacher

Although all of these are important to the ministry of the church, none is more important than proclaiming God's eternal Word. The apostles affirmed this when they declared:

> It would not be right for us to neglect the ministry of the word of God in order to wait on tables. Brothers, choose seven men from among you who are known to be full of the Spirit and wisdom. We will turn this responsibility over to them and will give our attention to prayer and the ministry of the word." So the word of God spread. The number of disciples in Jerusalem increased rapidly, and a large number of priests became obedient to the faith. (Acts 6:2–4, 7)

The apostles did not arbitrarily decide to make prayer and teaching their first priority. Rather, they were responding to an internal crisis in the infant church. "The Grecian Jews among them complained against the Hebraic Jews because their widows were being overlooked in the daily distribution of food" (6:1). The resulting antagonism threatened to splinter the fellowship. Something had to be done, and fast.

No one would have blamed the apostles if they had given their attention to this pressing need. After all, the Bible does teach us to care for widows and the needy—but not in place of prayer and the ministry of the Word. Thus, pastors need to appoint godly men and women to minister in these areas so they themselves can remain focused on preaching God's Word.

Lesson 4.1   Prioritize
Objective
4.1.1   Summarize several keys to setting biblical priorities.

Lesson 4.2   Prepare
Objectives
4.2.1   Describe how pastors should prepare to preach.
4.2.2   Explain how pastors should preach the major themes of the Scriptures and the whole will of God.

Lesson 4.3   Proclaim
Objectives
4.3.1   Explain the value of practicing your sermons.
4.3.2   Explain what it means to be "natural" when preaching.
4.3.3   Identify key aspects of delivery.
4.3.4   Analyze the value, risk, and method of open preaching.

4.1.1
OBJECTIVE
Summarize several keys to setting biblical priorities.

1 What does Acts 6:1–7 teach?

Prioritize

Acts 6:1–7 demonstrates that pastors should establish clear biblical priorities. As any pastor will tell you, the tyranny of the urgent constantly tempts a minister to forego the important. In setting priorities, pastors must discern both what God has called them to do and what He has called others to do.

That is, we must put first things first. More often than not, pastors will have to choose between two or more legitimate concerns. They are not choosing between good and evil—that would be easy. Rather, like the apostles, pastors must often choose between pressing needs and spiritual preparation. For example, should they make hospital calls, visit the shut-ins, or give themselves to prayer and the study of God's Word? When churches are small, pastors may have adequate time to do all of that and more. However, the larger a church grows, the more important it becomes for others to share in the ministry of the church.

I well remember facing that kind of dilemma some years ago. The congregation I was serving experienced significant growth and all the accompanying dynamics. We were building a new facility, adding more staff, and enlarging our ministries. My responsibilities were also expanding. With increasing frequency, I was invited to travel and minister throughout the country. Our radio ministry had expanded into more than 150 cities and was demanding more and more of my time. Often, the work of ministry crowded out my time for prayer and study. Soon, I found myself physically drained and emotionally depleted. Moreover, my preaching lacked the power it once had. I knew I had to do something, but what?

Admit Your Weaknesses

First, I had to admit that I was only human; I could not do it all. Then I had to decide what to do, what to delegate, and what to leave undone.

2 How does Philippians 4:13 relate to prioritizing?

For me, this first step was the hardest. All my life, I had been taught that I could "do everything through him [Christ] who gives me strength" (Philippians 4:13). Now I was forced to acknowledge my limitations. How could I reconcile this apparent contradiction? Then I realized something: I could do everything *God called me to do* because He would give me the strength to do it; but if I added to my God-given responsibilities, I had to rely on my own strength. I had to choose between a God-centered life and a need-centered one, between a divine assignment and a human-concocted opportunity.

A number of divine assignments filled my life at that point, but I had also cluttered my life with ministries I had taken upon myself. To remain effective in my calling, I had to recognize the difference and choose accordingly.

Determine Your God-Given Tasks

3 List four things God has called every pastor to do.

After admitting my limitations, I had to decide what to do—that is, what my assignments from God were. I had to discern which of my responsibilities were nonnegotiable, such as my personal relationship with Jesus Christ. If I did not maintain a vibrant spiritual walk, nothing else would work—not my ministry and not my life. Also, God had called me to be a good husband and father. No one else could fill those roles in my place.

As a senior pastor, I had certain other God-given responsibilities that no one else could do. I could not delegate all of my preaching and teaching responsibilities. I could share them, but since God had called me to serve by preaching to this congregation, I was responsible for it. In the same way, I could not abdicate my responsibility as the pastoral intercessor. God had charged me with praying for His people, and I would answer to Him. Yet all of my additional tasks were assignable to other people.

Decide Which Tasks to Delegate

4   What types of tasks can others in your church do?

After careful consideration, I decided to delegate the day-to-day administration of the church to my senior associate. He was gifted in this area, and I trusted him. Next, we called another minister and gave her the primary responsibility for pastoral care and counseling. We trained volunteers to help copy and edit tapes of the daily radio broadcasts. Finally, we gave each elder one task area with a written description of the duties involved. Although the ultimate responsibility for the administration of the church and its ministries still rested with me as senior pastor, now a capable group of gifted men and women helped me manage the work of the ministry.

Decide Which Tasks to Cut

Of course, a number of challenges arose as I implemented these changes, especially when it came to determining what to leave undone. While nearly everyone applauded my attempt to establish biblical priorities, most parishioners felt their situation was the exception to the rule. For example, in one board meeting, the elders unanimously agreed that I needed to restructure my workload and reduce my counseling and other one-on-one ministry. However, as soon as the meeting ended, two elders pulled me aside, one after the other, to urgently ask that I meet with each one about his pressing family issue. Neither man saw anything incongruous about requesting personal ministry from me only minutes after urging me to cut back in that very area. To them, the boundaries they set for others did not apply to themselves. Again, most people thought I should guard my time, giving myself to prayer and studying the Word, but no one thought I should do so at his or her expense.

Yet, to honor my commitment to biblical priorities, I had to resist the temptation to allow others' expectations to structure my ministry. It was not easy, but it was critical.

Once you recognize that your highest priority is to pray and study God's Word, you are responsible to schedule your time accordingly. An older, wiser mentor once told me that I would always have time for what I did first. Then he counseled me to make prayer and Bible study the *first thing* I did each morning.

I have not always been faithful to follow his advice, but when I have, it has paid rich dividends. Over the years, I have discovered the benefit of disciplining myself to rise early and go to my study for sermon preparation. Not only is my mind refreshed, but also the early hour means fewer distractions and interruptions. Obviously, early morning is not the only good time to prepare sermons, but it has always worked best for me. Whatever time you choose, you will need to guard it zealously.

4.2.1
OBJECTIVE

*Describe how pastors
should prepare to preach.*

5   How do pastors begin to
prepare their messages?

Prepare

As you prepare to preach, it is helpful to remember that you are preparing not only a message but also yourself. Even the best-prepared sermon lacks the power to convict and transform lives unless it comes from the spiritual overflow of a life submerged in the grace and power of the risen Christ. You simply cannot feed others what you have not partaken of yourself. Talent and charisma may entertain, but only the anointed Word of God can redeem and transform.

The personal spiritual preparation required of pastors—what I call *heart preparation*—is mainly accomplished through their devotional lives (see chapter 2). By spending time in God's presence, pastors submit themselves to the sanctifying work of the Holy Spirit. There, they address issues of pride and ambition, jealousy and greed, bringing each area into subjection to the Spirit's transforming power. They submit their thoughts to the eternal truths of God's holy Word. As a result, when pastors begin to prepare their messages, most of their personal spiritual preparation is already finished. Their hearts are aflame with passion for God and love for His people. Having prepared themselves in this way, pastors can now turn their full attention to preparing an effective message.

A Relevant, Fresh Message

The minister's first question must be, "What does God want to say to His people at this particular moment?" Nothing is more important than knowing you have received a fresh word to bring to the congregation. Bible studies are wonderful; sermons can be helpful; but nothing speaks to people's deepest spiritual issues like a fresh word from God.

By *fresh* word, I do not mean some new revelation, for nothing is new under the sun (Ecclesiastes 1:9). Rather, I refer to the great themes of Scripture—God's character, faithfulness, unconditional love, abounding grace, eternal salvation—with a fresh anointing. — *has to be a revelation of the Covenant.*

6   What should pastors do
to create relevant sermons?

To determine what message their people need to hear at a particular time, preachers must listen with both ears. With one ear, they listen to the Holy Spirit, and with the other, they listen to the heart cries of their congregation. Careful consideration of both sources enables pastors to develop messages that both remain true to God's purposes and speak to the deepest needs of the human heart.

Preachers or teachers hear the voice of God when they spend time with Him, particularly while immersing themselves in prayer and the Scriptures. By faithfully and systematically reading and studying the Word, pastors begin to understand more and more fully the timeless message God communicates to every generation.

7   What is a key to
understanding the Bible and
people?

At the same time, ministers hear the heart cries of their parishioners most clearly by spending time with them, especially when the people are facing a crisis. Be it a financial trial, a terminal illness, divorce, or the death of a child, the crisis will pose a host of difficult questions. By being attentive to these questions, pastors can prepare messages that bring the eternal truth of Scripture to bear on the most pressing human dilemmas. Those who choose not to spend time with their people soon find their preaching becoming abstract or separated from life; it drifts further and further away from people's needs. The pastor who does not study soon becomes trite. Therefore, the key to understanding the Bible and people is for pastors to spend time with both.

4.2.2
OBJECTIVE

Explain how pastors should preach the major themes of the Scriptures and the whole will of God.

Major Biblical Themes

Along with the Bible's wise proverbs and spiritual principles, the great stories of Scripture speak clearly to our human condition. Paul referred to Israel's history when he said, "These things happened to them as examples and were written down as warnings for us, on whom the fulfillment of the ages has come" (1 Corinthians 10:11).

As I have studied and preached on the Old and New Testament narratives, I have noticed that most contain both a major and a minor story. Each major story is about God, and each minor story pertains to people. For example, consider the fall of Adam and Eve. Any honest person can readily identify with their temptation, sin, and shame. All of us have heard the Tempter's voice, and no one is without sin. We have all known the bitter pain of regret. Like Adam and Eve, we may have tried to flee from God in shame and fear. This is the "minor" story of humanity's fall, and it is tragic.

8   Identify the major and minor stories in Genesis 3.

However, the larger story—the more important or major one—centers on God. Although He knew of Adam and Eve's sin, He did not abandon them. He still came to fellowship with them: "Then the man and his wife heard the sound of the Lord God as he was walking in the garden in the cool of the day, and they hid from the Lord God among the trees of the garden. But the Lord God called to the man, 'Where are you?'" (Genesis 3:8–9). That is the major story! No matter how miserably we fail, no matter how tragically we sin, no matter how far we fall, God still comes for us. He still covers our shame, forgives our sins, and restores us to fellowship.

Most, if not all, Bible stories follow this major story/minor story principle. However, pastors sometimes become caught in emphasizing one of the stories to the exclusion of the other. We tend to primarily preach on the minor story, leaving the congregation with an overwhelming sense of failure and need but with little awareness of God's unconditional love and eternal faithfulness.

Yet both major and minor stories are vital. As we develop our messages, we should consciously work to balance the two. Only as our hearers are brought face-to-face with their spiritual poverty (the minor story) can they fully appreciate the magnitude of God's grace (the major story). Thus, as I finish my sermon preparation, I always ask myself two questions:

1.   Is my message true to God's character?

2.   Does my message speak to the real needs of people?

If I can answer both questions in the affirmative, I am generally ready to proceed to the actual preaching moment.

God's Whole Will and Counsel

Pastors can become ensnared in maximizing the demands of the Christian life (what we do for God) while minimizing the benefits of the gospel (what God has done for us through the finished work of Christ) Some years ago, a missionary wrote to me after listening to several of my sermons on tape. He pointed out that although I continuously challenged the people to a deeper commitment, I seldom declared the good news of what God has done for us. After initially feeling offended, on further reflection I had to admit that he was right. Since then, I have consciously tried to make sure that the overriding theme of my preaching is God's grace—what He has done for us in Christ.

9 How do ministers benefit from regularly evaluating their preaching?

With this in mind, it is beneficial for pastors to regularly review their preaching to ensure they are faithfully declaring the whole counsel of God. Even the best of us easily fall into the habit of repeatedly proclaiming certain favorite themes at the expense of other equally valid truths. Further, while preaching from scriptural narratives is important, gleaning truths from the Bible's numerous proverbs and spiritual principles is just as essential. In particular, the New Testament epistles are packed with spiritual truth that the Holy Spirit inspired the apostles to write for the church.

We must also be careful to follow proper rules of interpretation and avoid focusing on one aspect of Scripture over another. For example, while God's Word teaches that God can and does deliver His people from trouble (see Hebrews 11:32–35), it also shows that He sometimes chooses to walk His followers through trials and hardships (see Hebrews 11:35–39). That is, in His sovereignty and omniscience, He does not opt to deliver His people every time.

Only by conscious discipline can we be sure we are staying true to the great themes of Scripture and declaring the whole will and counsel of God. At the end of our ministry, we want to be able to say with Paul, "You know that I have not hesitated to preach anything that would be helpful to you but have taught you publicly and from house to house . . . . I have not hesitated to proclaim to you the whole will of God" (Acts 20:20, 27).

10 What problems do you think all pastors should preach about?

To summarize, as we prepare to preach, we should ask ourselves these questions:

- Have I prepared myself to preach God's message? Have I fully yielded my heart and mind to the Holy Spirit?

- Do I have a fresh word from the Lord? Do I know God's will concerning the proclamation of this message?

- Am I in touch with my people? Do I truly understand the issues they are facing?

- Is my message scriptural and balanced? Is it relevant and true to the character of God?

11 When is a pastor ready to preach a sermon?

Only when we can answer these questions with reasonable certainty are we ready to proclaim God's Word.

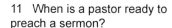

LESSON 4.3

4.3.1
OBJECTIVE
Explain the value of practicing your sermons.

Proclaim

The sermon does not actually become a "message" until it is preached. Until that moment, it is a sermon in name only, merely an outline or manuscript. Unfortunately, many preachers spend all their time preparing the sermon material without preparing for the actual proclamation. They give little thought to what will be required of them when they actually face the congregation and declare the Word of the Lord.

Practice Your Sermons

As a young pastor serving small, rural congregations, I had a considerably flexible schedule that afforded plenty of time for me to focus on my preaching. As a result, I disciplined myself not only in the message's preparation but also in its presentation. After completing each sermon, I practiced delivering it in the empty sanctuary at least twice, sometimes three times. In this way, I became both thoroughly immersed in the material and more comfortable with its presentation. When I actually delivered it to the congregation, then, I was familiar with it and relaxed enough to fine-tune or adapt the message based on the worshippers' response.

Although this routine has proved helpful to me and to many others, the vast majority of preachers remain averse to practicing their sermons. Many maintain that they are not actors and that preaching is not a performance to be rehearsed. I could not agree more. However, if actors care enough about their fictional lines to rehearse until they give the most convincing performance possible, how much more should we, the messengers of God, do everything within our power to speak "the very words of God" (1 Peter 4:11)? A weak presentation can undermine even the most carefully prepared sermon.

The more you practice a message, the more it is assimilated into your heart and spirit. And the better you know your message, the more the Holy Spirit can lead as you preach it.

Be Natural

When it comes to preaching, nothing is more important than the anointing of the Holy Spirit. Without it, the best efforts are simply futile. However, this does not mean that your part in the proclamation is unimportant. It means that your effectiveness depends on the Holy Spirit's anointing, not on your own efforts. Because God has chosen to speak through you, the most valuable gift you can bring Him is yourself, without trying to be someone different. The message God wants to speak through you is most effective when it flows naturally from who you are. That is, it flows most clearly from the context of all that has happened to you and all God has done in you.

Though it sounds contradictory, you are most fully yourself when you preach under the Spirit's anointing. Because you are most fully surrendered to the Holy Spirit at that moment, your preaching will be natural—it will flow out of who you are.

Of course, being natural does not mean that your preaching should be undisciplined or undeveloped. On the contrary, as you grow as a person and a minister, your preaching should develop as well. While still natural and still flowing, it becomes enlarged by your continued spiritual growth and your life experiences. Because you speak from your heart, you cannot help but speak to the heart of your congregation.

On the other hand, nothing undermines effective preaching more quickly than artificiality in the pulpit. Congregations easily detect when their ministers do not sound like their natural selves as they preach. Some preachers imitate a style they have heard others use and develop a "preaching tone." According to Wayne McDill, this preaching tone is characterized by "(1) a full volume projecting to the remotest hearer, (2) exaggerated articulation that is sound for the sake of sound, and (3) emotion that is overdone. . . . The ministerial tone is easily recognizable to most of us so that we say, 'He sounds like a preacher'" (1999, 117). Despite their good intentions, preachers who use anything other than their normal tone and way of speaking come across as contrived or phony.

The following chart was developed by McDill (1999, 121) to help preachers evaluate the effectiveness of their preaching style. Each continuum identifies a factor in determining how real you are when you preach. Generally, the more real you are, the more effective your preaching will be.

---

12 What can ministers do to make their sermons more presentable?

4.3.2
OBJECTIVE

Explain what it means to be "natural" when preaching.

13 Why should preachers be themselves and not imitate others?

4.3.3
OBJECTIVE

Identify key aspects of delivery.

Effectiveness of Preaching Style

less effective		more effective
Artificial	1 2 3 4 5 6 7 8 9 10	Natural
Stiff	1 2 3 4 5 6 7 8 9 10	Relaxed
Monotonous	1 2 3 4 5 6 7 8 9 10	Varied
Halting	1 2 3 4 5 6 7 8 9 10	Fluent
Timid	1 2 3 4 5 6 7 8 9 10	Confident
Harsh	1 2 3 4 5 6 7 8 9 10	Sympathetic
Flippant	1 2 3 4 5 6 7 8 9 10	Earnest
Obscure	1 2 3 4 5 6 7 8 9 10	Clear
Feeble	1 2 3 4 5 6 7 8 9 10	Energetic
Prosaic	1 2 3 4 5 6 7 8 9 10	Poetic

14 In which of the ten areas are you strongest and weakest?

Being "real" or natural in the pulpit does not mean behaving indiscriminately. McDill writes, "There is a line you don't want to cross, a line of decorum and good taste, a line of sensitivity to audience expectations. But too many preachers have such a limited idea of preaching style that they never express themselves in the most effective way" (1999, 127).

4.3.4
OBJECTIVE
Analyze the value, risk, and method of open preaching.

15 How can personality contribute to truth?

Be Open

As the famous nineteenth-century preacher Philip Brooks declared, "Preaching is truth through personality." In other words, the eternal unchanging truth of the gospel is seasoned with the minister's personality. Our mannerisms, ways of interacting with life, communication styles, and even our life experiences all become part of our message. In truth, our personal struggles—our own experiences with God's amazing grace—uniquely prepare us to speak to the deepest concerns of our congregations. And when they know that we deal with the same life issues they do, they inevitably perceive our preaching as more authentic, more real.

This is what makes the psalms so appealing, as they clearly reflect the psalmists' spiritual struggles and ultimate triumphs by the grace of God. Even the newest believer can identify with the psalms. The pain they express echoes our own. The psalmists' temptations, failures, and even sins are reflections of ours. And when they eventually overcome, their victories become a source of everlasting hope and encouragement.

16 What is open preaching?

As seen in the psalms, ministers do not need to hide appropriate personal information from the congregation. In fact, openly identifying with the audience is an effective method of preaching or speaking. I call it *transparent* or *open preaching.*

Share Past Struggles

However, although effective, open preaching is not without risks. You must use wisdom and sensitivity when disclosing your personal battles. When you make your congregation privy to your current temptations and struggles, you threaten them in a way; for in spite of everything they may say to the contrary, many parishioners expect you to be above the kind of issues they commonly face. If you are not, they reason, you should at least have the good sense not to mention your spiritual shortcomings in the pulpit. Therefore, the true power of open or transparent preaching lies not only in *what* you share but also in the *way* you share it. When you relate personal temptations, you must be careful to disclose them in a way that focuses the worshippers' attention not on your struggles but on God's grace.

17   What are the benefits of transparent preaching?

In general, I have found that I may be as open as I desire as long as the personal struggles and failures I disclose are in the past tense (or very nearly so). Sharing past issues accomplishes at least two things:

Rather than threatening my parishioners, it gives them hope because I have already worked through the situation. My experience provides practical insights for helping them deal with their own temptations, thus reinforcing their faith. As pastors reveal the wounds God has healed in their lives, they bring healing to others (Nouwen 1979).

Because my parishioners know that I share their common life experiences, they find my preaching more real and more palatable.

Admit Your Shortcomings

Yet revealing too much too soon is not the only pitfall ministers face when preaching out of their own life experiences. They must also resist the temptation to present themselves only in the best possible light. If our congregations always see us as heroes, conquering every foe, they will classify our preaching as self-preserving and our creditability as suspect. On the other hand, if they can see us as real people with real problems, they are more likely to take our preaching seriously.

To illustrate, a few years ago I preached a series of messages on parenting, one of which related to the mistakes parents make. While I wanted to be especially careful not to sound accusatory or condescending, I knew it was imperative that parents come to grips with their shortcomings. I solved my dilemma by sharing a personal experience in which I had failed as a parent: One evening when my daughter Leah accidentally caught a kitchen towel on fire, I lost control, and my angry outburst wounded and humiliated her in front of her friend. Approaching Leah afterward, I was tempted to make an excuse, but I realized that would still make Leah responsible for my behavior. Instead, I had to accept full responsibility for my sinful outburst, sincerely apologize to Leah, and ask her forgiveness, as well as apologize to her guest. I had to be willing to own my mistake and make restitution, thus restoring our relationship.

In sharing this painfully embarrassing incident with my congregation, I was able to position myself as just another parent. And like all parents, I make mistakes. By confessing my own sinful failure, I could highlight a common parental mistake without accusing anyone. Publicly owning my error allowed me to encourage other parents to accept responsibility for their own shortcomings as well. Finally, sharing from my own experience allowed me to present a model for making restitution for our parental failures without appearing to be self-serving.

Avoid Self-Focus

Perhaps the greatest challenge in transparent preaching is to avoid focusing on yourself. At first, this may seem contradictory. By its very nature, open preaching is somewhat autobiographical—full of personal accounts and experiences from your own life. How can you help but focus on yourself? Yet this method of preaching is not a contradiction but a demanding discipline. Sharing your experience in a way that helps the worshippers connect with the story and relate it to their own lives is preaching at its best.

Follow Jesus' Model

18 What is the key to helping people examine themselves spiritually?

Although transparent preaching cannot be reduced to a specific formula, it does involve some techniques. For instance, your stories should always address a common concern. You should share only those incidents with which everyone can identify. If you recount an experience so unique that it could never happen to anyone else, your congregation will have great difficulty applying it to their own lives. As a result, they will remember your story rather than getting in touch with their own.

19 Why is Jesus the best example of open preaching?

The best model for transparent preaching is Jesus himself. Most of what we know from the Gospels would be missing had Jesus not opened His life to His disciples. For example, how would we learn what occurred when Jesus went to the wilderness to fast for forty days? No one was with Him, yet both Matthew (4:1–11) and Luke (4:1–13) give a detailed account of what happened. While the Holy Spirit could have revealed it to them, it is more likely that Jesus spoke of His experience with the disciples to teach and encourage them. Jesus shared many personal things from His life. He did not hide the fact that He was human and had struggles. He spoke out of His own life experiences.

In the final analysis, preaching simply involves being witnesses to God's grace in our own lives. As He commanded the man whom He delivered from a legion of demons, Jesus asks us to go to our families and friends and "tell them how much the Lord has done for you, and how he has had mercy on you" (Mark 5:19).

Ministers have the privilege of fulfilling this command to their congregations. Frederick Beuchner writes,

The task of the preacher is to hold up life to us. . . . Drawing on nothing fancier than the poetry of his own life, let him use words and images that help make the surface of our lives transparent to the truth that lies deep within them, which is the wordless truth of who we are and who God is and the Gospel of our meeting. (1977, 16)

Test Yourself

Circle the letter of the *best* answer.

1. When setting priorities, ministers should first ask themselves what
a) must be done first.
b) God has called them to do.
c) the need is.
d) they do best.

2. *Delegate* means
a) "to put things first."
b) "to assign boring tasks."
c) "to empower others to do tasks."
d) "to do important work by oneself."

3. The first step in preparing a message is to
a) choose a text.
b) write an introduction.
c) select a topic.
d) prepare one's heart.

4. A pastor listens with both ears by hearing
a) the Spirit and people's needs.
b) both sides of an issue.
c) two people at the same time.
d) the advice of two wise leaders.

5. The minor story in a Bible passage is always about
a) people.
b) Israel.
c) children.
d) God.

6. Practicing your sermons will
a) improve your messages.
b) make you seem well educated.
c) give you a better preaching tone.
d) enable you to follow the biblical pattern.

7. When preaching, a minister should act
a) dignified.
b) spiritual.
c) natural.
d) simple.

8. Preachers are more effective when they are
a) passionate.
b) confident.
c) relaxed.
d) all of the above.

9. When preaching openly, ministers should emphasize
a) God's grace.
b) temptation's power.
c) their faults.
d) others' faults.

10. To help listeners connect to their stories, ministers should
a) tell stories in the present tense.
b) share about common struggles.
c) use stories everyone has heard.
d) use altered names in the stories.

Responses to Interactive Questions
Chapter 4

Some of these responses may include information that is supplemental to the IST. These questions are intended to produce reflective thinking beyond the course content and your responses may vary from these examples.

1 What does Acts 6:1–7 teach?

The apostles recognized that their primary task was the ministry of God's Word (Acts 6:2). They realized the necessity of putting first things first.

2 How does Philippians 4:13 relate to prioritizing?

Christ gives us strength to do what God calls us to do, but we all have limitations. Divine help does not apply to what we assign for ourselves.

3 List four things God has called every pastor to do.

(1) Walk daily with God. (2) Be a good spouse and family member (including a good member of the family of God). (3) Preach the Word of God. (4) Pray for people.

4 What types of tasks can others in your church do?

Answers will vary. Others can undertake tasks according to their God-given gifts and as they recognize the needs.

5 How do pastors begin to prepare their messages?

By allowing the Holy Spirit to prepare their hearts, making them responsive to God's message

6 What should pastors do to create relevant sermons?

Direct one ear toward what God has to say and the other toward the needs of the people.

7 What is a key to understanding the Bible and people?

Spending time with both, hearing more than speaking

8 Identify the major and minor stories in Genesis 3.

Major story: God's grace extended to fallen humanity. Minor story: Disobedience separated humankind from God.

9 How do ministers benefit from regularly evaluating their preaching?

It helps them to avoid emphasizing one biblical theme or aspect over others; that is, to preach the whole will and counsel of God.

10 What problems do you think all pastors should preach about?

Answers will vary.

11 When is a pastor ready to preach a sermon?

Answers will vary but should focus on the minister's spiritual preparation, an anointed word from God, the people's needs, and a scriptural and balanced perspective of the message.

12 What can ministers do to make their sermons more presentable?

Practice preaching them.

13 Why should preachers be themselves and not imitate others?

Trying to be someone else makes the minister sound unnatural and insincere.

14 In which of the ten areas are you strongest and weakest?

Answers will vary.

15 How can personality contribute to truth?

One of the most effective ways for ministers to communicate truth is to share from their own lives.

16 What is open preaching?

Messages that share personal experiences of spiritual struggles and triumphs to drive home the sermon's point

17 What are the benefits of transparent preaching?

Personal testimony of victory gives hope; you become a personal example of overcoming temptation; and your preaching will seem more real.

18 What is the key to helping people examine themselves spiritually?

Using illustrations or stories about common struggles that most anyone could relate to

19 Why is Jesus the best example of open preaching?

He did not hide His humanity or struggles; He opened His life to His disciples.

The Pastor as Worship Leader

By calling pastors *worship leaders*, I refer to their responsibility for the overall direction of the church service. Like their parishioners, ministers live in the "real world" with its pressing demands and distractions; but unlike the congregation, pastors are expected to focus on spiritual matters. While others may straggle in to the worship service beset with the cares of life, ministers are expected to come tuned and sensitive to the eternal. They are responsible to set the tone for worship, to create a spiritual atmosphere that turns the congregation's attention toward God, by reading Scripture, selecting worship songs, leading congregational prayer, and preaching the Word. This is particularly true of churches that lack the luxury of adequate staff to distinguish these roles.

Worship cannot be forced, but it can and must be encouraged. Although the Holy Spirit's presence cannot be manufactured, worshippers must be taught to recognize His nearness and accommodate His manifestations. This is the true purpose of liturgy. Liturgy in itself is not worship, but it prepares the congregation to worship. True worship occurs only as we "see" God. It is an act of our will—"a sacrifice of praise" (Jeremiah 33:11)—that sensitizes us to God's immanence.

Pastors can encourage people to be more sensitive to God's presence, but the people themselves must choose to be active participants. To illustrate, a friend told me of a time he boarded a small airplane and sat directly behind a mother and her small son, about two to three years old. Fascinated by the unfamiliar surroundings, the boy's attention was focused on examining the seat belts and reaching for briefcases and other eye-catching carry-ons. The young mother certainly had her hands full. To complicate matters, she was trying to persuade the boy to wave good-bye to his daddy. First she asked; then she tried coaxing; and finally, she ordered him—all to no avail. She could not divert her son's attention from the new, exciting world inside the plane. Having exhausted all forms of persuasion, the mother resorted to gentle force. Wrapping one arm around the boy's waist, she grasped his wrist and turned him toward the window, awkwardly waving good-bye with his stiff arm. Yet the boy resisted, squirming and twisting until he broke free. With renewed determination, the mother again took hold of him, pressed his face close to the plane's small window, and forced his reluctant arm to wave. Then, suddenly, everything about the boy's manner changed. He caught sight of something. Pressing his face against the window, he cried excitedly, "Daddy! I see Daddy!" Now he was waving both chubby arms eagerly, almost frantically.

Like the boy's mother, pastors direct their congregations in acts of worship designed to wrestle their attention away from the distractions of the world. In effect, pastors press the people's faces against the window of eternity. At first, the people do not "see" anything and merely go through the motions of worship. Then, suddenly, they catch sight of God, and their mechanical motions transform into reality, into true worship. Now God's presence is undeniable, and without further prompting, their hearts respond of their own accord, crying: "'*Abba*, Father.' [For] the Spirit himself testifies with our spirit that we are God's children" (Romans 8:15–16).

Lesson 5.1   The Holy Spirit's Leading

Objective

5.1.1   Explain the value of yielding control to the Spirit.

Lesson 5.2   The Holy Spirit's Gifts

Objectives

5.2.1   Describe how to make room for spiritual gifts in a service.

5.2.2   Explain four steps in teaching people to use spiritual gifts.

Lesson 5.3   The Worshipper's Decision

Objectives

5.3.1   Explain why a pastor should always give an invitation.

5.3.2   Describe why the altar time is important.

5.1.1
OBJECTIVE

Explain the value of yielding control to the Spirit.

1   Describe a worship service you attended in which the Holy Spirit preempted the scheduled order.

The Holy Spirit's Leading

Even if pastors do not have a written order of worship, they usually enter services with a clear idea of how things will go. Generally, the order of worship includes an opening prayer, public Scripture reading, congregational singing, an offering (worship in giving), special music, pastoral prayer, the sermon, and an altar service. Of course, all of this is (or should be) subject to the leading of the Holy Spirit. Should the Spirit direct the service in another way, the pastor must be quick to respond to His leading.

In one of my worship experiences some years ago, the Holy Spirit did just that. As I stepped to the pulpit to pray, I was suddenly, overwhelmingly, aware of God's presence. Even now, I can hardly speak of it. As wave after wave of God's glorious love washed over me, I was overcome with weeping. I could not stand. I fell to my knees and pressed my forehead to the floor. God's overwhelming holiness was all around me, and never have I felt so unclean. Like Isaiah, inwardly I cried, "Woe to me! . . . I am ruined! For . . . my eyes have seen the King, the Lord Almighty" (Isaiah 6:5). While every shortcoming, every failure, was shamefully obvious, I did not feel condemned. As paradoxical as it may sound, I felt absolutely unworthy yet totally accepted.

This continued for more than thirty minutes, although it seemed far less. An awesome sense of the Lord's presence had filled the whole sanctuary, touching everyone present. The praise team continued to lead the congregation in worship through song, and there was an ever-increasing liberty.

When I regained my composure, I briefly shared with the people what I could about what had happened. Then we began to worship again—a worship so free that I have not experienced anything like it ever since. As one person, several hundred worshippers passionately praised the Lord. The intensity of our praise was literally overpowering, yet never has worship been so effortless, so spontaneous. We sang of God's holiness and majesty. We encouraged one another to "be bold, be strong; for the Lord thy God is with thee." We sang militant songs about spiritual warfare: "I hear the sound of the army of the Lord. . . . It's the sound of praise, the sound of war." With each song, the sense of the Lord's presence and power increased.

Aware of the late hour, we tried to stop two or three times, but each time, the congregation picked up the song and began to sing again. Then, about four hours into the service, as we sang "Be Bold" yet again, the trumpet player took off on an inspired solo. A recent convert and former jazz musician, he simply stood there crying out his testimony through his trumpet. It took very little imagination to see where he had been, for years of drug and alcohol abuse had left their scars. No doubt about it, he had suffered. But now he was redeemed, and his music had a different theme. His joyous celebration held us spellbound at first, and then we found ourselves caught up with him in it. We sang and danced before the Lord with all of our might. It was uninhibited but not disorderly; spontaneous, but not out of control. It was Spirit-directed. It was worship!

Imagine how impoverished that service would have been had I resisted the Holy Spirit's leading and insisted on maintaining my predetermined order of worship. Only God knows how many times we have missed His richest blessings because of our insensitivity to the improvisation of the Spirit. And only God knows how blessed we will be—whether one person or hundreds of people—when we do obey the Spirit's promptings.

One Sunday in another service, I sensed the Holy Spirit's speaking to me while the associate pastor led the congregation in prayer. The Spirit directed my attention to a young couple on the front row who were visitors at our church. As I looked at them, a thought burst into my mind: *This woman has suffered a serious medical complication following the birth of her second child. The Lord will heal her if I will pray for her.*

When the associate pastor finished praying, I walked over and motioned to the couple, asking, "May I minister to you?" Before they could respond, the Holy Spirit came upon the young woman, and she fell backward onto her seat. I quickly moved to them, and leaning close to her, I described what the Holy Spirit had revealed to me about her medical condition. Then I prayed a simple prayer asking the Lord to completely heal her and restore her health. When I finished praying, we continued with the service.

Later, I learned that after their second child's birth, the woman's thyroid stopped working, causing serious physical and emotional complications. Medication prescribed by her doctors was doing little to no good.

On Monday morning, the woman called her doctor, told him what had happened, and informed him that she had stopped taking the medicine. (This was her decision, not something I as the pastor had told her to do.) When he recommended against that, she replied, "I am not asking you to recommend anything. I am simply informing you of what I have done. If God has not healed me and I experience a medical crisis, I simply wanted you to know that I have not had any medication since early Sunday morning."

When she returned to her doctor the next week, he ran a battery of tests that simply confirmed what she already knew: She was healed! She gave me a copy of her medical records for my files. On them, the doctor states, "Thyroid is normal. This is a miracle."

I share these two experiences to illustrate the importance of allowing the Holy Spirit to direct our worship. Again, only God knows how much eternal good has been lost because pastors have been insensitive or unresponsive to the Spirit's prompting. While the order of worship may provide structure and direction, it is the Holy Spirit who gives life to our worship and to our ministry.

5.2.1
OBJECTIVE
Describe how to make room for spiritual gifts in a service.

2 Identify three Scripture passages that encourage the use of spiritual gifts.

3 Why do some pastors hinder spiritual gifts?

5.2.2
OBJECTIVE
Explain four steps in teaching people to use spiritual gifts.

teaching f learning Same word in Hebrew.

The Holy Spirit's Gifts

Spirit-filled pastors should not only seek to follow the Holy Spirit's leading when directing worship but should also structure the worship service to give spiritual gifts a chance to operate. According to Romans 12, we are all one body in Christ, and each one of us has "different gifts according to the grace given us" (vv. 4–6). Thus, pastors are responsible to encourage and train believers in the use of their spiritual gifts.

Make Room for Spiritual Gifts

First Corinthians 12:7–11 lists several gifts that the Spirit gives to believers. The Scriptures teach us to "eagerly desire spiritual gifts" (1 Corinthians 14:1) and to "fan into flame the gift of God" (2 Timothy 1:6). Yet some pastors so tightly control their services that it is nearly impossible for the Holy Spirit to minister through spiritual gifts.

Such rigid control is unbiblical. Paul instructs, "Do not put out the Spirit's fire; do not treat prophecies with contempt" (1 Thessalonians 5:19–20). Why, then, do some sincere, Spirit-filled pastors hinder the manifestations of spiritual gifts? Their resistance may stem from a number of issues, but the primary reason usually involves past negative experiences with the gifts of the Spirit and/or lack of understanding regarding their operation in a church service.

Misuse of the gifts is nothing new. The New Testament church—particularly the church at Corinth—had to deal with this very issue. In facing obvious abuse of spiritual gifts, however, Paul did not discourage or forbid their use. On the contrary, he taught the church how to use them properly (1 Corinthians 14), encouraging the believers to "excel in gifts that build up the church" (1 Corinthians 14:12).

Train People to Minister with Their Gifts

Like Paul, Spirit-filled pastors should instruct their people concerning the gifts of the Spirit. This may be awkward at first, and some ministers may feel unprepared to teach about this subject. But teaching is the best way to learn.

Teaching on spiritual gifts is similar to teaching a person to ride a bicycle in that it involves both information and application. Teaching and learning must go hand-in-hand. That is, teaching has not taken place until learning has occurred, and learning has not occurred until the student has climbed on the bicycle and ridden it. Facts are of little importance; people must engage in the experience themselves for true learning to occur.

In the same way, the amount of the worshippers' knowledge about spiritual gifts matters little if they are not allowing the Holy Spirit to operate in and through them. Until the worshippers act on what they know, it is only information, not application. Therefore, our purpose in teaching about the gifts is to help people reach the place where they regularly minister in the power and gifts of the Spirit. Only then has true learning taken place.

Experience has taught me four basic steps in the teaching process:
1. Instruction: Tell them.
2. Demonstration: Show them.
3. Participation: Let them do it with you.
4. Ministry: Let them do it.

Let us consider these four steps specifically in relation to training about spiritual gifts.

Instruction

4 Summarize the steps in training people to use spiritual gifts.

This phase should include identification of the gifts (1 Corinthians 12:7–11), definition of the gifts, and an explanation of how the gifts operate. Obviously, this material falls into the information category. When you complete this step, your congregation will know a great deal about the gifts, but for the most part, they will not have used them. Thus, you must lead them further into application.

Demonstration

During the demonstration phase, you should provide an opportunity for ministry so the gifts can be exercised. Then the congregation will be able to witness firsthand what you have been teaching.

When I taught about spiritual gifts in the church I served (see chapter 8 for more discussion of our training program), I ended each session with a time of ministry. That is, following the teaching, I prayed and asked the Holy Spirit to show us how He wanted to minister. At this point, the Lord would usually give me or someone on the ministry team a word of knowledge or a prophecy (1 Corinthians 12:8, 10).

One time, the Lord gave a ministry team member a word of knowledge about a woman with a serious back injury. When the team member shared this word, a young woman in the meeting shouted, "No way!" She told us that, being a very skeptical person, she had just prayed, "Lord, if this stuff is real, let him describe my back injury." When she added that she was scheduled for major back surgery, we invited her to come forward for prayer. The Lord completely healed her, and her doctor later confirmed that she was totally well.

Participation

5 How did Jesus involve His disciples in spiritual gifts (Matthew 14:16–21)?

The participation phase is the time for you to ask the Holy Spirit to speak and minister through members of the local body. That is, you should encourage believers to practice the gifts of the Spirit.

I understand this step best when I recall how my wife taught our daughter, Leah, to ride her bicycle. After some final instruction from my wife, Leah climbed onto the bicycle. At first, Leah could not keep her balance, so my wife ran behind her and steadied the bike. As Leah became more proficient, however, my wife began to release her hold on the bicycle for longer and longer periods of time. She still ran beside Leah, but she no longer steadied the bike. Finally, Leah was speeding down the street completely by herself.

When I reach this stage in my teaching on spiritual gifts, after we have prayed, I ask if anyone senses that the Holy Spirit wants to speak or minister through him or her. In one meeting, a woman responded, "I sense the Holy Spirit telling me that there is a person here who has an abnormal fear of dying. Though this person is young, he or she is tormented with thoughts of dying and leaving his or her children."

Almost immediately, a young man began to weep. He explained, "Both of my parents died before they were fifty years old. Just this week, my brother was diagnosed with terminal cancer. Now, all I can think about is my own death. I cannot sleep. I have lost my appetite. I feel like I am losing my mind."

We invited him to come forward for prayer. I asked the woman who had shared the word of knowledge to join me in praying for the man. Finally, I invited anyone else who would like to minister in this way to help us pray. After a few minutes of intense prayer, the young man's countenance changed as God's peace flooded his soul.

6 How did the author let people minister to others with their spiritual gifts?

Yet what happened in the hearts and lives of those who prayed for him was of nearly equal significance. Now that God had used them to minister to someone, they realized that the ministry of the Holy Spirit is not reserved for a select few but is available for every believer (see 1 Corinthians 12:4–11).

Ministry

The fourth and final phase of the learning process involves solo ministry—the time to release those you have been teaching into the work of ministry. Jesus did this with the twelve disciples (Matthew 10) and with the seventy-two others He sent out (Luke 10:1–24). It is important to let believers minister spiritual gifts without you.

At the church I served as pastor, we scheduled a formal commissioning service for this purpose. We laid hands on each person and released them to minister in the gifts and power of the Holy Spirit (Acts 13:3). These anointed ministers then prayed for others during prayer time and in the altar services. Usually, thirty to fifty of them stood at the front of the church at prayer time, enabling a significant number of hurting people to receive personal ministry during a relatively short time. Having been trained in the ministry of the gifts of the Holy Spirit, our prayer leaders ministered "with a demonstration of the Spirit's power" (1 Corinthians 2:4). In service after service, God worked through these ordinary men and women to bring healing and grace to others. For a number of years, hardly a week went by without a miracle of some kind, be it physical or spiritual.

Establish a Model for the Gifts' Operation

7 On what should ministers focus when establishing procedures for the operation of spiritual gifts?

As they structure services to provide opportunity for the manifestation of spiritual gifts, pastors should also establish a working model through which the gifts are exercised "in a fitting and orderly way" (1 Corinthians 14:40). At our church, for example, before a person could give a prophecy, a message in tongues, or an interpretation, he or she had to come to a microphone at the front of the church and be recognized by a pastoral staff member. This served three purposes:

It allowed us to maintain order while encouraging manifestation of the gifts of the Spirit.

By formally granting the floor to the person exercising the gift, we were able to add the weight of pastoral recognition to the ministry.

From a practical standpoint, using a microphone enabled everyone in a large auditorium to hear the message.

8 How can a pastor help new believers to use spiritual gifts?

On the other hand, if the individuals giving the prophecy, message in tongues, or interpretation lacked spiritual maturity, a member of the pastoral staff consulted with them before releasing them to speak at the microphone. On rare occasions, permission might be refused, or the staff member might feel it would be better if he or she shared the word with the congregation. In any case, the pastoral presence gave the congregation a sense of security.

9 How should a pastor help visitors when spiritual gifts are evident in a service?

In a growing church with new worshippers attending almost every service, the operation of a spiritual gift should be used as a teaching moment. It gives the pastor an opportunity to provide brief scriptural basis for the gift and to explain the guidelines governing its use in the local body. Although we will never eliminate misuse of spiritual gifts, by closely adhering to principles like these, we can minimize the abuse of the gifts without limiting the free flow of the Holy Spirit in our services.

The Worshipper's Decision

Of all the pastor's responsibilities as worship leader, none is more important than bringing the worshippers to a spiritual decision.

Invite Everyone to Respond to the Message

5.3.1
OBJECTIVE
Explain why a pastor should always give an invitation.

10 How do people respond to messages?

Regardless of where they may be in their spiritual pilgrimage, all worshippers need to be challenged and encouraged to take the next step. For unbelievers, this means taking the first step in their journey with Christ. Thus, the pastor must lead unbelievers to a place where they can choose to accept Jesus as Lord and Savior. Mature believers, however, will need to grow in other areas. While God may guide some to give time or money to the Kingdom, He may call others to commit to a church leadership role. Whatever the situation, worship should bring each person face-to-face with God and the claims God is making on the worshipper's life at that moment. That is, worship should be a time for obedience and growth.

Never close a sermon without inviting people to respond to your message! Every sermon should be presented to (1) solve a problem, (2) meet a need, or (3) improve something or someone. After you preach, you should invite the people to immediately make a decision about the truths presented. According to Larsen, closing a sermon without an invitation is like netting a fish, then dropping the net and letting it escape (1992, 99). Although preachers cannot force people to act, their duty is to bring people to a point of decision.

Invite People to Pray at the Altar

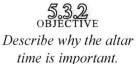

5.3.2
OBJECTIVE
Describe why the altar time is important.

11 Why are many spiritual decisions made at the altar?

While individuals certainly can respond to God at any time in the service, they most frequently make life-changing spiritual decisions during the altar service. For that reason, regardless of the nature of the service, pastors should *always* give opportunity for unbelievers to receive Jesus as their Savior. They should also encourage believers to deal with the issues presented in the sermon. Of course, the Holy Spirit can communicate to the worshippers' hearts and minds, but He often uses pastors' words to articulate His call in a way that clearly defines the choice being asked for.

If pastors preach on healing, they should invite the sick to come to the altar for prayer (James 5:14–15). If their topic was the baptism in the Holy Spirit, they should call to the altar those who need to be filled with the Spirit (Acts 2:38–39). Whatever the sermon addresses—total commitment, baptism, discipleship, the call to full-time ministry, spiritual guidance, repentance, forgiveness, stewardship, or so forth—the pastor has a God-given responsibility to press for a decision.

12 What principle concerning people's response can ministers learn from 1 Samuel 8:7?

If no one responds to an invitation, some preachers may believe they have failed, thinking it reflects on their ability as ministers. Yet nothing could be further from the truth! The altar call is not about the pastor or the pastor's ability. He or she must not take the rejection personally. The person who resists the appeal of the Spirit is rejecting God, not the minister. When Israel's clamoring for a king sparked the prophet Samuel's hurt and displeasure, God responded, "It is not you they have rejected, but they have rejected me as their king" (1 Samuel 8:7).

13 What balances some individuals' rejection of the message?

On the other hand, nothing affirms a pastor more than to see lost men and women receive Christ. Dr. Haddon Robinson, professor at Gordon-Conwell Theological Seminary and prolific author, tells of preaching a joint series of meetings to several churches in a small Minnesota town. From his perspective, the results seemed to be minimal. However, several years later on the West Coast, Robinson met a man who asked if he remembered those meetings. When Robinson indicated that he did, the man added, "Do you remember that on a Wednesday night two guys came forward? Well, I was one of them. My friend and I came that night, and we did two things: we trusted Christ, and we decided that if He was worth trusting, He was worth giving our lives to. I'm now in the ministry, and my friend is a missionary in Africa" (Robinson, personal communication).

Thank God that Dr. Robinson did not allow the humble setting or the small crowd to discourage him. And thank God he did not assume that everyone in attendance was already a believer. Had he done so, those two men might have remained lost, along with all those they had reached through their own ministry.

Although every worshipper shares some responsibility for the service, none is more responsible than the pastor. Therefore, pastors must prepare their hearts and minds through prayer to become more sensitive to the Holy Spirit. From beginning to end, they must follow the Spirit's leading, accommodate the ministry of spiritual gifts, and move the worshipers to some type of spiritual decision. Having done this, ministers can say with Paul, "I was not disobedient to the vision from heaven" (Acts 26:19).

Test Yourself

Circle the letter of the *best* answer.

1. As a worship leader, the pastor is responsible for
a) guiding the service.
b) planning the songs.
c) causing people to respond.
d) staying on schedule.

2. When pastors yield control of the service to the Holy Spirit,
a) people listen to their sermons.
b) people pay their tithes.
c) their ministry is more effective.
d) their personalities change.

3. A pastor can make room for spiritual gifts by
a) encouraging people to use them at home.
b) teaching people about spiritual gifts.
c) planning time for multiple prophecies in the service.
d) all of the above.

4. After showing people how to use spiritual gifts, pastors should
a) explain what spiritual gifts are.
b) show them how to prophesy.
c) teach about spiritual fruit.
d) allow them to use their gifts.

5. When we create a model for using spiritual gifts, we
a) keep order in the service.
b) limit the freedom of the Spirit.
c) reduce the spiritual to the natural.
d) maintain our service schedule.

6. Teaching about spiritual gifts involves information and
a) application.
b) skill.
c) discipline.
d) common sense.

7. Pastors should seek what result from their preaching?
a) Guilt
b) Excitement
c) Church growth
d) Change

8. Pastors should give invitations
a) on the first Sunday of each month.
b) at the close of each sermon.
c) after preaching about salvation.
d) when they see new people at church.

9. Altar time is important because it
a) helps people make spiritual decisions.
b) shows whether the sermon was anointed.
c) allows people to fellowship with others.
d) gives pastors time to greet visitors.

10. A successful altar service requires
a) leading people to a private room.
b) subsequent house calls from the minister.
c) the guidance of the Holy Spirit.
d) a vision from heaven.

Responses to Interactive Questions
Chapter 5

Some of these responses may include information that is supplemental to the IST. These questions are intended to produce reflective thinking beyond the course content and your responses may vary from these examples.

1 Describe a worship service you attended in which the Holy Spirit preempted the scheduled order.

Answers will vary.

2 Identify three Scripture passages that encourage the use of spiritual gifts.

(1) 1 Corinthians 12:7–11 admonishes pastors to allow for the gifts of the Spirit during the service; (2) 2 Timothy 1:6 admonishes pastors to fan into flame the gifts of God by encouraging their use; (3) 1 Thessalonians 5:19–20 admonishes believers not to quench the Spirit's ministry.

3 Why do some pastors hinder spiritual gifts?

They may not want to give up control; they may fear misuse of the gifts; or they may neglect to teach how the gifts should be used.

4 Summarize the steps in training people to use spiritual gifts.

(1) Instruction involves teaching what the gifts are and how they operate. (2) Demonstration provides a service context with liberty for the gifts to be used. (3) Participation is nurturing the people to use their gifts, as the Spirit of God enables them. (4) Ministry is encouraging the believers to exercise the gifts by themselves as often as the opportunity and leading of the Spirit allow.

5 How did Jesus involve His disciples in spiritual gifts (Matthew 14:16–21)?

He gave the disciples the chance to work with Him in bringing about the miracle of the multiplied bread and fish. This illustrates the participation stage of teaching believers how to operate in the gifts.

6 How did the author let people minister to others with their spiritual gifts?

He had an altar call specifically for those who desired to be used in spiritual gifts, where the pastor and elders laid hands on, anointed, and prayed for the Lord to use the people. Then they were commissioned to go forth and minister. In other words, the pastor sanctioned their desire and believed with them for God to use them.

7 On what should ministers focus when establishing procedures for the operation of spiritual gifts?

They should focus on giving opportunity, maintaining order, and providing the best possible means for all to hear so that all are edified by the blessing of God's visitation among them.

8 How can a pastor help new believers to use spiritual gifts?

The pastor should instruct new believers about spiritual gifts when he or she feels they are ready. If new believers feel the need to give a message before such instruction occurs, however, the pastor should gently consult with them about the direction of the message, perhaps speaking in their stead or occasionally prohibiting them from speaking.

9 How should a pastor help visitors when spiritual gifts are evident in a service?

The pastor should explain what Scripture teaches about them, giving some guidelines for their use in the church.

10 How do people respond to messages?

Some for salvation or rededication to follow Jesus; others in commitment to some service or special use by God

11 Why are many spiritual decisions made at the altar?

People associate the altar with making spiritual decisions and commitments according to what they have heard during the preaching. They recognize the altar call as a time to commune with God.

12 What principle concerning people's response can ministers learn from 1 Samuel 8:7?

If the pastor has preached the truth of God's Word, the people's response to the invitation does not reflect acceptance or rejection of the preacher; rather, it is each person's response to or rejection of God.

13 What balances some individuals' rejection of the message?

The encouraging reality that new life comes to some who respond and that their step of faith changes the entire direction of their lives, perhaps extending the pastor's ministry through their own

The Ministry of Pastoral Care

Pastoral care refers to the ministry a pastor gives to people in crisis. While most often related to sickness or death, such crisis includes tragedies of all types: job loss, family conflict, divorce, pregnancy out of wedlock, illegal activity, drug or alcohol addictions, abuse, depression, and so forth. Virtually every crisis carries with it a sense of loss followed by grief. Because of this, the fundamentals of pastoral care—presence, empathy, and caregiving—remain the same whatever the difficulty or trial.

Lesson 6.1   Presence

Objectives

6.1.1   Explain the value of a pastor's presence to a person in crisis.
6.1.2   Summarize two mistakes that pastors make in crises.

Lesson 6.2   Empathy

Objectives

6.2.1   Define empathy.
6.2.2   Explain the stages of the grieving process.

Lesson 6.3   Caregiving

Objectives

6.3.1   List four things that a person in a crisis might appreciate.
6.3.2   Explain three keys for relating to a person in a trial.

6.1.1
OBJECTIVE
Explain the value of a pastor's presence to a person in crisis.

1   Describe a time in your life when a pastor's or friend's presence comforted you.

Presence

The ministry of pastoral care is relatively simple—not easy, but simple—because the most helpful thing you can do is to just be there. The Holy Spirit will minister strength and comfort through the gift of your presence. Since the effects of a crisis linger long after the actual event has passed, the persons most directly impacted will continue to need pastoral care until they have had a chance to completely work through their feelings. This process will most likely take several weeks or months.

The True Comfort of Presence

While hurting individuals may have many questions, they do not really seek answers; rather, they crave stability, friendship, and comfort. Too often, we try to say something, such as a Scripture verse or trite comment, that will make their pain go away. In doing so, we usually just make matters worse. We try to explain away the tragedy when the only thing the hurting person needs and wants to hear is, "I'm so sorry." Our efforts to comfort are often fumbling at best. In reality, ministers and others who come to simply hold the hand of the person in crisis because they cannot think of anything to say generally provide more help than a dozen Scripture-quoting friends.

Please do not misunderstand me. I am not making light of Scripture or its value. I am merely pointing out that there is a time to speak and a time to be silent (Ecclesiastes 3:11). At times, quoting Scripture passages will comfort and sustain as nothing else will. But that seldom occurs during the early stages of a crisis when the persons involved are still numb from shock and grief. The beginning of a tragedy is a time to simply be there, a time for an arm around the shoulder and a supporting hand.

My introduction to pastoral ministry was literally a baptism by fire, or perhaps I should say by sickness and death. During the first four weeks I served as pastor, I preached at three funerals and spent many long hours in the hospital with the sick and their families.

Nothing in my training or experience had prepared me for this. At the hospital, I felt like an intruder, as though the doctors merely tolerated my presence in a place where science and medicine reigned. I felt intimidated. What good could I possibly do? Of what value were Scripture and prayer compared to the advances and knowledge involved in modern medicine?

Still, I faithfully visited the sick, sitting with their families while the patient was in surgery and during the critical hours when things could go either way. I did the things I had been taught to do—administer Scripture and prayer—as well as a number of other things no one had ever mentioned, such as simply being there and listening without saying anything. Generally, I felt pretty useless.

Then, I began receiving thank-you notes from the people I had visited in the hospital. They wrote, "It meant so much to have you there when I was facing surgery," or "I cannot tell you how much strength I gained from your visit." I could not believe it. I felt as though I had not done anything special. Yet despite my inabilities, people were genuinely touched by my visits. Knowing that the Holy Spirit was working through me to bring comfort gave me more confidence the next time I made hospital calls.

About two years later, a crisis occurred that helped me understand this even better. Nine days after our daughter Leah was born, my wife began hemorrhaging so much that she was nearly unconscious from blood loss by the time we reached the emergency room. After watching the staff wheel her into surgery and signing the necessary forms, I was left alone with my thoughts and fears. Imagining a host of terrifying possibilities, I paced the floor in agitation. Comfort came only when my mother joined me. Although I do not recall her saying anything, I felt better just knowing she was there. Somehow her presence strengthened and encouraged me.

For the first time, I realized that when a crisis arises, small acts of kindness make a huge difference. Simple things like an encouraging word, the touch of a hand on your shoulder, or just another's presence have a profound impact. Even the bravest and most self-reliant experience an inner strengthening from the presence of a compassionate friend or minister. While the circumstance may be just as grim, somehow they do not seem as foreboding.

The Value and Power of Presence

6.1.2
OBJECTIVE
Summarize two mistakes that pastors make in crises.

2   What two errors can pastors make when caring for others?

Few pastors are especially gifted in the area of pastoral care. By nature, most of us feel the need to do something when confronted with a crisis. If we cannot "fix" the problem, we feel useless. This leads to two types of tempting mistakes: (1) premature and/or ineffective ministry or (2) absence or abandonment.

One young woman, in the hospital with cancer, told me that her pastor breezed in and out of her room, chatting the whole time, hardly giving her a chance to speak. Although he always asked how she was doing, he never asked in a way that encouraged her to respond honestly. After two or three minutes, he would pray and immediately leave, pleading a busy schedule. While she was thankful for his visit, it provided very little ministry.

When this pattern continued for several visits, the woman determined to do something about it. Arriving for his next pastoral call, he swept in with his usual chatter and superficial questions: "How are you feeling today? Did you sleep well? Are you having much pain?" When he paused for a breath, she told him exactly—not angrily but honestly—how she was feeling: "The pain is absolutely unbearable. I'm afraid of dying. I pray day and night, but God never answers me; He never makes His presence known. As far as I'm concerned, the heavens have turned to brass, and God has turned His back on me."

This admission made the pastor visibly uncomfortable. When she broke down in sobs, he quickly said, "Let's pray." The woman replied, "Do not do that to me! You are always using prayer like some sort of escape hatch. Every time I try to tell you what it is really like to be barely thirty years old, the mother of two children, and dying with cancer, you want to pray. That is not real prayer. It is just religious words, a smoke screen, so you do not have to deal with my feelings. Today you are going to hear me out; you are going to walk with me through this valley of the shadow of death. That is what you are supposed to do. That is why you are here—so I do not have to face death alone."

The pastor stayed and listened to her until she was finished, but he did not visit her again for a long time. Although a conscientious pastor, he succumbed to both temptations. That is, he used prayer prematurely and for the wrong reasons and, when his desperate parishioner confronted him about it, he simply stopped visiting her.

I share that incident not to discredit the pastor or the ministry but to graphically illustrate what happens when we use prayer and Scripture too soon while ministering to people in crisis. This is probably not a conscious choice; more likely, we naturally gravitate to prayer when we find ourselves facing challenging or impossible situations. And in most cases, this is a good response.

Yet in the situation above, prayer effectively isolated the dying woman—something it was never meant to do.

3   How can pastors make prayer more meaningful?

Thus, the keys are timing and sensitivity. One grieving father said, "I know all the 'right' biblical passages, but the point is this: While the words of the Bible are true, grief renders them unreal." This could be said about prayer. Nothing is more powerful than prayer, yet suffering and grief can render it unreal too, at least for a time. I am not saying that prayer has no place in the sickroom. I simply mean that prayer is more effective *after* we have listened deeply and compassionately to the honest concerns of the person in crisis and his or her family. It is our presence that makes prayer real for them.

Some years ago, I ministered to a grieving mother, Joyce, whose teenage son had died in a tragic accident. Through her tears, she shared an experience that illustrates the power of presence. One morning when she was feeling particularly low, the doorbell rang. She momentarily wrestled with the idea of ignoring it since her eyes were red from crying, her hair was a mess, and she was not dressed for the day. But when the doorbell rang again, Joyce forced herself to open the door.

The visitor, a friend from church, walked right in and said, "I've come to talk with you." Noting Joyce's disheveled appearance, she quickly added, "And if you don't feel like talking, I'll just sit with you. If you want to cry," she continued, brandishing a box of tissue, "I'm prepared to cry with you." While she spoke, the uninvited guest made her way to the kitchen and prepared the coffeemaker.

The two friends spent the rest of the morning sharing coffee laced with conversation and tears. As they talked, Joyce began to feel better. Although still sad, she was no longer alone with her sorrow. A friend had come to help her bear it. This somehow reassured her that God was present too, comforting her.

As she related the story to me, Joyce concluded almost wistfully, "If only there were more people like her. And she brought her own tissue! Can you believe that?"

4   How does 2 Corinthians 7:5–6 relate to pastoral care?

This is the ministry of presence. It is what Paul alluded to when he wrote, "For when we came into Macedonia, this body of ours had no rest, but we were harassed at every turn—conflicts on the outside, fears within. But God, who comforts the downcast, comforted us by the coming of Titus" (2 Corinthians 7:5–6).

Presence in the Face of Death

Many pastors avoid pastoral care for the sick and dying because it is so emotionally draining. Watching a person die, whether it takes a few hours or several weeks, is painful. Death seems to mock us; it seems to render our best efforts, the latest medical technology, and even our most earnest prayers impotent. Moreover, the sickroom brings us face-to-face with our own mortality. In the rush of living, we can keep it at arm's length, but the death of someone else brings our mortality into focus, demanding our attention.

Jesus looked into the face of death in the Garden of Gethsemane. Perceiving a hostile, lonely, cruel death ahead, He turned to His closest friends for strength (Matthew 26:36–45). He confessed to them, "'My soul is overwhelmed with sorrow to the point of death. Stay here and keep watch **with me'**" (26:38). Yet they failed Christ by sleeping during one of His greatest hours of need.

The ministry of presence, especially around sickness and death, can be difficult. When we are used to getting things done, we find it hard to sit and wait, powerless, for death to come. Our need to do something, anything, is almost unbearable. Taking some sort of action gives us the illusion of being in control, thus making us feel better. Yet as we allow our discomfort to initiate action, we usually do the wrong thing. For instance, when Jesus tried to explain His impending death to His disciples, "Peter took him aside and began to rebuke him. 'Never, Lord!' he said. 'This shall never happen to you!'" (Matthew 16:22).

5 What are the advantages of letting the dying talk about their impending death?

Peter's reaction reminds me of some pastors who ignore or reject the cues many dying people try to give. Often, patients say such things as, "I don't have much to look forward to anymore," or even, "I think I'm going to die soon." Well-meaning but misguided pastors might respond by changing the subject or downplaying the comment: "Don't talk that way! You're going to live for years. In fact, you'll probably outlive me." While the intent may be to bring cheer, it rarely works. Instead, these remarks effectively isolate the patient. By refusing to allow dying individuals to talk honestly about their impending death, pastors leave them to face it alone.

A better response is to take their hand, saying, "Would you like to talk about it?" or "How does that make you feel?" Questions like these give dying or hurting people a chance to talk about their true feelings, even the ones they think they should not have. This is what hurting people are looking for. They need a safe place and a safe person with whom they can grieve without being misunderstood or rebuked. They want someone who will allow them to be real; someone who will let them weep or rage when they need to; someone who will not try to explain the unexplainable or fix everything with a prayer.

Those who are hurting do not seek theological explanations. They simply want our presence—nothing more, nothing less. That is what they need the most.

6.2.1
OBJECTIVE
Define empathy.

6 What is empathy?

Empathy

To minister effectively to people in crisis, pastors must have some understanding of what the individuals are experiencing. That is, pastoral care requires empathy. Empathy is the ability to share in others' emotions or feelings, to feel what they are feeling to some degree.

Learning Empathy

Although we learn best by experience, we do not have to go through every crisis to empathize with the people we minister to. The individuals themselves can teach us. By observing and listening to them, we can gain an understanding of what they are experiencing.

We can imagine ourselves in the place of sick individuals, considering what is happening to them and how it might make them feel. People who are very ill may feel unrelenting pain and weakness, undermining their morale and perhaps their faith. Psychologically, the ill also feel a loss of power. Their familiar surroundings are gone, replaced by an environment in which they have little or no control over their own lives and bodies. They can no longer set their own schedule or make everyday decisions. They may be subjected to humiliating procedures. Although all of this may lead to healing, in the meantime it can be demoralizing.

7 What general fears grip the sick?

However, the most debilitating emotion is likely fear. Those who are sick generally fear the unknown as well as mundane worries: What is going to happen to me? Will I get well? Will I be able to provide and care for my family? How will I pay the hospital bills? Will I still have a job when I recover?

OBJECTIVE

Explain the stages of the grieving process.

8 How do most people first react when told they are dying?

9 Read Job 3. What stage of grief do you think Job is exhibiting?

10 What can help prepare you to visit a hurting person?

The Grieving Process

Interlaced with the other fears is the underlying, perhaps unspoken possibility that recovery may not happen. Should the worst fears of the sick be confirmed—that they suffer from a terminal illness—they will experience a host of emotions as they prepare for their own death. Dr. Elisabeth Kübler-Ross, known for her studies on death and dying, identifies five stages in dealing with the trauma of a fatal illness:

- **Denial:** This stage includes thoughts such as, "It can't be true. The doctors must be wrong. Someone made a mistake." In the denial stage, many patients go to doctor after doctor seeking a favorable diagnosis. If they believe in divine healing, they may refuse to even consider the possibility of death so as not to "doubt" and thus undermine their faith and the healing it can bring.

- **Anger:** During the anger stage, individuals may ask questions such as these: "Why, God? Why me? Why not someone else? Why should I suffer? Haven't I served You faithfully, Lord? Why would You heal others and not heal me? It's not fair."

- **Bargaining:** Once their anger has subsided, terminally ill patients may try to reason with God: "God, if You heal me, I will live the rest of my life for You. I will give 20 percent of my income to the church. If You will let me live to see my son grow up . . . my daughter get married . . . the birth of my first grandchild (and so on), I will die without complaining."

- **Depression:** Here, the patient realizes that nothing has worked— not denial, anger, or bargaining. Illness and pain are real, and death looms near. During this stage, patients often turn inward and become noncommunicative. They essentially give up, feeling hopeless, and may resist medical treatment.

- **Acceptance:** In this final stage, dying people learn to accept the reality of their death and are usually no longer resigned. To be resigned is to lose all hope, to give up, saying that nothing can change. To accept, on the other hand, is to acknowledge reality without losing hope. People at this stage realize that death is inevitable without a medical breakthrough or divine intervention, but they do not give up. Nor do they waste the precious time they have left in anger or denial. During this stage, people begin preparing for the end, getting things in order, and saying good-bye (Kübler-Ross 1997, 51–146).

To minister effectively under these circumstances, pastors need to understand the spiritual and emotional dynamics experienced by the patients and their families. In addition, pastors must be able to identify and respond to the various emotional stages in which the patients find themselves. Sometimes, pastors need to simply listen nonjudgmentally as the patients pour out their troubles; at other times, pastors need to offer encouragement from the Scriptures. When appropriate, pastors should pray. Above all, they should always strive to follow the Spirit's leading.

Some pastors have an innate gift for the ministry of pastoral care. With little or no training, they intuitively know how to relate to hurting people. However, the rest of us must discipline ourselves to be spiritually and emotionally prepared each time we minister. In that regard, I have found it helpful to pause before entering the sickroom to set aside whatever concerns might keep me from being fully present emotionally. I consciously put myself in the suffering person's place. I identify with him or her as completely as I can. Then I ask the Holy Spirit to direct and anoint everything I do. Only when I have done all of this am I ready to minister.

6.3.1
OBJECTIVE

List four things that a person in a crisis might appreciate.

Caregiving

Identifying with People in Crisis

People in severe trials or crises have multiple needs—physical, emotional, and spiritual. Most of us, especially early in our ministry, have no firsthand knowledge regarding the trauma others have experienced. We have never been diagnosed with a terminal illness. We have never lost a child to death. We have never been divorced or fired from a job or forced into financial ruin. We have never discovered that our child is hooked on drugs. The list of situations we have never experienced may be virtually endless. As a result, we have little idea what individuals in such crises are feeling or what they want or expect from us.

With that in mind, perhaps it is best to begin with the perspective of those in crisis. Perhaps we need to let them tell us what is going on in their lives and how we can minister to them and their families.

Years ago, I discovered a small pamphlet that proved invaluable to me. The author was Wendy Bergren, a young breast cancer patient and mother of three children. When her doctor discovered the enormous malignancy, Wendy underwent surgery, chemotherapy, and intensive radiation in a last-ditch effort to stave off imminent death. The chemotherapy produced every possible side effect and confined her to bed two weeks per month for over a year and a half. Although a host of caring friends tried their best to help, they simply did not know what to do. In one of her darkest moments, Wendy wrote some ideas to give her friends (and us) a glimpse of what people like Wendy and their families need during such times:

1. Visit frequently, but call before you come. Don't stay away so I can get my rest. Companionship is often more important than rest.
2. Ask me whom I would like to see, and invite them to come along. Sometimes I'm too tired to talk, but it's nice to listen.
3. Take snapshots of my children over the months so I don't feel I've totally missed out on this part of their lives.
4. Offer to run two small errands a week for the family.
5. Allow me to feel sad and prepare for the worst.
6. Tell me a joke. Even if it's not funny, I'll laugh!
7. Touch me. The isolation of being an invalid makes love's touch sweeter.
8. Say the word *cancer* around me so I can feel normal.
9. Tell me how good I look, considering everything I've been through. (Someone told Wendy she had to be the best-looking bald woman in town, and she loved it!)
10. Offer to babysit—even if my husband and I stay home. This gives us the freedom of a private adult life in a place my illness can cope with.
11. Encourage your husband to come over to visit my husband in the evenings. My illness has eliminated many of his pleasures. How happy I am when I hear him laughing with a friend!
12. Pray for me, and tell me that you're praying.
13. Talk to me about the future. Planning for the future, birthdays, graduations, etc., increases my faith. (Bergren 1982)

Of course, pastors cannot be expected to meet all of these needs themselves, but they can make their congregations aware of them. They can also develop a formal system to train and mobilize caring laypeople for this ministry.

11 What are the most pressing needs of dying people?

Review Wendy's list for a moment. When I did, I realized that eight of the thirteen suggestions relate to her emotional needs. She asked people to visit her, to allow her to feel sad, joke with her, touch her, and so on. Four items dealt with her family's needs, and one dealt with her spiritual need for prayer.

Another victim of cancer, Janet Britton, emphasized the same point. Although her church family prepared meals, cleaned her house, did laundry, and helped care for her children, none of that compared with the love and care they showed her personally. She said:

> Their greatest gift, though, was touching—physically and emotionally. Friends sat beside me, as I lay exhausted on our couch. They touched my shoulder, held my hand, kissed my cheek, hugged me; their touch cushioned me. They shared with me, as they always had, their marital problems, occupational problems, and personal difficulties. Their continued confidence reminded me that although physically impaired I was not mentally or emotionally damaged. (Britton 1985, 82–83)

OBJECTIVE

Explain three keys for relating to a person in a trial.

12 What are the keys to relating to those who suffer?

Responding to People in Crisis

Crises, in whatever form they take, are emotionally wrenching. They produce not only a host of emotional needs but also much hurt and anger. Hurting people invariably lash out, perhaps doing and saying things we do not necessarily expect Christians to do or say.

Our response to hurting individuals in that moment goes a long way toward determining the effectiveness of our pastoral care. If they sense our disapproval, they may hide their true feelings and say the "right" things instead of the "real" things. That is, they may begin to say what they think they *should* say rather than what they *need* to say. While this may be more comfortable for us, it limits our ministry of pastoral care.

How should you respond to people in crisis, especially if they express a lot of hurt and anger? Let Jesus be your model:

Absorb Anger

Following Lazarus's death, Jesus went to minister to his sisters. When Martha heard that He was coming, she rushed to meet Him and immediately began pouring out her heart. "Lord," she cried, "if you had been here, my brother would not have died" (John 11:21). Thus, her first response was hurt and despair. She essentially accused Jesus of not caring, of ignoring them in their hour of greatest need.

How did Jesus respond? He listened and absorbed her anger and hurt without rebuking her. He understood how circumstances must have seemed from her limited perspective, how much she loved her brother, and how deeply she hurt.

Reflect Faith

Yet Martha's response continued, rising above her confusion and hurt. Even in her grief and anger, she expressed her faith: "I know that even now God will give you whatever you ask. . . . I know he [Lazarus] will rise again in the resurrection at the last day. . . . I believe that you are the Christ, the Son of God, who was to come into the world" (John 11:22, 24, 27).

When Martha moved from anger to faith, Jesus met her there and built on her confession. He replied, "I am the resurrection and the life. He who believes in me will live, even though he dies; and whoever lives and believes in me will never die. Do you believe this?" (11:25–26). Martha responded by crying, "Yes, Lord" (11:27).

Mourn Together

Mary expressed her grief differently than Martha did, however. She too was hurt and angry but also very sensitive. "When Mary reached the place where Jesus was and saw him, she fell at his feet and said, 'Lord, if you had been here, my brother would not have died.' When Jesus saw her weeping, . . . he was deeply moved in spirit and troubled. . . . [and] Jesus wept" (John 11:32–33, 35).

13 Why did Jesus not discuss theology with Mary?

Notice that Jesus also met Mary at her point of grief, both spiritually and emotionally. There was little or no faith in her confession beyond the faith to tell Jesus how she felt. Somehow, even in her sorrow, pain, and disappointment, she believed He would understand. And He did. For her, Jesus had no theological pronouncements, no revelation about resurrection life, and no discourse about His divine Sonship.

He excluded these things not because they were any less true but because He knew Mary was not ready to receive them. Nothing was in her heart but sorrow and tears, so He met her there. Jesus wept with her.

I use the account of Jesus with Martha and Mary simply to say this: When ministering to people in crisis, meet them where they are, spiritually and emotionally. If they express honest faith, reflect honest faith back to them. If they rage, pouring out their hurt and anger, absorb it without rebuke. Do not censor them. And do not attempt to explain why this terrible tragedy has happened to them. Listen with love. Cry with them. Remember that it is all right to say, "I don't know." Life is filled with mysteries, and no one—not even a pastor—has all the answers.

Pastoral care is an ongoing ministry, and the healing it provides is gradual. This slow process will likely include times of supernatural visitation, but for the most part, the healing occurs more like the coming of spring after a long winter. Caring pastors understand this and remain patient; the assurance of their presence gives the person in crisis the comfort and strength to continue. During these critical moments, may your testimony be "we were gentle among you, like a mother caring for her little children" (1 Thessalonians 2:7).

Test Yourself

Circle the letter of the ***best*** answer.

1. The most special gift pastors can give those in crisis is
a) money or food.
b) advice.
c) presence.
d) explanations.

2. A pastor should pray with people in crisis, but not too
a) soon.
b) often.
c) loudly.
d) boldly.

3. When ministering to people in crisis, many pastors err by
a) reading the Bible to them.
b) visiting them in the hospital.
c) making them feel useless.
d) avoiding them.

4. Sharing in another person's feelings is called
a) grief.
b) empathy.
c) association.
d) role-play.

5. Sick people often struggle with
a) a fear of the unknown.
b) a loss of control.
c) feelings of loneliness.
d) all of the above.

6. A grieving person questions God in the stage of
a) denial.
b) anger.
c) depression.
d) bargaining.

7. The last stage of the grieving process is
a) death.
b) forgiveness.
c) acceptance.
d) empathy.

8. We should begin showing care to people in crisis by
a) giving advice.
b) reading Scripture.
c) teaching.
d) listening.

9. If grieving people express anger, we should
a) gently rebuke them.
b) reflect it back.
c) absorb it.
d) discuss it.

10. The key to ministering to people in crisis is to
a) relate to them.
b) show them pity.
c) talk to them.
d) do things for them.

Responses to Interactive Questions
Chapter 6

Some of these responses may include information that is supplemental to the IST. These questions are intended to produce reflective thinking beyond the course content and your responses may vary from these examples.

1 Describe a time in your life when a pastor's or friend's presence comforted you.

Answers will vary.

2 What two errors can pastors make when caring for others?

(1) Attempting to minister prematurely or ineffectively, or (2) avoiding or abandoning the hurting person altogether

3 How can pastors make prayer more meaningful?

Be sensitive to the right timing and the person's feelings. Prayer means the most after the pastor has listened deeply and compassionately to the hurting family.

4 How does 2 Corinthians 7:5–6 relate to pastoral care?

In shows that Paul knew firsthand the comfort of having Titus' presence nearby.

5 What are the advantages of letting the dying talk about their impending death?

As you allow them to talk of death, they cease to feel so alone in the experience. They can honestly express pent-up feelings and fears that are often brought into perspective when heard aloud in the comfort of someone who is accepting.

6 What is empathy?

The ability to share in another person's emotions or feelings

7 What general fears grip the sick?

Fear of the unknown, day-to-day concerns, and perhaps the possibility of death

8 How do most people first react when told they are dying?

In denial

9 Read Job 3. What stage of grief do you think Job is exhibiting?

Probably either anger or depression

10 What can help you prepare to visit a hurting person?

Pausing before entering the room to set aside your own troubles and consciously put yourself in the hurting person's place; praying for wisdom, direction, and anointing from the Holy Spirit

11 What are the most pressing needs of dying people?

Their emotional concerns; the need to be listened to, to be touched, to be allowed to feel, and so forth. They want to feel as much a part of their friends' and families' lives as possible.

12 What are the keys to relating to those who suffer?

(1) Absorb their anger. (2) Reflect their honest faith and build on it. (3) Mourn with them.

13 Why did Jesus not discuss theology with Mary?

He knew that this was the time for mourning with Mary, not teaching. She was not ready to hear a theological discussion.

UNIT PROGRESS EVALUATION 2

Now that you have finished Unit 2, review the lessons in preparation for Unit Progress Evaluation 2. You will find it in the Essential Course Materials section at the back of this IST. Answer all of the questions without referring to your course materials, Bible, or notes. When you have completed the UPE, check your answers with the answer key provided in the Essential Course Materials section, and review any items you may have answered incorrectly. Then you may proceed with your study of Unit 3. (Although UPE scores do not count as part of your final course grade, they indicate how well you learned the material and how well you may perform on the closed-book final examination.)

The Pastor's Responsibilities Part 2

Unit 3 continues with the duties and work of the ministry. Chapters 7–9 include a growing emphasis on equipping the saints for ministry. Blessed are the pastors who do not try to do everything themselves, for they shall guide each member of the body to do its part! As the whole body builds itself up, the needs of each member will be met.

No course on pastoral ministry would be complete without a chapter on special services. Chapter 10 is not just theory; rather, it provides a step-by-step guide of services related to the special events of life.

The Pastor as a Leader

Other than obvious character defects or moral failure, nothing limits the effectiveness of pastors' ministry more than lack of leadership. Some of the most gifted preachers serve struggling congregations, while some of the most dynamic churches led by pastors who are ordinary preachers at best. All other factors being equal, this suggests that leadership is more important than preaching when it comes to growing a thriving congregation.

To be effective leaders, pastors must follow the Holy Spirit's leading. They must know what God wants for their particular congregation. Like Jesus, pastors should do only what they see the Father doing (John 5:19); in other words, "seeing" comes before "doing." Only when pastors see God's plan for their congregation can they lead the people in the way they should go.

Once pastors receive a vision, they are responsible to communicate it to the body. Habakkuk 2:2 says, "Write down the revelation and make it plain on tablets so that a herald may run with it." Using both the pulpit and one-on-one meetings with lay leaders, wise pastors clearly define their goals and objectives, enabling their congregations to see and feel what the pastors themselves are seeing and feeling. In this way, the pastor's vision becomes the people's as well.

Finally, wise pastors use their gifts and influence to motivate the congregation to invest their resources and thus see the vision become reality. In this, as in all areas, pastors should lead by example. Their leadership will encourage others to follow the pastors' example as they follow the example of Christ (1 Corinthians 11:1).

Lesson 7.1   Discerning God's Will
Objective
7.1.1   Summarize ways in which God speaks to people.

Lesson 7.2   Communicating the Vision
Objective
7.2.1   Explain principles for sharing a vision with people.

Lesson 7.3   Motivating the Congregation
Objectives
7.3.1   Explain how pastors lead with actions.
7.3.2   Contrast faith and presumption.

7.1.1
OBJECTIVE

Summarize ways in which God speaks to people.

1 Why must pastors know God's will for their congregations?

2 What is the first thing pastors should do to know God's will?

3 List several ways in which God speaks.

Discerning God's Will

Clearly, leaders cannot lead unless they know where they are going. Only God knows the future, and only He knows the plans He has for each congregation (Jeremiah 29:11). Therefore, pastors must search the mind of God and seek His direction. Only as they discern God's **vision** and His direction for the congregation can they truly lead the people under their care.

How can we know God's vision for our people? Although we cannot point to absolute ways, we can consider several key principles. For instance, I find great comfort in knowing that God will take the initiative to communicate His will. We can be assured that He wants us to know His will even more than we want to know it. However, experience has also taught me that He seldom reveals His plans simply to satisfy our curiosity. He most often reveals them to people who are fully committed to *doing* His will.

With that in mind, the first task for pastors is to surrender all of their own dreams and desires. Like Jesus in Gethsemane, they must pray, "Not my will, but yours be done" (Luke 22:42). Having thus surrendered themselves to Christ's plans and purposes, pastors can have confidence that the Spirit will guide them as they lead their congregations. God is well able to unfold His direction and vision to the pastor who surrenders fully to God, and then seeks God's direction for a specific congregation. Vision and direction are not instantaneous, but will grow out of an onging surrender to the will of God.

A word of caution may be in order here: Do not try overly hard to hear God's voice. When you do, it is too easy to imagine that God is speaking when He is not. Instead, the best way to hear God's voice is to simply be attentive when you pray and worship. Be sensitive to the thoughts and impressions that come to you as you go about your duties. Pay special attention to any thoughts or impressions that often reoccur.

Usually, God's guidance comes in the ordinary course of our lives. Moses was doing nothing especially spiritual when God spoke to Him from a burning bush; he was simply tending sheep as he had done hundreds of times before (Exodus 3:1–4).

More specifically, God generally reveals His will through one of four ways or a combination thereof:
1. The Scriptures
2. An inner witness of the Holy Spirit
3. Providential circumstances or wise counsel
4. Special spiritual manifestations such as dreams and visions

God Speaks through the Scriptures

The Bible says much to pastors concerning leadership of local churches. Paul told Timothy, "Although I hope to come to you soon, I am writing you these instructions so that, if I am delayed, you will know how people ought to conduct themselves in God's household, which is the church of the living God, the pillar and foundation of the truth" (1 Timothy 3:14–15). Later he taught, "All Scripture is God-breathed and is useful for teaching, rebuking, correcting and training in righteousness, so that the man of God may be thoroughly equipped for every good work" (2 Timothy 3:16–17). Therefore, an awareness of God's voice speaking through the Scriptures is essential for effective church leadership.

God Speaks in Other Ways

In 1 Corinthians 2:6–16, Paul assures us that the Holy Spirit's wisdom is available to us. It is the Spirit who reveals to each believer the truth of redemption through Christ. He is our Counselor, the Spirit of truth who "will teach [us] all things and will remind [us] of everything" Jesus taught (John 14:16–17, 26). Jesus said that the Holy Spirit would guide us "into all truth. . . . He will bring glory to me by taking from what is mine and making it known to you" (16:13–14). Thus, through the Spirit, "we have the mind of Christ" (1 Corinthians 2:16).

During the years I served as senior pastor at Christian Chapel, in Tulsa, Oklahoma, the church grew from a struggling congregation of fewer than 100 members to a thriving fellowship of nearly 1,000. We purchased several acres of land, built the church's first building, and became generously involved in world missions. We established an institute to train lay ministers, a counseling center, and a crisis pregnancy outreach. We also hosted a nationwide call-in radio program as well as a daily teaching broadcast.

However, God did not direct us to do all of these at once; He instead led us to develop one ministry at a time. First, He taught us to make world missions our number one priority. In this case, the word of the Lord came to me through a conversation with my brother, Don, a missionary in Argentina. Don sensed that God wanted our congregation to put world missions first and to initiate a missionary-in-residence program that would become a model for other churches.

At the time, lacking a building of our own, we held Sunday services in a school. Moreover, we had defaulted on a mortgage of nearly $600,000. While Don's idea seemed like a good one, I was sure it was not for Christian Chapel. There simply was no way we could do what he thought the Lord was calling us to do.

4 How does God speak through the inner witness of the Spirit?

Little did I know the plans God had for us, however. Over the next several weeks, the idea took root in my spirit. As much as I tried to ignore it, this inner witness of the Spirit would not go away. Finally, I shared it with the church board, and God quickened it to their hearts as well.

Making this vision from God a reality required several steps. (1) We amended our constitution and bylaws to reflect our commitment to world missions. (2) We made a "faith promise" to increase our monthly missions giving by $500 every three months. (3) We agreed to provide a fully furnished home at no cost to missionaries when they were in the area on furlough. We would also give a minimum monthly pledge of $1,000 for each missionary-in-residence.

Because of our circumstances, these commitments seemed almost ludicrous. Yet almost immediately, God began to supply our needs in supernatural ways. A piece of undeveloped property we owned suddenly sold, enabling us to pay off all our debt. On hearing about our vision to provide a home for missionaries, a man offered to buy a house for us, and as a result, three months later we owned a sizeable home, debt-free. Another man gave our church a $30,000 Christmas gift. However, the greatest miracle came fourteen months after our decision to make missions our first priority: In August 1982, some stock in an oil company was sold in the church's name, and we received a check for $429, 444.79. As believers often quote, "Where God guides, He provides!"

A natural outgrowth of our mission's emphasis was our national radio ministry. God communicated this vision to my heart through the inner witness of the Holy Spirit. Over several months, I felt a growing desire to minister on the radio. Once again God orchestrated people and events to make the impossible

possible, and in just a few weeks, we began broadcasting the call-in counseling program live via satellite. Not only were we reaching a national audience, but the Lord also used this ministry as a primary tool to help grow our own congregation.

With the growth came ever-increasing demands. To meet these needs, the church board and I felt led to establish a training program to equip believers to do the work of the ministry. We needed lay ministers to help us. This time, God spoke to us through a young seminary student who was interning at our church.

Afterward, we entered a season in which we felt led to emphasize signs and wonders and prophetic ministry. In this way, God made His direction known through the gifts of the Spirit. During the nearly four years of this season, ministers came from many parts of the nation to experience the wonderful manifestations of God's supernatural power. Hardly a week went by without a special healing or some other manifestation of the Spirit's presence.

In my final three years at Christian Chapel, our congregation emphasized intercessory prayer, evangelism, and Spirit-directed social action to transform the institutions of society. God's guidance for this came in a variety of ways: national events focusing our attention on our nation's needs, conversations with other spiritual leaders, and an ever-increasing inner witness of the Spirit.

As we focused on each new area of ministry, we did not disband our earlier emphases but built on them. Rather than replacing an earlier ministry, we simply added to it as the Lord directed us to do so.

As I review my years at Christian Chapel, three things stand out to me.
1. God will give us wisdom for every situation if we ask Him (James 1:5).
2. Obedience is mandatory. It does little good to receive divine direction if we are not willing to follow it.
3. Like Abraham, who "obeyed and went, even though he did not know where he was going" (Hebrews 11:8), we must step out even when we do not know how things will turn out. As I have heard it said, "God never gives us more light until we walk in the light we have."

The Bible Provides Many Examples

While personal experiences are encouraging, nothing is as helpful as the Scriptures. We can learn much about leading our congregations by considering the various ways God led the New Testament church.

5 In what ways does the Lord give wise counsel today?

In Acts 6, He directed them through wise counsel inspired by the Holy Spirit:

So the Twelve gathered all the disciples together and said, "It would not be right for us to neglect the ministry of the word of God in order to wait on tables. Brothers, choose seven men from among you who are known to be full of the Spirit and wisdom. We will turn this responsibility over to them and will give our attention to prayer and to the ministry of the word." This proposal pleased the whole group. (Acts 6:2–5)

By following the Holy Spirit's leading, the apostles not only solved a difficult situation but also enabled the church to advance: "So the word of God spread. The number of disciples in Jerusalem increased rapidly, and a large number of priests became obedient to the faith" (6:7).

When it was time for His church to take the gospel to the Gentiles, God spoke in a more dramatic way. He allowed persecution to scatter the early believers and gave visions and dreams, such as Cornelius's and Peter's. To those who criticized him for preaching to the uncircumcised,

Peter . . . explained everything to them precisely as it had happened: "I was in the city of Joppa praying, and in a trance I saw a vision. I saw something like a large sheet being let down from heaven by its four corners, and it came down to where I was. I looked into it and saw four-footed animals of the earth, wild beasts, reptiles, and birds of the air. Then I heard a voice telling me, 'Get up, Peter. Kill and eat.' I replied, 'Surely not, Lord! Nothing impure or unclean has ever entered my mouth.'

"The voice spoke from heaven a second time, 'Do not call anything impure that God has made clean.' This happened three times, and then it was all pulled up to heaven again.

"Right then three men who had been sent to me from Caesarea stopped at the house where I was staying. The Spirit told me to have no hesitation about going with them. These six brothers also went with me, and we entered the man's house. He told us how he had seen an angel appear in his house and say, 'Send to Joppa for Simon who is called Peter. He will bring you a message through which you and all your household will be saved.'

"As I began to speak, the Holy Spirit came on them as he had come on us at the beginning. Then I remembered what the Lord had said: 'John baptized with water, but you will be baptized with the Holy Spirit.' So if God gave them the same gift as he gave us, who believed in the Lord Jesus Christ, who was I to think that I could oppose God?"

When they heard this, they had no further objections and praised God, saying, "So then, God has granted even the Gentiles repentance unto life." (Acts 11:4–18)

6   How did God guide Peter to Cornelius in Acts 10?

Thus, God made His plan known to Peter in a combination of ways: prayer, a vision, providential circumstances, and the voice of the Spirit. That is, while Peter prayed, he fell into a trance and saw a vision (11:5). Providentially, the three men Cornelius had sent arrived at that exact moment. And immediately the Spirit said to him, "Simon, three men are looking for you. So get up and go downstairs. Do not hesitate to go with them, for I have sent them" (10:19–20).

7   Why does God speak in unusual ways at times?

Experience has taught me that God most often speaks in extraordinary ways when He knows we will face unusual challenges in carrying out His directions. Knowing that Peter would be breaking years of tradition and risking his peers' disapproval, God made His will emphatically clear. Had His direction been less dramatic, Peter may not have had the necessary courage to respond as he did.

We see the same principle at work in the life and ministry of Paul and his missionary team. Luke writes:

Paul and his companions traveled throughout the region of Phrygia and Galatia, having been kept by the Holy Spirit from preaching the word in the province of Asia. When they came to the border of Mysia, they tried to enter Bithynia, but the Spirit of Jesus would not allow them to. So they passed by Mysia and went down to Troas. During the night Paul had a vision of a man of Macedonia standing and begging him, "Come over to Macedonia and help us." After Paul had seen the vision, we got ready at once to leave for Macedonia, concluding that God had called us to preach the gospel to them. (Acts 16:6–10)

Several things stand out to me when I read this account. At first, Paul and his friends had difficulty discerning the mind of God regarding their next assignment. However, they did not just sit around and wait for something to happen (Horton 2001, 279). They tried to go to the province of Asia, but the Holy Spirit restrained them. Then they attempted to enter Bithynia to the north, but the Spirit of Jesus kept them from going there too. In each instance, it was God himself—not the enemy—who closed the door to ministry.

8 What truths from Acts 16:6–10 can comfort church leaders?

I take comfort in the struggles of these people of God. If a spiritual giant like Paul had to try three times before discerning God's direction for his next step, I do not feel so bad when I struggle to know the mind of God about a matter. The fact that God did not give up on them also encourages me. He kept working with them until they finally understood His plan.

Based on God's clarity of direction through the vision, we might assume that Paul immediately experienced tremendous success when ministering in Philippi, Macedonia's chief city. Although Paul was doing exactly what the Lord wanted him to do, he still faced unbelievable opposition. He was eventually able to plant a small church in Philippi, but not until he had been beaten and thrown in prison (Acts 16:22–24). Yet his clear vision from God enabled him to remain faithful through all of the trials.

Note that Paul's companions bore witness to the direction God had given him: "After Paul had seen the vision, we got ready at once to leave for Macedonia, concluding that God had called us to preach the gospel to them" (Acts 16:10). Many times, the Lord will confirm His word to spiritual leaders through their advisers or lay ministers. These advisers must be trustworthy, strong enough to speak the truth in love, and wise enough to discern between God's wisdom and their own opinion. Ideally, they provide an inner circle of spiritual support and protection for ministers.

7.2.1
OBJECTIVE
Explain principles for sharing a vision with people.

9 According to Acts 7:25, what was Moses' mistake?

Communicating the Vision

Knowing the will of God does little good if pastors cannot communicate the vision. In fact, it can become a source of extreme frustration for both the pastor and the congregation. If pastors know what God wants to do but cannot communicate it in a way that enables the people to catch the vision, conflict is inevitable.

Assume Nothing

I experienced considerable difficulty in this area early in my ministry. No matter how much I prayed and sought the mind of God, it appeared to have little impact on my ability to communicate the vision to the congregation. They seemed to resist my most determined efforts to lead them. As a result, I struggled with anger and resentment.

One day while studying the life of Moses, I came across Stephen's account in Acts 7:23–29:

When Moses was forty years old, he decided to visit his fellow Israelites. He saw one of them being mistreated by an Egyptian, so he went to his defense and avenged him by killing the Egyptian. Moses thought that his own people would realize that God was using him to rescue them, but they did not. The next day Moses came upon two Israelites who were fighting. He tried to reconcile them by saying, "Men, you are brothers; why do you want to hurt each other?"

But the man who was mistreating the other pushed Moses aside and said, "Who made you ruler and judge over us? Do you want to kill me as you killed the Egyptian yesterday?" When Moses heard this, he fled to Midian, where he settled as a foreigner and had two sons.

Although I had read this passage many times, I had never connected it with leadership. Suddenly, I realized that, like Moses, I assumed my congregation would understand what God was attempting to do in and through me. Of course, most of the time they did not.

Studying this passage brought things into focus. I often wrestled for months in prayer to come to a reasonable understanding of God's direction for our church. Only after I felt it was perfectly clear did I share it with the congregation. When they did not immediately accept it as the "word of the Lord," I tended to conclude that they were spiritually deaf. Now I saw my mistake: I expected them to instantly accept what had taken me weeks and sometimes months to process.

Involve Leaders

10 Why should pastors share new ideas early with key leaders?

Once I understood this, I determined to change my leadership style. As soon as the Lord began dealing with my heart regarding His direction for the church, I shared it with the elders and other key leaders in the body. I readily acknowledged that I was merely in the earliest stages of the decision-making process and encouraged their input. By seeking their prayers and advise, I enabled them to participate in the process.

If an idea lost its appeal after prayer and counsel, we concluded that it was not from the Lord. On the other hand, when an idea burned in our hearts and seemed to take on a life of its own, we concluded that it was, in fact, from God.

Promote Ownership of the Vision

Rather than undermining the elders' confidence in my leadership, this process actually enhanced it. And because they had been part of the process, they took ownership of the vision. Now it was not "my" vision; it was "our" vision.

11 Describe three steps pastors can take when proposing a change for their congregations.

For example, as one congregation I served prepared to move into new facilities, I sensed that God wanted us to restructure our meeting schedule. Realizing the sensitivity of this issue and its impact on the whole family, I first decided to involve both the church board members and their wives. We prayed about it for thirty days and then had a lengthy discussion. While several interesting ideas emerged, we could not agree and decided to pray for another thirty days. At our next meeting, people presented only a few ideas, yet we still could not agree. When we met for the third time, after another thirty days of prayer, we were in complete agreement.

The second step was to involve the small group leaders and all of the Sunday school teachers. We met with them and explained the new schedule, describing the process we had used to develop it. After a brief discussion, they too accepted it as God's plan for our church.

The third step was to announce the plan to the entire church body. Again, I carefully explained the process the leaders had used to reach our decision. Although we had no time to discuss it in the service, the congregation readily accepted the new schedule. Those with questions or concerns took them to their small group leaders or a board member. Because the leaders had been involved in the process and saw the vision as their own, they were able to address these concerns.

Shortly after moving into our new facilities, our congregation doubled in number. Only then did we see the wisdom of the new service schedule. Had we not made the change before growth occurred, we would have experienced tremendous pressure and time constraints to do something. That would have made the decision much more difficult and could have caused division among the people.

12 List three ways to keep parishioners aware of a vision.

As a congregation grows, communicating the church's vision to those being added to the body becomes increasingly important. This can be accomplished in a number of ways. For instance, at Christian Chapel, we gave every visitor a cassette tape with two sermons on it: a message explaining our ministry and vision on one side, and a message about God's provision toward our missions emphasis on the other. In addition, one of the pastors taught an eight-week class that introduced people to the ministries and vision of our church.

To visually communicate our commitment to world missions, we decorated our sanctuary and foyer with banners and flags from around the world and hung a world map along with pictures of the missionaries we supported. We also printed our fourfold vision—missions, the Word, worship, and relationships—on our letterheads, bulletins, and newsletters. We wanted everything people saw and heard to reinforce our vision.

13 Do pastors usually receive a complete vision for their congregations? Explain.

God's vision for the church usually comes through the pastor, but it is seldom complete when he or she receives it. As the pastor shares it with other key spiritual leaders, they become involved in its development. Together, they fast and pray, dream and discuss, until they are in complete agreement regarding God's direction for the church.

Generally, pastors are the primary communicators of the vision to the congregation. They use services and small group meetings to bring the vision into focus for their people. Other leaders use their influence to reinforce the pastor's efforts. Together, they create an atmosphere of faith and expectancy, releasing the congregation to follow the Holy Spirit's leading.

LESSON 7.3

7.3.1
OBJECTIVE
Explain how pastors lead with actions.

Motivating the Congregation

Vision does not become reality until it is translated into Spirit-directed action. And the congregation seldom takes action until they see the pastor and other spiritual leaders stepping out in faith. In other words, pastors lead by example. They lead both by what they say and by what they do.

This leadership principle is taught throughout the Scriptures. For example, when Israel entered the Promised Land, the ark of the covenant went before them. God commanded the priests to step into the Jordan River first. When the people saw their spiritual leaders step out in faith, they were quick to follow.

> When the people broke camp to cross the Jordan, the priests carrying the ark of the covenant went ahead of them. Now the Jordan is at flood stage all during harvest. Yet as soon as the priests who carried the ark reached the Jordan and their feet touched the water's edge, the water from upstream stopped flowing. It piled up in a heap a great distance away, at a town called Adam in the vicinity of Zarethan, while the water flowing down to the Sea of the Arabah (the Salt Sea) was completely cut off. So the people crossed over opposite Jericho. The priests who carried the ark of the covenant of the Lord stood firm on dry ground in the middle of the Jordan, while all Israel passed by until the whole nation had completed the crossing on dry ground. (Joshua 3:14–17)

14 What principle does Joshua 3:14–17 illustrate?

Notice that God did not step in to help until the priests stepped out in obedience; the waters raged until their feet touched the edge. God spoke, the priests obeyed, and then God helped.

7.3.2
OBJECTIVE
Contrast faith and presumption.

At this point, we would be wise to consider the difference between faith and **presumption**. Pastors who walk in faith wait for God to speak and then respond in obedience. God is the initiator, and faith is our obedient response. In Joshua 3, the priests did not just step into the Jordan. God commanded them to do so: "And the Lord said to Joshua, '. . . Tell the priests who carry the ark of the covenant: "When you reach the edge of the Jordan's waters, go and stand in the river"'" (3:7–8).

Presumption, on the other hand, is humankind's attempt to force God to act. Self seizes the initiative and takes action without waiting for God to speak. Presumptuous pastors may sincerely think they are moving in faith, but they will reap the consequences of their unwise actions. Those who act before God speaks are moving in presumption, not faith.

When the congregation sees their pastor obeying the Lord's direction in faith, they are encouraged to do the same. This principle is true both in the day-to-day life of your parishioners and in the moments of daring obedience. If you want your congregation to pray, let them see you praying. If you want them to be faithful givers, set the example. If you want your people to serve one another, let them see you serving. Pastors are to "set an example for the believers in speech, in life, in love, in faith and in purity" (1 Timothy 4:12).

Leading by example is even more vital in times of crisis. When people are confused or discouraged, it is important for the pastor to demonstrate confidence in God's faithfulness. Consider how Paul encouraged his fellow passengers and crew on a ship in the face of a storm. For more than two weeks, they had been battered by hurricane-force winds, forcing them to dump the cargo in hopes of saving themselves. When clouds blocked the sun and stars for many days and the storm continued to rage, their hopes were completely dashed. Yet at this critical moment, Paul demonstrated his leadership skills in encouragement:

> Just before dawn Paul urged them all to eat. "For the last fourteen days," he said, "you have been in constant suspense and have gone without food—you haven't eaten anything. Now I urge you to take some food. You need it to survive. Not one of you will lose a single hair from his head." After he said this, he took some bread and gave thanks to God in front of them all. Then he broke it and began to eat. They were all encouraged and ate some food themselves. (Acts 27:33–36)

15 In Acts 27, why do Paul's actions show faith and courage instead of presumption?

The people were encouraged by Paul's words, but even more so by his actions. When they saw him eating, they began to eat too. When your congregation see you trusting God no matter how severe the storm, they will also learn to trust Him.

John H. Johnson, founder of Johnson Publishing Company, and other achievers indicate that the key to success is to start with a small achievement, dream big, and work hard. With that in mind, I challenge you to

- start small. If you are faithful in the small things, God will entrust you with greater responsibility (Matthew 25:21).

- dream big dreams for your congregation. Dream God-given dreams that are worthy of Him "who is able to do immeasurably more than all we ask or imagine, according to his power that is at work within us" (Ephesians 3:20).

- work hard. "Whatever you do, work at it with all your heart, as working for the Lord, not for men, since you know that you will receive an inheritance from the Lord as a reward. It is the Lord Christ you are serving" (Colossians 3:23–24).

Test Yourself

Circle the letter of the *best* answer.

1. The first task for a pastor to know God's vision for the congregation is to
a) look to visionary leaders for inspiration.
b) immerse him- or herself in vision literature.
c) surrender his or her own dreams and desires to God.
d) consult the key leaders of the congregation.

2. Where should pastors go first for guidance?
a) Other pastors
b) The Scriptures
c) Their spouses
d) Counselors

3. God speaks to believers through
a) circumstances.
b) wise people.
c) the Spirit's inner-witness.
d) all of the above.

4. God led Paul to Macedonia through
a) an inner-witness.
b) a biblical truth.
c) wise counsel.
d) a vision.

5. Moses made the mistake of not
a) seeking God's guidance for a vision.
b) waiting for people to accept the vision.
c) obeying the wise counsel of others.
d) allowing people to ask questions.

6. Pastors should share their vision early with
a) key leaders.
b) other pastors.
c) new believers.
d) everyone.

7. Pastors can reinforce their vision by
a) writing it on banners.
b) talking about it often.
c) teaching it to new members.
d) all of the above.

8. For a vision to become reality, pastors must
a) set the example.
b) urge others to take the first step.
c) preach several sermons about it.
d) wait and watch.

9. When the Israelites crossed the flooded Jordan, who stepped in first?
a) Joshua
b) The priests
c) The soldiers
d) Children

10. Which word describes *presumption?*
a) Faith
b) Obedience
c) Overconfidence
d) Ignorance

Responses to Interactive Questions
Chapter 7

Some of these responses may include information that is supplemental to the IST. These questions are intended to produce reflective thinking beyond the course content and your responses may vary from these examples.

1 Why must pastors know God's will for their congregations?

God has a definite plan for each local church. If the pastor is to effectively lead in that direction, he or she must know and communicate God's vision.

2 What is the first thing pastors should do to know God's will?

Surrender all their personal dreams and desires, and embrace God's plan.

3 List several ways in which God speaks.

Through the Scriptures; an inner witness of the Holy Spirit; providential circumstances or wise counsel; and spiritual gifts, dreams, or visions

4 How does God speak through the inner witness of the Spirit?

Once the Lord has gotten your attention regarding His will, the Holy Spirit will not let it be pushed aside until you have accepted or rejected it. God confirms with results when we obey.

5 In what ways does the Lord give wise counsel today?

Answers will vary but may include the ideas of Scripture, spiritual leaders, words of knowledge and wisdom, and so on.

6 How did God guide Peter to Cornelius in Acts 10?

Prayer, a vision, circumstances, and the voice of the Spirit

7 Why does God speak in unusual ways at times?

To prepare our hearts and stir our faith for exceptionally difficult trials that lie ahead

8 What truths from Acts 16:6–10 can comfort church leaders?

(1) Paul too had to persevere through the struggle to discern God's will, and (2) God never gives up on us as we seek His will. Often, if not for the vision for the church, knowing and doing God's will would not be enough for the pastor to endure the difficulties that must be faced.

9 According to Acts 7:25, what was Moses' mistake?

He assumed his own people would realize that God was using him to rescue them, but they did not.

10 Why should pastors share new ideas early with key leaders?

It enables others to be a part of the process and thus to take ownership of it.

11 Describe three steps pastors can take when proposing a change for their congregations.

(1) Inform and pray through to unity with the board members. (2) Inform and pray through with other key leaders in the body. (3) Present the change, with an explanation of the process, to the entire church.

12 List three ways to keep parishioners aware of a vision.

(1) Allow other leaders to have input and a chance to spread the vision in their sphere of influence. (2) Share the vision with new members as part of their orientation to the church. (3) Use as many means as possible to expose everyone to the vision.

13 Do pastors usually receive a complete vision for their congregations? Explain.

No. As pastors share and invite other leaders to pray with them, the others' input and suggestions usually flesh out the vision.

14 What principle does Joshua 3:14–17 illustrate?

God speaks; we obey; then God steps in to help.

15 In Acts 27, why do Paul's actions show faith and courage instead of presumption?

God had told Paul that no one on the ship would die. Therefore, Paul words and actions were based on God's initiative, not Paul's.

The Pastor as an Equipper

In many congregations, pastors are the only ones who are paid for serving. Everyone else who serves in any capacity of ministry is a volunteer. Even in congregations that are able to pay the pastoral staff and support personnel, the vast majority of ministry is still accomplished by unpaid volunteers. History suggests that no matter how large a local church becomes, it still depends on volunteers to do much of the ministry to meet all of the congregation's needs.

Of greater concern is the reality that pastors are often the only persons with any training to prepare for the work of the ministry. Volunteers are often recruited on the basis of need rather than competence. As a result, churches are frequently staffed by well-meaning but unqualified people or, worse yet, talented but uncommitted people.

Clearly, it is unrealistic to expect volunteers to go to Bible school to receive training. Nearly all of them have families and other responsibilities such as finances and their occupations. What is the solution, then?

To resolve this issue, pastors may need to rethink the way they minister. Too many pastors have seen themselves as spiritual experts and have been reluctant to share their skills or responsibilities. To prepare our congregations for ministry, however, we must begin to think of ourselves as equippers. We must become spiritual leaders who impart our knowledge and expertise to others so they can share the work of the ministry.

Although this may sound like a new idea, it is not. The apostle Paul said:

It was he [Jesus] who gave some to be apostles, some to be prophets, some to be evangelists, and some to be pastors and teachers, to prepare God's people for works of service, so that the body of Christ may be built up until we all reach unity in the faith and in the knowledge of the Son of God and become mature, attaining to the whole measure of the fullness of Christ. Then we will no longer be infants, tossed back and forth by the waves, and blown here and there by every wind of teaching and by the cunning and craftiness of men in their deceitful scheming. Instead, speaking the truth in love, we will in all things grow up into him who is the Head, that is, Christ. From him the whole body, joined and held together by every supporting ligament, grows and builds itself up in love, as each part does its work. (Ephesians 4:11–16)

According to this passage, Jesus gave the fivefold ministry gifts to the church "to prepare God's people for works of service, so that the body of Christ may be built up" (4:12). In Paul's mind, one of the pastor's primary responsibilities is to train and equip the laity to do the work of the ministry. Therefore, the question is not *whether* pastors should equip their congregations for ministry, but *how*.

Lesson 8.1   Developing a Biblical Model
Objective
8.1.1   Explain the basis of a scriptural training model.

Lesson 8.2   Selecting Materials
Objective
8.2.1   Analyze the parts of a training program.

Lesson 8.3   Implementing Training
Objective
8.3.1   Describe methods for the implementation of training in churches.

8.1.1
OBJECTIVE

Explain the basis of a scriptural training model.

1 What is a primary task for pastors (Ephesians 4:11–12)?

2 Why do pastors need to share the ministry?

3 Before training anyone, pastors should examine each potential worker in what areas?

4 What signs indicate that a person is spiritually mature enough to engage in ministry?

5 According to 1 Timothy 3:6, why should a recent convert not be a minister?

6 List some signs of good Christian character.

Developing a Biblical Model

As we noted in chapter 1, a shared ministry is both a practical necessity and a biblical imperative. Circumstances demand it, and the Scriptures teach it. The principles of shared ministry are at least threefold:

It is the only way the church can hope to minister to the whole spectrum of its constituency.

It is the only strategy that affords spiritual leaders the time and energy needed to develop the quality ministry the church has a right to expect.

It concentrates on discovering and developing the ministry gifts and potential of all the people in the church body.

Once pastors become convinced that shared ministry is both biblical and expedient, they are then faced with the logistics. Who can they use in lay ministry? How do they begin? What are the qualifications for the people to be trained, and how will pastors make their selections? How can they implement the biblical concepts into their congregations?

Again, the Scriptures provide the most workable model. In Exodus 18:21, Moses' father-in-law, Jethro, directed him to "select capable men from all the people—men who fear God, trustworthy men who hate dishonest gain." As seen in this verse, a good standard is to evaluate each potential participant in three areas: (1) spiritual maturity, (2) character, and (3) capabilities or giftedness.

The apostles established a similar standard for the New Testament church. To oversee ministry to widows, the apostles instructed the people to select individuals who were "known to be full of the Spirit and wisdom" (Acts 6:3).

Spiritual Maturity

When choosing people to train, pastors must first consider the individuals' spiritual maturity. Do they fear God? Are they full of the Spirit? Do they have a solid understanding of the Scriptures? How do they view God? Is their image of Him in harmony with the Father whom Jesus revealed? Their perception of God is critical because they will emulate this understanding as they relate to others, especially in ministry situations.

Personal and emotional maturity are also factors. Are the individuals emotionally stable and generally free from mood swings? Have they demonstrated faithfulness in their personal lives and to the church?

If a candidate does not meet the spiritual qualifications, proceed no further. A person's gifts and abilities are not truly an asset unless they are undergirded and reinforced by a consistent spiritual walk. When considering talented people, the temptation to overlook or at least minimize spiritual flaws is not unusual. However, beware! Gifted but uncommitted, unfaithful participants have rendered many church ministries largely ineffective. Pastors can avoid much disappointment and frustration by steadfastly adhering to this principle.

Character

After spiritual maturity, the next consideration is individuals' character. Are they honest, trustworthy people? Do they have a good self-image? If not, they will be continually tempted to use the ministry to meet their own needs.

Further, are the individuals loyal, or are they motivated by selfish ambition? Are they able to work with people? Do others trust these individuals? Do they relate well to others, and do others respond positively to them? Are they sincere?

Gifts and Abilities

Only if potential trainees meet the qualifications for spiritual maturity and character should pastors consider their gifts and abilities. Are the individuals wise? Are they capable? At this point, pastors become coaches or scouts. Pastors determine the individual's gifts and abilities so they can train him or her to do ministry in the area of his or her God-given gifts.

8.2.1
OBJECTIVE
Analyze the parts of a training program.

7   Moses was to train others in what three areas (Exodus 18:20)?

Selecting Materials

As a pastor, you hope to eventually train every member for service, but initially, you should choose only the most qualified. When you have selected these individuals, the actual training will begin. Again, Moses' experience in Exodus 18 provides an example, as his father-in-law instructed, "Teach [the Israelites] the decrees and laws, and show them the way to live and the duties they are to perform" (v. 20). Thus, Moses was to train the people he led in three areas:

1. The laws of God
2. The way to live
3. The duties they were to perform

Based on this model, your training program should have three tracks:

a biblical track,

a life skills track, and

a ministry track.

Biblical Track: Teach God's Word

Before believers can be trained to do the work of the ministry, they must be grounded in the Scriptures. Everything they do in ministry is based on their understanding of God and how He relates to us. An accurate understanding can come only through God's Word, making basic biblical knowledge an absolute necessity.

8   With what should pastors begin when training others?

First, you should instruct your trainees with an overview of Scripture. (In our church's program, this entailed a sixteen-week introductory course.) Teach them when the Bible was written and by whom. Explain why we consider it to be the divinely inspired Word of God. Describe what Scripture teaches about God, humankind, salvation, and life after death. Also teach them how to study the Bible for themselves. This may seem elementary, but pastors do well to remember that many believers—especially new believers—have little or no idea how to study God's Word.

Additional courses of study should include survey courses on both the Old and New Testaments. Expository studies of various books of the Bible are always helpful, as is studying the life of Christ. Lessons based on the accounts of men and women in Scripture can be life-changing. And a good course on Bible doctrines is a must.

Pastors can design the biblical track to address their congregations' needs, as they are in the best position to determine those needs. Since a healthy church is always growing, the pastor will need to continually monitor the level of the people's biblical literacy and adjust the training curriculum accordingly. The pastor should also research and be aware of good, biblical sources for curriculum materials.

Life Skills Track: Teach Principles for Living

To be effective in ministry, believers need to know how to live the Christian life. The way they relate to others, both inside and outside the church, will impact their ability to minister. Clearly, a person's actions and way of living speak more loudly than his or her words. A Christian walk that does not measure up to biblical standards limits effectiveness in ministry. Not only will others question such a believer's right to minister, but the believer will also be distracted by the confusion in his or her own life.

9   Identify several life lessons pastors should teach.

Therefore, topics in the life skills track should address issues such as these:

- Devotional life
- Relationship building
- Good stewardship of time and money
- Marriage and family
- Spiritual formation for young families
- Parenting skills

While these subjects relate directly to life skills, they should all be based on biblical principles. Those who have built their personal and business relationships on a solid foundation are in a much better position to minister to others.

Ministry Track: Give Instruction for Duties

10   What is the purpose of ministry training?

The ministry track is especially designed for more mature believers. Its purpose is to equip believers to do specific ministry tasks. For example, Christian Chapel's ministry track was designed to train small group leaders, Sunday school teachers, and prayer workers to minister at the altar. We also had classes on intercessory prayer, spiritual warfare, and the gifts of the Holy Spirit.

When I resigned as senior pastor at Christian Chapel, we had trained and certified more than two hundred lay ministers. A significant number of those had been certified as ministers of prayer, which enabled us to minister to many people in a relatively short time each Sunday. An added benefit of the prayer ministry was that it focused on and grew from the body of believers instead of the pastor.

11   How does ministry training help the local church body?

We trained and certified all of our small group (or home fellowship group) leaders in pastoral care so that they formed the front line of that ministry. In other words, we gave these lay leaders the responsibility of visiting people at home and in the hospital and conducting telephone counseling. They were also responsible to arrange meals for families in times of sickness and death, hosting potluck suppers, and planning bridal and baby showers. Obviously, through these leaders the pastoral ministry of Christian Chapel multiplied many times over. Without their ministry, numerous people would have received little or no personal ministry.

To function effectively, this kind of shared ministry requires open communication, well-defined task descriptions, and accountability. When Moses appointed people to help him in Exodus 18, he gave each one a specific job with clearly defined limits: "He chose capable men from all Israel and made them leaders of the people, officials over thousands, hundreds, fifties and tens. They served as judges for the people at all times. The difficult cases they brought to Moses, but the simple ones they decided themselves" (vv. 25–26).

8.3.1
OBJECTIVE

Describe methods for the implementation of training in churches.

Implementing Training

The idea of implementing a program for training lay ministers may seem overwhelming. The task truly is enormous, and the logistics can be staggering. Where and how do you begin? Who prepares the materials? Who should teach? Who will select the participants?

As I consider all the details, I am reminded of the question, "How do you eat an elephant?" The answer is, "One bite at a time." So it is with launching a ministry training program—one class or course at a time.

When we began the lay ministry training institute at Christian Chapel, about 150 people attended our congregation. Thankfully, these included a number of mature believers who were well grounded in the Scripture and well adjusted in their life skills. As a result, the first class we established, "Lay Ministry 1," was in the ministry track and was designed to train our small group leaders how in the ministry of pastoral care.

Using the Exodus 18 model, I chose twenty-five possible candidates, sending each of them a personal letter inviting them to participate in a sixteen-week training course on pastoral care. I told them that the training was by invitation only and that I had selected them based on their spiritual maturity and aptitude for ministry. I then outlined the course requirements:

1. Class attendance
2. Outside reading assignments
3. Written reports
4. Supervised ministry assignments

In conclusion, I urged them to participate, but only if they were committed to completing the training course.

Since I could not find what I felt were suitable materials, I decided to prepare my own. Each week, I developed a lesson plan and outline. I collected other materials to copy and distribute to each participant. The trainees were required to read the selected material and write a brief report. I also invited them to join me when I made hospital calls and other pastoral visits and required them to make an unsupervised hospital visit and describe it in a written report. Those who successfully completed the training requirements were certified as lay ministers in pastoral care and released to do ministry.

Once the first class was complete, I invited another twenty-five people to join me for the sixteen-week course. This time, I chose a person from the first group to serve as my co-teacher, preparing him to teach the third session so I could begin another class. Therefore, when the third session began, we would have two classes—Lay Ministry 1: Pastoral Care, and Lay Ministry 2: Prayer Ministry and the Gifts of the Spirit.

After the second session of Lay Ministry 1, then, I invited graduates from the first two classes to participate in Lay Ministry 2, another sixteen-week course. This training course focused on the gifts of the Spirit and how they operate during ministry. Again, I prepared a lesson plan and outline for each week. I selected various teaching tapes and reading materials for outside study and required each participant to prepare written reports. We concluded each class session with prayer, and most of the time, the gifts of the Holy Spirit ministered during this closing time.

Those who successfully completed the course requirements for Lay Ministry 2 were certified as ministers of prayer and began their ministry during prayer time at each service. Many of the healings and other supernatural manifestations I described in lesson 5.2 (see "Train People to Minister with Their Gifts") occurred through their ministry. Of course, we encouraged those who completed the class to also be alert to any opportunity to minister to hurting people in the course of their day-to-day lives.

I remember a young man named Greg, an executive in an oil company, who did just that. One day as he met with the company's loan officer at the bank, he noticed that one side of her face drooped. When she talked or smiled, that side of her face did not move. Since they had worked together for more than two years, Greg felt free to ask about her condition. She explained that doctors had diagnosed it as Bell's palsy and that it should correct itself over the next several weeks. However, she was planning to get married in ten days.

Greg sensed the Holy Spirit directing him to pray for this woman. When he asked her permission, she hesitated for a moment but then replied, "Please do." Bowing his head, Greg prayed quietly but intensely for two or three minutes, asking God to totally heal her. While he could discern no visible improvement when he finished praying, all of her symptoms disappeared that night. This demonstrates only one of our graduates' many opportunities to minister to hurting people, both during services at the church and in the world outside of church.

After finishing the first session of Lay Ministry 2, I again selected a graduate of the class to be my co-teacher. As before, my intent was to train him to teach Lay Ministry 2 so I could launch another class.

It was a slow process, requiring six months to get a single course in place. However, as our pastoral staff grew, the other pastors launched additional classes in the other two tracks, thus speeding the process.

12 Summarize five guidelines for training believers to share ministry.

I refer to Christian Chapel's program only as an example of the possibilities. The Lord may direct you in an entirely different way as you implement a training program for your congregation. However, the principles for lay ministry training are universal:

1. Select qualified people.
2. Train them.
3. Give them a written task description.
4. Establish clear lines of accountability.
5. Release them into ministry.

Your method of implementing these principles in your local church will vary depending on your unique situation. As you ask the Lord for wisdom (James 1:5), He will show you the best way to train your people.

Keep in mind that a shared ministry does not diminish a pastor's office, but it does change his or her role. Pastors become facilitators, training and motivating others, in effect reproducing their ministry exponentially. They still have a special responsibility before God (Exodus 18:19). They remain shepherds of the flock (1 Peter 5:2–4) and the principal teachers and spokespersons for God (Exodus 18:20). Still, a shared ministry multiplies their effectiveness while not dividing their authority.

As trained members of the congregation begin to find their place in ministry, Romans 12:5–8 becomes a reality, and the church functions as God intended:

> In Christ we who are many form one body, and each member belongs to all the others. We have different gifts according to the grace given us. If a man's gift is prophesying, let him use it in proportion to his faith. If it is serving, let him serve; if it is encouraging, let him encourage; if it is contributing to the needs of others, let him give generously; if it is leadership, let him govern diligently; if it is showing mercy, let him do it cheerfully. (Romans 12:5–8)

Test Yourself

Circle the letter of the *best* answer.

1. Ephesians 4 encourages pastors to
a) discipline their children.
b) rejoice with those who rejoice.
c) care for widows and orphans.
d) share ministry responsibility.

2. When choosing disciples, the most important aspect is their
a) spiritual maturity.
b) character.
c) gifts and talents.
d) Bible knowledge.

3. Who illustrates how pastors should select leaders for shared ministry?
a) Joseph
b) Moses
c) David
d) Jeremiah

4. Gifts and abilities are useless unless the person
a) is intelligent.
b) has a good reputation.
c) demonstrates spiritual maturity.
d) has a Bible college education.

5. What should disciples learn first?
a) Counseling techniques
b) Ministry training
c) Bible study
d) Life skills

6. In the first phase of a training program, a disciple should learn about
a) doctrines of the Bible.
b) the leaders of the Bible.
c) how to study the Bible.
d) all of the above.

7 Which is an example of a life skill?
a) Praying for the sick
b) Managing money
c) Studying the Bible
d) Discipling others

8. In Lay Ministry 1, students learned the basics of
a) pastoral care.
b) spiritual gifts.
c) church business.
d) music ministry.

9. What did students study in Lay Ministry 2?
a) Leadership strategies
b) Principles of preaching
c) The Great Commission
d) The gifts of the Spirit

10. The best way to start a church training ministry is to
a) implement a little at a time.
b) implement the whole program at once.
c) poll the congregation to determine interest.
d) wait until other pastoral staff are hired.

Responses to Interactive Questions
Chapter 8

Some of these responses may include information that is supplemental to the IST. These questions are intended to produce reflective thinking beyond the course content and your responses may vary from these examples.

1 What is a primary task for pastors (Ephesians 4:11–12)?

To train and equip other believers for ministry

2 Why do pastors need to share the ministry?

To effectively reach and minister to the whole church body, to improve the quality of ministry, and to help develop gifts in other believers

3 Before training anyone, pastors should examine each potential worker in what areas?

(1) Spiritual maturity, (2) character, and (3) capabilities

4 What signs indicate that a person is spiritually mature enough to engage in ministry?

The spiritually mature know and obey the Scriptures, are people of integrity and faithfulness, walk with the Holy Spirit, and have a healthy view of God.

5 According to 1 Timothy 3:6, why should a recent convert not be a minister?

A new convert has yet to be grounded in God's Word of God and might misguide other believers; the position and privilege of being a leader could cause the new convert to become haughty.

6 List some signs of good Christian character.

Answers may vary but could include these ideas: honesty, trustworthiness, loyalty, faithfulness to God in spirit and possessions.

7 Moses was to train others in what three areas (Exodus 18:20)?

(1) The laws of God, (2) the way to live, and (3) the duties they were to perform

8 With what should pastors begin when training others?

An overview of Scripture and its basic teaching and principles, as well as how the people can study the Bible for themselves

9 Identify several life lessons pastors should teach.

A good devotional life, relationship building, good stewardship of God-given resources, marriage and family, parenting skills, spiritual formation for young families, and so on

10 What is the purpose of ministry training?

To equip mature believers for ministry; to help them learn and use their skills according to the church's needs and mission

11 How does ministry training help the local church body?

It develops the members' skills and gifts in a way that honors God, allowing the body of Christ to function more efficiently. It makes people feel included and unforgotten. It can also help draw unbelievers to the church and ultimately to the Lord Jesus himself.

12 Summarize five guidelines for training believers to share ministry.

(1) Select qualified people; (2) train them; (3) give them clear instructions; (4) establish accountability measures; and (5) send them into ministry.

Developing Small Groups

Small groups wear many labels in the church. Dr. David Yonggi Cho, pastor of Yoido Full Gospel Church in Seoul, South Korea, calls them *cell groups.* Others call them spiritual growth groups, support groups, home fellowships, or just small groups. No matter how we identify them, small groups represent a group of believers (usually about eight to sixteen in number) who meet for the purpose of New Testament-type fellowship and personal spiritual growth.

Although a significant number of highly effective churches utilize small groups, many pastors still hesitate to embrace them. Their reasons vary but generally fall into two or three categories:

1. They do not recognize the need for small groups.

2. The models they are familiar with would not work in their congregation.

3. They feel they lack the expertise to begin a small group ministry.

This chapter will address each of these issues.

The size of the group is often eight to nineteen. If a group is too small, people may feel like they are under pressure. If a group is too big, there is less fellowship. The purpose of those in a small group is to enter into a spiritual covenant—like believers did in the New Testament—so they can have fellowship and grow spiritually.

Lesson 9.1   Recognizing the Need
Objectives
9.1.1   Describe needs that small groups meet.
9.1.2   Contrast worship with fellowship.

Lesson 9.2   Designing an Appropriate Model
Objective
9.2.1   Discuss small group principles related to goals, guidelines, belonging, sharing, and pastoral care.

Lesson 9.3   Establishing Group Guidelines
Objective
9.3.1   Write a job description for a small group leader.

9.1.1
OBJECTIVE
Describe needs that small groups meet.

1 How do small groups provide a uniquely common ground for pastoral staff and laity?

9.1.2
OBJECTIVE
Contrast worship with fellowship.

✱ He is saying we are too focused on Christ and not ourselves?!

Recognizing the Need

A small group ministry is the best venue to address a number of the church's needs, including personal ministry, fellowship, pastoral care, discipleship, and evangelism. Of course, the most obvious of these needs is the overwhelming burden of personal ministry.

Personal Ministry

The pastor and/or the pastoral staff simply cannot meet all the needs of a local church body. To attempt such a thing is futile. Every pastor is well advised to consider Jethro's observations and advice to Moses:

> What you are doing is not good. You and these people who come to you will only wear yourselves out. The work is too heavy for you; you cannot handle it alone. Listen now to me and I will give you some advice, and may God be with you. You must be the people's representative before God and bring their disputes to him. Teach them the decrees and laws, and show them the way to live and the duties they are to perform. But select capable men from all the people—men who fear God, trustworthy men who hate dishonest gain—and appoint them as officials over thousands, hundreds, fifties and tens. Have them serve as judges for the people at all times, but have them bring every difficult case to you; the simple cases they can decide themselves. That will make your load lighter, because they will share it with you. If you do this and God so commands, you will be able to stand the strain, and all these people will go home satisfied. (Exodus 18:17–23)

Each member of the body of Christ—the church—has a role to fulfill. Paul writes: "From him [Jesus] the whole body, joined and held together by every supporting ligament, grows and builds itself up in love, as each part does its work" (Ephesians 4:16). To this end, small groups are ideal, for they allow most everyone to have a part and to help each other grow spiritually.

Fellowship

A second need is to provide a place where people can experience genuine New Testament fellowship. The world is full of individuals who are desperate, not to join, but to belong. A host of social factors contribute to this longing, including the break-up of traditional communities, the tendency for businesses to become larger and therefore more impersonal, the mobility of modern life, and the generation gap. The result is a great hunger for contact, belonging, and a need to overcome feelings of alienation and estrangement.

Sadly, the church—which God intended to be a holy community—seems to add to this mounting frustration. Far too often, the church's primary focus is on the worship service and little else. Desperate for real fellowship, worshippers come and are offered little or no opportunity to bond with each other. In fact, the very structure of worship prohibits this. Its focus is on celebration, not community.

In light of this, let us ask ourselves some demanding questions. Suppose we were outsiders looking in, feeling isolated and lonely, as though we do not belong anywhere. Would the church attract us by the quality of its fellowship? Would we feel that we had finally come home, that this is where we truly belong? Unfortunately, the answer is probably no.

The usual worship service is foreign to outsiders. The songs are unfamiliar, the music is different, and the language is strange. Even if they are vaguely

WOWZERZ

familiar with the order of worship, they will not truly feel like they belong. And this painful experience is not unique to the unchurched. Undoubtedly, many regular attendees leave worship with the same empty feelings.

Why is that? One reason is that most congregations are too large to be conducive to fellowship. According to sociologists, individuals can become personally acquainted with as many as sixty persons but will tend to feel isolated in groups larger than sixty. Thus, in a church setting, if they do not see a familiar face, if no one remembers their name, they will feel left out no matter how vibrant the worship. If this happens week after week, it will undermine their personhood, and they will begin to doubt their own value and self-worth.

This sense of isolation can occur in small churches as well. The problem is not size but mind-set or attitude. When members of a congregation are comfortable and all their needs are being met, they tend to enjoy the fellowship to the exclusion of new persons. Sometimes people perceive church growth as a threat, but most often, they are merely insensitive to the newcomer's needs.

Over the last few decades, concerned church leaders have attempted to address these issues. Many have gone to great lengths to restructure their worship services. They encourage more lay involvement in various ways, including the use of ministry gifts and perhaps dialogue in the sermon. While some of these changes were superficial and temporary, others have proved enormously effective. Still, they have done almost nothing to meet the church's need for true fellowship.

Simply put, the church cannot solve its need for community by changing its style of celebration. Such methodology is like trying to cure one patient by treating another.

Forcing a worship service to equally accommodate celebration and community does not work. Celebration and community are not rivals vying for equal time during the worship service; rather, they are complementary manifestations of the true church. They are different in purpose but equal in value.

Celebration focuses primarily on God; it is the church ministering to the Lord. Although celebration causes believers' spiritual needs to be met, their need for fellowship, the need to belong, usually remains. Celebration may include community, but its main focus is on worship, not relationships.

2   What is the best context for effectively meeting needs in a church?

The worship service clearly cannot provide the quality of fellowship our hearts hunger for, nor should it. Sunday school classes, sometimes called adult Bible fellowships, provide a measure of community, as do potluck dinners and church socials. However, the depth of fellowship we long for will elude us unless we consciously plan for it. It cannot be forced, but it can and must be cultivated. The best place for this to occur is in small groups.

The ministries of pastoral care, discipleship, and evangelism are natural outgrowths of this fellowship. They flow out of relationship and are most effective when the individuals' fellowship needs are being met.

9.2.1
OBJECTIVE

Discuss small group principles related to goals, guidelines, belonging, sharing, and pastoral care.

3   Identify some guidelines for establishing small groups.

4   Small groups can be based on what areas of interest? What must they include?

5   Physically, what speaks *inclusion* to each group member?

Designing an Appropriate Model

Creating the right small group model for a particular congregation involves five keys.

Key 1: Set Goals

The first step in developing an appropriate model for your small group ministry is to identify your goals: What do you want the small group ministry to accomplish in your church? What specific needs do you want it to meet? When you have identified your goals, you can design a small group ministry to address them. In general, the small group ministry should develop community, disciple believers, provide pastoral care, and evangelize the lost.

Key 2: Set Guidelines

Some churches have a rigid small group program. Their small groups are based on geography, and participants are required to attend the nearest group. They set specific limits on each group's size, when it meets, and what is taught. Often, the pastor of a pastoral staff member meets with all the small group leaders to teach them that week's lesson, which they in turn teach to their respective small group.

Other churches use a more flexible model. Their small groups form around mutual interests or needs. Some areas of interest are what you might expect: intercessory prayer, Bible study, worship, marriage and/or parenting. Others do not appear spiritual at first glance: sports, scrapbooking, hiking, rock climbing, and so on. Yet these "less spiritual" groups often become the most evangelistic because they have more appeal to the unchurched. The ministry philosophy of this approach maintains that discipleship and outreach flow out of relationships and that the unique makeup of each small group causes it to excel in a specific area. These small group meetings center on the area on interest and include at least one spiritual component—worship, prayer, Bible study, or a testimony.

Key 3: Make People Feel Welcome

If the first goal of small group ministry is to meet individuals' belonging needs, the most important element in a small group is tone. Many factors contribute to a group's tone, but none is more significant than the leader's attitude. Small group leaders can, simply through the furniture arrangement or method of structuring the meetings, create an open or closed environment. By placing the furniture in a circle, leaders encourage eye contact and interaction within the group. The leaders should be relaxed and at ease. They should demonstrate a genuine interest in each individual and model the kind of interaction that reflects true New Testament fellowship or *koinonia*. It is crucial that leaders not perceive their primary role as that of teacher, lest the meeting become just another "class" where community is lost in the traditional teacher-lecturer, student-listener structure.

As we formulate our models for small group ministry, we should consider Bruce Larson's analogy: "The neighborhood bar is possibly the best counterfeit there is to the fellowship Christ wants to give his church" (Larson and Miller 1977). A bar is usually characterized by regular clientele who know and trust one another, who are willing to listen to each other without criticism or judgment. We need to cultivate this nonjudgmental, noncritical atmosphere in the church,

[handwritten margin note: Pray freely to Christ. — Somethings we just dont need to know what they think.]

particularly in small groups. We need to create a place where individuals know and trust one another and are able to talk freely—an atmosphere of belonging.

Key 4: Create an Environment for Sharing

A small group must be a place where people can share without fear of judgment or jealousy. It must encourage sharing not only of achievements and growth but also failures and discouragement. David R. Mace writes, "We can somehow endure pain, provided we can grasp a loving hand and be supported by a familiar arm. We can live through failure if only one dear companion goes on believing in us. But what we can not endure is the experience of being utterly alone, without anyone to love us or care about us" (1973, 5).

6 What creates an atmosphere in which all feel safe to share their feelings?

Small group leaders facilitate this kind of sharing by opening their lives to the group and modeling transparency. Jesus is the best model, for He practiced this type of relationship with the Twelve. They shared His successes, miracles, and even spiritual experiences such as the Transfiguration. They were also part of His painful struggles. They were with Jesus when many disciples deserted Him (John 6:66–67), and they were with Him in Gethsemane when He said, "My soul is overwhelmed with sorrow to the point of death" (Mark 14:34).

Even when they did not participate in the actual experience, Jesus made them part of it by speaking candidly about it, sharing His thoughts and feelings. For instance, no one witnessed Jesus' temptation in the wilderness. He was alone there for forty long days. Yet Matthew, Mark, and Luke all wrote about the experience. Where did they get their information? Is it not likely that Jesus told them about it?

Jesus revealed things to the Twelve that He did not share with the multitudes that thronged Him. Further, He shared things with Peter, James, and John that He did not share with the other disciples. He was not being secretive or choosing favorites; He was simply showing sensitivity to each disciple's spiritual and emotional maturity. In John 16:12, He said, "I have much more to say to you, more than you can now bear."

It is critical that small group leaders demonstrate this same sensitivity. They should not share indiscriminately because they may offend "weaker" members. However, they can share almost any past experience they have overcome. Such a disclosure does two things: (1) It communicates an open honesty, a way of saying, "I'm one of you. I struggle with life just like you do. I understand." (2) It communicates hope because the leader has, in fact, overcome. It reaffirms faith in God's sufficiency.

Leaders must be responsive without letting the group manipulate them. They must direct without dominating. While they should encourage everyone to share both pain and joys, they must be careful not to allow one person to monopolize the group's time. People often need to talk, that is, need someone to listen with love; however, if they are not guided, the group will feel used. It is sometimes helpful to make a comment such as this: "It sounds like you are really hurting. How can we help?" Moreover, leaders must not allow the meeting to become bogged down with sadness and despair. The opportunity and freedom to share struggles and hurts must always be in an atmosphere undergirded with faith and ministry.

Small group leaders need to be responsive, accepting, and affirming to each person in the group. They must try to get to know each person individually, which is possible only according to their willingness to invest time on a one-on-one basis outside the group. However, leaders must guard against only answering people's questions and telling them what to do or believe instead of guiding the individuals to think and discover truth for themselves. Leaders should strive to support the group members in their efforts to grow toward wholeness.

Of course, the small group will achieve its full potential only as the individual members catch the vision and begin to relate to each other as the leader relates to them. When they do, New Testament-type fellowship begins to take root, thus fulfilling the small group ministry's primary goal in the life of the church.

Key 5: Encourage Pastoral Care

Another ministry of small groups is to provide the first line of pastoral care, a natural outgrowth of New Testament fellowship. In Acts 2:44–45, Luke records, "All the believers were together and had everything in common. Selling their possessions and goods, they gave to anyone as he had need." Relationships and responsibility—love and duty—go hand in hand.

Each small group accepts the responsibility of providing primary pastoral care for its members. Because the group is small, no one is left out. If someone is absent from the small group meeting, he or she is missed. The group members notice if a member misses Sunday worship because they make a special effort to sit together or at least look for each other. And the group takes responsibility for contacting the absentees. They never apply pressure or inflict guilt; they simply express love and concern.

7 What can small group members do for and with one another?

Through personal contact, small group members are more likely to be aware of individual needs, whatever their nature. By being in relationship with each other, they naturally feel a responsibility toward one another and reach out accordingly. They may host bridal and baby showers, celebrate birthdays and anniversaries, and do many little caring things for each other. They might get together for coffee, talk by phone, or form prayer partnerships.

In short, they are "there" for each other. If sickness or death strikes a member of the group, the others rally around to offer comfort and love. The leader or an appointed delegate contacts the church office to ensure that the pastoral staff is informed, and then they begin making the necessary arrangements. This may include baby-sitting and meals as well as hospital visits. If the illness is lengthy and the needs exhaust the group's limited resources, they then enlist the church at large to help.

Bill Hybels, senior pastor of Willow Creek Community Church near Chicago, Illinois, relates an experience that illustrates how this works:

> One Sunday morning, at the conclusion of the service, a young couple approached him and asked him to pray for their baby. The father then handed the blanketed baby to him.

> As he prepared to pray, the mother pulled back the blanket that covered the baby's face. Hybels said, "I felt my knees begin to buckle. I thought I was going to faint. Had the father not steadied me, I may well have keeled over. In my arms was the most horribly deformed baby I had ever seen. The whole center of her tiny face was caved in. How she kept breathing I will never know."

> The parents told him that the doctors gave the baby about six weeks to live. "We would like you to pray that before she dies, she will know and feel our love."

> After praying together, Hybels returned the baby to her parents. "Is there anything we can do for you?" he asked. "Any way that we as a church can serve you during this time?"

"Bill, we're okay," the father responded. "Really, we are. We've been in a loving small group for years. Our group members knew that this pregnancy had complications. They were at our house the night we learned the news, and they were at the hospital when Emily was delivered. They helped us absorb the reality of the whole thing. They even cleaned our house and fixed our meals when we brought her home. They pray for us constantly and call us several times every day. They are even helping us plan Emily's funeral."

Just then, three other couples stepped forward and surrounded Emily and her parents. One of them said, "We always attend church together as a group." After prayer together, they all walked up the aisle toward the lobby. (Hybels 2002, 22–23)

Can you imagine the stress a pastor would feel if he or she were responsible to provide all the pastoral care that couple needed? What would it be like if the pastor had to arrange for someone to prepare the meals and clean the house as well as provide spiritual and emotional support? Now multiply that responsibility many times, because a pastor is responsible not just for a single family but for the entire congregation.

In light of situations like this, small group ministry is the best solution. It releases pastors to focus their energies on the needs of the whole church while providing the best possible ministry to individuals in need.

9.3.1
OBJECTIVE
Write a job description for a small group leader.

8   Name three considerations when choosing small group leaders.

Establishing Group Guidelines

When you have recognized the need for a small group ministry and determined the appropriate model for your congregation, it is time to implement the program. With any new ministry, it is best to think in terms of birthing rather than creating. To give birth means to start small and grow, whereas creating focuses more on the finished product than the process. In regard to small group ministry, this means you will likely best serve your vision by starting with two or three small groups rather than trying to involve the whole congregation from the beginning.

Choose a Mature Leader

To launch a small group ministry, you must begin with the leaders. Depending on which model you choose for your congregation, the qualifications of a small group leader may be rigid or flexible. Of course, even the most flexible model will include certain leadership requirements.

Again, both Exodus 18:21 and Acts 6:3 provide excellent guidelines regarding the qualifications for those who would serve in ministry. As with any other spiritual leaders, pastors must evaluate small group leaders in three areas: spiritual maturity, character, and capabilities or giftedness (see Lesson 8.1).

It may be helpful to think of these qualifications as a way to identify potential leaders rather than to screen out the unqualified. Remember, perfect people do not exist. You are looking for people who love the Lord and are committed to serving His church. Often, these people are already involved in pastoral care, discipleship, and evangelism, not through a recognized ministry of the church, but in their day-to-day relationships.

Describe the Ministry of the Leader

Written Agreement

When you are ready to invite individuals to become small group leaders, you should give them a detailed task description and a list of the responsibilities required of such a leader. I have found it best to present these in written form to minimize the chance of misunderstanding (see the sample small group form at the end of this chapter). The written form should include a statement indicating the candidates' willingness to do the following:

- Help fulfill the congregation's mission and vision
- Adhere to a lifestyle honor code
- Support and teach the doctrines of the church
- Fulfill the job description of a small group leader

Only when potential leaders understand what is required of them are they able to decide whether or not to serve. Should they decide to become small group leaders, have them sign two copies of the agreement. Give one copy to the candidate, and keep the other for the church records.

Job Description

You should tailor the task or job description to fit the goals and expectations of your congregation's small group ministry. It should be simple and straightforward. The description should include (1) the details of when, where, and how often the small group will meet; (2) the general format of the meeting; and (3) the small group's responsibilities to its individual members and to the overall ministry of the church.

For example, at our church, one of the primary responsibilities of our small group ministry was pastoral care. Therefore, the job description included hosting bridal and/or baby showers for members of the group as well as providing meals and/or childcare in case of sickness or hospitalization. Of course, providing prayer and counsel in times of crisis was also part of the task description.

Communication and Accountability

9 What communication issues need to be considered concerning small group leaders?

Finally, be certain to maintain open communication and clear lines of accountability. Regardless of the flexibility and openness of your system, it will still require a certain amount of structure. For instance, who provides pastoral oversight and care for the small group leaders? Who answers their questions, and who provides wise counsel when they face a situation beyond their expertise? Who administers discipline if needed? These are the kinds of issues that structure addresses. In the earliest stages, each small group leader may report directly to the pastor, but as the ministry grows and develops, that will likely change.

An effective church growth paradigm that takes its cue from Jesus is based on small groups and the relationships between people who share interests, talents, or needs. By taking ministry outside the church building and setting people free to live their faith while doing the things they love to do, leaders see church growth occur naturally.

A small group organizational model must provide clear and specific accountability relationships for the group leaders. The size of the congregation and the community and the availability of qualified leaders will determine the accountability structure. Regardless of their position in the small group system, all individuals must know who provides their spiritual covering and to whom they are accountable.

Whatever you wish to call them—cell groups, spiritual growth groups, home fellowships—small groups formed the heart of the New Testament church, and they are vital for the twenty-first-century church as well. Although the Scriptures do not include a definitive model for small group ministry, they do provide clear principles, including community, discipleship, evangelism, and pastoral care (Acts 2:44–47). Other than being relational in nature, the New Testament model is deliberately vague, allowing each local church to develop the model best suited to its needs. Small group ministry is essential for giving us a place to know and be known, making New Testament fellowship (*koinonia*) a reality even in our impersonal world.

Sample Small Group Form

Job Description/Agreement for a Small Group Leader

Church Name: _____

Date: _____

Pastor: _____

Group Leader: _____

Name of Group: _____

Goals for Group: _____

_____

_____

_____

I, _____ **, the new leader, commit to:**

-

-

-

-

Details about the Group:

- It will meet each _____ (week or month) on
  _____ (day)
  from _____ to _____ (time) at
  _____ (place/address).
- This is what will happen in a normal meeting:

  _____

  _____

  _____

  _____

- Some things small group members will do *for* and *with* each other
  include:

  _____

  _____

  _____

Guidelines for Communication:

- _____ cares for the small group leader.
- The small group leader will communicate weekly with _____
  .
- _____ will answer the questions that the
  small group leader may have.
- _____ gives advice when a leader has a
  difficult problem.
- _____ gives discipline if it is needed.

The guidelines of this written form are agreed to by:

_____ (Group Leader)
Date _____

Signed in the presence of:

_____ (Pastor)
Date _____

_____ (Witness)
Date _____

Test Yourself

Circle the letter of the *best* answer.

1. Small groups primarily meet the needs of fellowship and
a) worship.
b) friendship.
c) evangelism.
d) personal ministry.

2. Close fellowship at church is limited by
a) the size of the church.
b) the structure of the service.
c) the mind-set of the people.
d) all of the above.

3. Worship and fellowship are
a) different in purpose and value.
b) equal in purpose and value.
c) different in purpose, but equal in value.
d) equal in purpose, but different in value.

4. Before planning for small groups, a pastor should
a) set goals and guidelines.
b) choose qualified leaders.
c) plan a Sunday night service.
d) do all of the above.

5. The first goal of a small group is to
a) create an attitude of worship.
b) study a Bible lesson.
c) make people feel welcome.
d) start and end on time.

6. Leaders can create a setting for sharing by
a) telling a Bible story.
b) sharing their struggles.
c) playing soft music.
d) sitting on the floor.

7. Small group leaders must
a) allow each member to talk as long as he or she desires.
b) downplay their own struggles and weaknesses.
c) keep themselves apart from the other group members.
d) encourage an atmosphere of faith and ministry.

8. A natural result of close relationships is
a) dependence.
b) commitment.
c) disagreement.
d) competition.

9. The most important quality in a small group leader is
a) spiritual maturity.
c) spiritual gifts.
b) experience.
d) character.

10. A leader's job description would **NOT** include
a) a statement of commitment.
b) guidelines for communication.
c) information about salary.
d) details about the group.

Responses to Interactive Questions
Chapter 9

Some of these responses may include information that is supplemental to the IST. These questions are intended to produce reflective thinking beyond the course content and your responses may vary from these examples.

1 How do small groups provide a uniquely common ground for pastoral staff and laity?

With training, the general membership shares the opportunity to minister with the pastor(s).

2 What is the best context for effectively meeting needs in a church?

A well-planned small group centered around Christian interaction

3 Identify some guidelines for establishing small groups.

Encourage members to commit to a particular group. Limit group size. Formulate a group around a common interest or purpose, remembering the church's mission. Ensure that leadership approves the topics. Establish group leadership training.

4 Small groups can be based on what areas of interest? What must they include?

Answers may vary. Students should consider that believers and unbelievers have an interest in addressing felt needs along with spiritual topics.

5 Physically, what speaks *inclusion* to each group member?

A circle that allows all to participate in a context of face-to-face interaction

6 What creates an atmosphere in which all feel safe to share their feelings?

The group leader sets the tone of the discussion by wisely sharing his or her own struggles and victories to the group.

7 What can small group members do for or with one another?

Stay informed of and support one another in spiritual nurturing and the growing events of life, such as celebrations or private struggles, times when prayer and love-in-action are treasures. Details may vary.

8 Name three considerations when choosing small group leaders.

(1) spiritual maturity, (2) character, and (3) talents and abilities

9 What communication issues need to be considered concerning small group leaders?

Communication issues include these: Who provides pastoral oversight and care for the small group leaders? Who answers their questions, and who provides wise counsel when they face a situation beyond their expertise? Who administers discipline if needed?

Special Services of the Church

Pastors have the opportunity to share in many of life's most significant experiences. Among them are weddings, funerals, baby dedications, water baptism, and Holy Communion. These events are momentous in the lives of believers. Because of their character, these services are sometimes described as *sacraments*—literally, "sacred things" or "oaths consecrated by a sacred rite"; they are also referred to as ***ordinances*** because they are ceremonies "ordained by the Lord Himself" (Pearlman 1950, 25).

As pastors, we have the responsibility to conduct these special services in ways that both honor the Lord and edify the worshippers. They must never become common or ordinary to us. Each one is an act of worship and should be approached and conducted accordingly.

To assist them in the discharge of these duties, pastors should have a minister's service book, which contains ceremonies and orders of service for almost every occasion, including weddings, baptisms, child dedication, installation of officers and deacons, Communion, and funerals. While you will likely modify each order of service to meet the needs of your individual situation, the service book provides a helpful overview. Some of the most used volumes are these:

- *Abingdon Marriage Manual*, rev. ed., by Perry H. Biddle, Jr. (Nashville: Abingdon Press, 1987).

- *Minister's Manual*, Volumes 1–3, compiled and edited by William E. Pickthorn (Springfield, MO: Gospel Publishing House).

- *The Star Book for Ministers*, 2nd rev. ed., by Edward T. Hiscox (Valley Forge, PA: Judson Press, 1994).

However, there is more to the success of a special service than the instructions, samples, and prayers. What happens before these services is paramount to their success.

Lesson 10.1   Conducting Ceremonies

Objectives

10.1.1 Explain guidelines for church weddings.

10.1.2 Summarize in writing the order of a wedding service.

10.1.3 Describe the purpose of baby dedications and how to involve the parents and the church.

10.1.4 Explain the pastor's role concerning funerals.

Lesson 10.2   Administering the Ordinances

Objectives

10.2.1 Summarize scriptural teachings regarding water baptism.

10.2.2 Describe the pastor's role concerning water baptism.

10.2.3 Explain the pastor's role concerning Communion.

Conducting Ceremonies

Weddings

Although a wedding is normally a joyous occasion, it is also an extremely stressful time, particularly for the bride and her mother. If their needs and desires for the wedding conflict with the spoken and unspoken guidelines for use of the church, the pastor and the church can be placed in a difficult position.

Having a written policy manual already in place can minimize such misunderstandings. The manual should cover such things as availability of the sanctuary and/or fellowship hall; fees for the sound technician, janitorial service, and so forth; and the rental fee for non-members (active members should be able to use the facilities at no cost). The policy manual should also set guidelines regarding for whom the pastor or a member of the pastoral staff may conduct a wedding. For instance, at Christian Chapel, the pastoral staff would not marry any couple who had not completed twelve weeks of premarital counseling.

While the groom customarily gives the minister a monetary gift for his or her services, some pastors provide their services at no charge to church members. If the couple is not part of the congregation, it may be wise to also include the minister's fee in the fee schedule included in the policy manual.

As you and other church leaders compose the guidelines in your church's written policy manual, it is helpful to review manuals from other, perhaps larger, churches. These can serve as an excellent resource to assist you in preparing your own.

Counseling

Premarital counseling should touch on basic teachings of the faith, biblical guidelines for marriage, finances, medical requirements, pregnancy, temperaments, and communication. Some churches use trained laity to conduct premarital counseling for engaged couples and to provide one year of mentoring for the newlyweds. In that way, since the newlyweds have already bonded with the couple who provided their premarital counseling, it is natural for them to continue the relationship after they marry. The mentoring couple and the newlyweds meet at least once per month, usually for lunch or dinner. This provides a scheduled time when they can talk about the joys and difficulties of marriage. Of course, the mentoring couple is available at other times as well, especially in times of marital crisis.

Planning

Regardless of who does the premarital counseling, the pastor should meet with the engaged couple to review the ceremony and assist in planning the wedding. The couple's perspective of their wedding not only affects the ceremony's structure but also helps determine its spirit. Couples often view the wedding primarily as a celebration of their love and plan the service accordingly. However, the pastor is responsible to help the engaged couple understand that their wedding is first and foremost an act of worship.

The pastor must also help the couple understand that their marriage is a covenant both with each other and with God. The vows they exchange are holy promises not only to each other but also to God. Numbers 30:2 states, "When a man makes a vow to the Lord . . . he must not break his word but must do everything he said." The pastor should carefully review the vows with the couple to ensure that they fully understand the holy promises they are making.

10.1.1
OBJECTIVE

Explain guidelines for church weddings.

1 What can a church provide to help wedding plans go smoothly?

2 Aside from premarital counseling, what is the pastor's primary task before the wedding?

Communion

Many couples wish to receive **Communion** during their wedding ceremony. I have found it best to celebrate this immediately after the couple has exchanged their vows, making it their first act as a married couple. Communion give the minister a special opportunity to share some thoughts about marriage. For instance, the pastor might say:

> Bill and Faye have chosen Communion as their first act as a married couple to signify their sincere desire to put Jesus first in their marriage and to serve Him all the days of their lives. Not only is receiving Communion a wonderful demonstration of Bill and Faye's commitment to our Lord, but it also provides an apt picture of the selfless love that marriage requires. When Jesus took the bread and broke it, He was demonstrating the kind of love that willingly lays down its life for the beloved. In marriage, both of you will be required to give unreservedly of yourselves. You will have to lay down your lives for each other. Without this kind of sacrificial love, your marriage can never become all God intends it to be.
>
> The cup symbolizes the high cost of forgiveness. Jesus said, "This is my blood . . . which is poured out . . . for the forgiveness of sins" (Matthew 26:28). As unbelievable as it may seem at this moment, you will sin against each other. You may do it accidentally, out of ignorance, or you may do it deliberately, out of anger. But of one thing you may be sure: You will sin against your love. When that happens, only one thing can save your marriage—the cup of forgiveness.
>
> Receive with thankful hearts the love and mercy our Lord has provided through the gift of himself, but learn from it as well. Determine that you will love each other as the Lord loved you and that you will graciously forgive each other just as the Lord has forgiven you. Do this all the days of your lives, and your marriage will be all God intends marriage to be.

Service Order

10.12
OBJECTIVE

Summarize in writing the order of a wedding service.

3   Who should receive a detailed order of the wedding service?

Because even the simplest church wedding is a logistical challenge, a typed order of service should be ready and available at the rehearsal. Those who need copies of the order of service include the wedding coordinator (if there is one), minister, musicians, singers, and the sound technician. The order of service should contain a diagram of where the minister, bride and groom, and the wedding party will stand during the ceremony. It should also include details about the ceremony such as the order in which the parents are seated, when the attendants will enter, and the order of special music and the recessional at the end of the wedding. If the bride does not have a wedding coordinator, the responsibility of coordinating the various elements should be given to a knowledgeable person.

Along with the order of service, a pastor must have a copy of the service itself. This includes the introduction, message to the guests, Scriptures to read to the couple, and the vows to repeat. The minister's book contains samples of wedding services, with vows for the bride and groom to repeat.

Careful planning and clear communication are key to a memorable wedding. Since this is usually the first wedding for the bride and groom, they will look to the pastor for guidance and direction. The pastor's knowledge and expertise provide guidelines to help a couple plan a wedding that is truly an act of worship even as it reflects the unique characteristics of their relationship. When this is done well, nothing is more meaningful, and the pastor will have a special place in the couple's hearts.

OBJECTIVE

Describe the purpose of baby dedications and how to involve the parents and the church.

Baby Dedications

Few things in life are more special than the dedication of a baby, especially to the parents and grandparents. For this reason, pastors need to approach this service with sincere devotion. Neither a meaningless ritual nor simply a religious form, a baby dedication is an act of worship. It is important both to the Lord and to the family; therefore, it must be important to pastors as well.

Some pastors of larger churches dedicate babies only once a month or less. They plan a single service in which they dedicate a number of babies at once. While I understand the logistical advantages of doing it this way, I feel that group dedications detract from the spiritual significance. I strongly recommend that pastors dedicate only one baby at a time, even if it means they have a baby dedication in every service.

The Purpose

4 What is the purpose of a baby dedication?

Unlike those who practice infant baptism, we do not believe that a child receives salvation through being dedicated to the Lord. Rather, baby dedication is an act of worship in which the parents humbly acknowledge that the child is not theirs but the Lord's. Like Hannah, who brought Samuel to the temple, the parents give their child back to the Lord. With Hannah, they declare, "For his whole life he will be given over to the Lord " (1 Samuel 1:28).

The Process

First, the pastor invites the parents and grandparents (if present) to bring the baby and join him or her on the platform. However, this moment is not just for the parents; the whole congregation should be involved in the dedication, which is a significant event in the child's life. The dedication serves as a public acknowledgment that this child is a gift from God.

During the baby dedication, pastors may want to remind the congregation of these truths from Scripture:

- Children are a heritage from the Lord. The fruit of the womb is His reward (Psalm 127:3, NKJV).

- Mary and Joseph presented baby Jesus to the Lord in the temple (Luke 2:22–24).

- Jesus instructed His disciples to "let the little children come to me, and do not hinder them" (Mark 10:14).

- Jesus "took the children in his arms, put his hands on them and blessed them" (Mark 10:16).

5 When dedicating a baby, why should the pastor include a charge to the congregation?

Pastors should admonish the parents and all others present in the child's godly upbringing, for it is both the parents' and all believers' responsibility to teach and correct the child in accordance with God's Word. Also, pastors should note to everyone that children are a blessing and that, while the upbringing of a child is a great responsibility, it is also a subject of praise. While these charges and reminders can be taken from the script of a minister's manual, I have found it very meaningful and more personal when pastors simply share the truths and admonitions God lays on their hearts for each family.

After addressing the parents and congregation, pastors should pray a prayer of dedication for the child, asking the Lord to fulfill His purposes for him or her. Again, these prayers are more meaningful when pastors specifically pray the things God places in their hearts for each individual child.

At the end of the dedication, the parents traditionally receive a certificate and a gift from the church that communicates the sacredness of the moment and reminds them of the commitment they have made. A Bible is usually an excellent choice for such a gift. It is also helpful to later give the parents a CD, video, or DVD of the service to commemorate the occasion.

Funerals

10.1.4
OBJECTIVE
Explain the pastor's role concerning funerals.

Just as weddings and baby dedications are first and foremost acts of worship, so are funerals. During weddings and baby dedications, the church rejoices with those who are rejoicing; during funerals, the church mourns with those who mourn (Romans 12:15). Yet whether we are rejoicing or mourning, we are worshipping. When tragedy strikes, like Job who "fell to the ground in worship," we can say, "Naked I came from my mother's womb, and naked I will depart. The Lord gave and the Lord has taken away; may the name of the Lord be praised" (Job 1:21).

Preparation

Pastoral ministry to the bereaved often begins before the death of the loved one. In cases of chronic or terminal illness, pastors will likely spend considerable time with both the patient and his or her family. This special opportunity to bond with the family enables pastors to minister more effectively at the funeral.

As soon as pastors learn of a death, they should immediately go to the home of the bereaved to offer comfort and condolences. Even the bravest, most self-reliant, faith-filled individuals experience an inner strengthening through the presence of a compassionate pastor. Seemingly small things such as an encouraging word or the touch of a hand on the shoulder have a profound impact on a grieving person. Reading Scripture and praying are appropriate, but they are most effective after the bereaved have had the opportunity to express their sorrow.

Planning

6   Define *obituary* and *eulogy*.

At the appropriate time, pastors need to determine the family's wishes regarding the funeral service, such as time, place, special music, special Bible passages, the obituary (brief biography of the deceased), the eulogy (the part of the service that honors the deceased), and so forth. During this critical time, tactful pastors may help the family make difficult decisions like whether to have an open or closed casket, whether to request donations in lieu of flowers, and, if so, where to direct the donations. Once these matters are determined, pastors are prepared to turn their attention to the service itself.

The Service

7   Of what value is a pastor's officiating at the funeral of an unbeliever?

The funeral service gives pastors a unique opportunity to affirm both the comforting presence of Father God (Psalm 23:4) and the hope of eternal life through Jesus Christ (John 11:23–27). If the deceased was a believer, pastors can personalize the message to reflect the person's faith and relationship with Jesus. If the deceased was not a known believer, the pastor can still focus on the eternal truths of Scripture, comforting the bereaved with the promise of the Lord's presence while clearly proclaiming the promise of eternal life through faith in the Lord Jesus Christ. Whatever the circumstances, the message should always provide both comfort and hope.

After the service, if the family has requested an open casket, pastors should stand at the head of the casket as friends and family of the deceased pass by. In this way, pastors can offer a brief word of condolence to those who appear to take the death especially hard. They should also remain by the casket as the family views the deceased for the last time, not to be intrusive, but to offer a comforting word, a supporting arm, or a quick hug. Such compassion and sensitivity will minister greatly to the grieving family.

When the casket has been closed, it is a good idea for the pastor to walk ahead of the pallbearers as they carry the casket to the hearse and to remain there as the casket is placed in the hearse for transport to the cemetery. At the cemetery, the pastor should go immediately to the hearse so he or she may precede the casket to the grave.

The pastor should conduct the graveside service to fit the customs of the people. In some countries, the grave is the place for eulogies—for many people to say kind things about the deceased. In other places, such as most of the United States, the graveside service is traditionally brief. It may include a few Scripture verses, a prayer to commit the loved one to God, and a closing prayer. The pastor should then speak briefly with each of the immediate family members before leaving.

Ministry to the bereaved is one of the highest callings for pastors. The most helpful thing they can do is just be there for those who are grieving. The Holy Spirit will minister strength and comfort through the gift of the pastor's presence.

Remember that grief lingers long after the funeral is over. The persons most directly impacted by a death—usually the immediate family—will continue to need pastors' ministry until they have finished grieving. This process will likely take several months or even two or three years. (Review chapter 6 for guidelines about ministry to the grieving.)

8 Define *ordinance*, and name the two instituted in the New Testament.

Administering the Ordinances

Jesus instituted two ordinances, or religious ceremonies, for the church: (1) **water baptism** (Matthew 28:19) and (2) Communion, sometimes called the **Lord's Supper** or the Lord's Table (Matthew 26:26–29; Mark 14:22–26; Luke 22:17–20; 1 Corinthians 11:23–26). Since Jesus himself gave only these two ordinances to the church, they have special significance in believers' lives, and pastors should treat them accordingly. Thomas Oden observes:

The ministry that misunderstands these decisive sacramental acts or relegates them to a secondary position does a grim disservice to the Christian community. . . . Life in Christ begins with a cleansing bath of repentance and pardon; it continues with nurturing food and drink. . . .These lowly earthly things—bread, wine, and water—are freely used by God to convey that which is highest: divine mercy, covenant faithfulness, and suffering love. . . . They are signs of God's mercy to us and of God's immediate presence in our midst. (1983, 106–107)

According to Myer Pearlman,

Water baptism is the rite of entrance into the Christian church and symbolizes spiritual life begun; the Lord's Supper is the rite of communion and signifies spiritual life continued. The first pictures faith in Christ; the second pictures fellowship with Christ. The first is administered only once, for there can be but one beginning of the spiritual life; the second is administered frequently, teaching that spiritual life must be nourished. (1950, 25)

Summarize scriptural teachings regarding water baptism.

Water Baptism

Timing

While some churches have a baptismal service only once or twice a year, that was not the practice of the New Testament church. The book of Acts—the earliest history of the church—indicates that under most circumstances, water baptism immediately followed conversion. Consider these passages:

> Peter replied, "Repent and be baptized, every one of you, in the name of Jesus Christ for the forgiveness of your sins. . . ." Those who accepted his message were baptized, and about three thousand were added to their number that day. (Acts 2:38, 41)

> Then Philip began with that very passage of Scripture and told him the good news about Jesus. As they traveled along the road, they came to some water and the eunuch said, "Look, here is water. Why shouldn't I be baptized?" Philip said, "If you believe with all your heart, you may." The eunuch answered, "I believe that Jesus Christ is the Son of God." And he gave orders to stop the chariot. Then both Philip and the eunuch went down into the water and Philip baptized him. (8:35–38)

> While Peter was still speaking these words, the Holy Spirit came on all who heard the message. The circumcised believers who had come with Peter were astonished that the gift of the Holy Spirit had been poured out even on the Gentiles. For they heard them speaking in tongues and praising God. Then Peter said, "Can anyone keep these people from being baptized with water? They have received the Holy Spirit just as we have." So he ordered that they be baptized in the name of Jesus Christ. (10:44–48)

> The jailer called for lights, rushed in and fell trembling before Paul and Silas. He then brought them out and asked, "Sirs, what must I do to be saved?" They replied, "Believe in the Lord Jesus, and you will be saved—you and your household." Then they spoke the word of the Lord to him and to all the others in his house. At that hour of the night the jailer took them and washed their wounds; then immediately he and all his family were baptized. The jailer . . . was filled with joy because he had come to believe in God—he and his whole family. (16:29–34)

9 When do you think a new convert should be baptized?

Based on this New Testament model, I would suggest that pastors baptize new believers immediately following their conversion. Some dynamic churches have water baptism as part of every Sunday evening service. What a powerful testimony that is, and what an encouragement to evangelism.

Although many churches schedule water baptism at the very end of a service, others have found it to be a source of inspiration for worship when conducted at the very beginning. Regardless of its placement in the service, water baptism is both a sacred act and a spiritual experience; therefore, every part of water baptism should be done with the utmost reverence.

Describe the pastor's role concerning water baptism.

Preparation

Prior to a baptismal service, the pastor or another qualified spiritual leader should talk to each candidate, ensuring that he or she has received Jesus Christ as Lord and Savior and understands the significance of water baptism. The pastor or leader should also give each candidate clear instructions about the logistics of the service, including appropriate attire, location of dressing rooms, and any other pertinent information.

Procedure

When the baptismal candidate enters the water, the pastor should ask questions pertaining to the participant's belief in Jesus Christ as the Son of God and Savior of the world. "Salvation is found in no one else, for there is no other name under heaven given to men by which we must be saved" (Acts 4:12). The pastors should also specifically refer to Christ's work on the cross and His resurrection.

The new believer is expected to make a public confession of faith by responding to the questions or taking active part in the dialogue. Since the participant's purpose in being baptized is to make a confession of faith, the pastor should lead and guide him or her in the confession. Following the participant's testimony, the pastor will completely immerse him or her in the water, saying, "Upon your public confession of faith in the Lord Jesus Christ and your determination to follow Him, I now baptize you in the name of the Father, the Son, and the Holy Spirit."

10 During a baptismal service, what truths should a pastor reinforce with all present?

Afterward, pastors should explain to new believers that "all of us who were baptized into Christ Jesus were baptized into His death. We were therefore buried with Him through baptism into death in order that, just as Christ was raised from the dead through the glory of the Father, we too may live a new life" (Romans 6:3–4). The book of Galatians further indicates that all who are baptized into Christ have clothed themselves with Christ (Galatians 3:27).

It is the blood of Christ—not water—that saves people. Myer Pearlman notes: "Water baptism in itself has no saving power; people are baptized not in order to be saved but because they are saved. Therefore, we cannot say that the rite is absolutely essential to salvation. But we can insist that it is essential to full obedience" (1950, 28).

OBJECTIVE

Explain the pastor's role concerning Communion.

11 How often do you think a church should receive Communion?

Communion

Although Assemblies of God churches customarily observe Communion once a month, there is no scriptural reason for not observing the ordinance more often. In fact, some congregations celebrate Communion every time they worship. Others contend that receiving Communion at every service makes it too commonplace and routine. But does praying every day reduce prayer's significance? Of course not! If anything, the more we pray, the more precious prayer becomes. Perhaps we would more fully appreciate the true significance of the Lord's Supper and its spiritual benefits if it were given a more prominent place in our worship.

To come to a clearer understanding of Communion's purpose and importance, it may be helpful to review the Scriptures. Consider Matthew 26:26–29:

> While they were eating, Jesus took bread, gave thanks and broke it, and gave it to his disciples, saying, "Take and eat, this is my body." Then he took the cup, gave thanks and offered it to them, saying, "Drink from it, all of you. This is my blood of the covenant, which is poured out for many for the forgiveness of sins. I tell you, I will not drink of this fruit of the vine from now on until that day when I drink it anew with you in my Father's kingdom."

When Jesus broke the bread (1 Corinthians 11:24), He was depicting the physical suffering He would endure: He would be brutally beaten not only as punishment for our sins but also for our physical healing. Isaiah declares, "He was pierced for our transgressions, he was crushed for our iniquities; the punishment that brought us peace was upon him, and by his wounds we are healed" (53:5).

With the cup, Jesus reminds us that He suffered and died for our sins, pouring out His lifeblood, for "without the shedding of blood there is no forgiveness" (Hebrews 9:22). As Peter writes, "It was not with perishable things such as silver or gold that you were redeemed . . . but with the precious blood of Christ, a lamb without blemish or defect" (1 Peter 1:18–19).

Each time we partake of the bread (or crackers) and cup (usually grape juice) of Communion, we reaffirm our faith in the new covenant in which Jesus' blood cleanses us from all our sins (1 John 1:7). The Lord's Supper and its emblems remind us of the spiritual and physical benefits that come to us from the Lord's suffering, death, and resurrection. These blessings include forgiveness of sins, peace with God, and physical healing.

12 What is the difference between an open and a closed Communion service?

Some churches practice **closed Communion**, where they allow only members of their church to take part. Although we practice **open Communion** in the Assemblies of God, in that people do not have to be members of the church to share in the Lord's Supper, we do not approach Communion casually. Paul warns, "Whoever eats the bread or drinks the cup of the Lord in an unworthy manner will be guilty of sinning against the body and blood of the Lord" (1 Corinthians 11:27). Therefore, each person "ought to examine himself before he eats of the bread and drinks of the cup. For anyone who eats and drinks without recognizing the body of the Lord eats and drinks judgment on himself" (11:28–29).

13 What encourages believers to examine their spiritual lives before taking Communion?

By the mandate to "examine" ourselves before receiving Communion, Paul referred to our approaching the Lord's Supper in faith, recognizing that we are about to partake of the Lord's body. With this in mind, we must examine our lives for any area that could be in rebellion against God. If such a sin exists, we need to confess it, turn away from it, and receive forgiveness. Communion is a wonderful time to receive grace. Only those who refuse to repent and believe should not take the Lord's Supper (Menzies and Horton 1993, 115). Remember, "the blood of Jesus, his Son, purifies us from all sin. . . . If we confess our sins, he is faithful and just and will forgive us our sins and purify us from all unrighteousness" (1 John 1:7, 9).

Thus, the Lord's Supper reminds us to look in three directions:

- *Back* to the Lord's death
- *Within* to ensure peace in our hearts
- *Forward* to Christ's second coming (1 Corinthians 11:25–26)

Procedure

As pastors prepare for the actual Communion service, they should ensure that those who will assist them (usually the elders or deacons) know exactly what to do. As they prepare to distribute the emblems (the bread and cup), pastors should give the congregation clear instructions about how Communion is to be received. For instance, the people need to know that they do not have to be a member of that particular congregation to take part; however, they must have a relationship with Jesus Christ. Parishioners also need to know that they should hold the emblems until everyone has been served.

14 Summarize the instructions pastors should give at Communion.

Once each person has been served, pastors should direct the congregation in the partaking of Communion. For example, I often remind the worshippers that our Lord's body was bruised and broken for their healing. When I pray over the bread, I ask the Lord to heal those who are sick and afflicted. Finally, I instruct the congregation to receive the bread by faith, believing for their healing as they do.

In much the same way, I remind the worshippers that the Lord shed His lifeblood to atone for our sins. I tell them, "God made him (Jesus) who had no sin to be sin for us, so that in him we might become the righteousness of God" (2 Corinthians 5:21). I remind them that Jesus endured the shame of the cross so we never have to bear the shame of our sin (Hebrews 12:2). Then, I invite anyone who has not received Jesus as Savior to do so as we partake of the cup together. When I pray over the cup, I thank the Lord for becoming a human and dying on the cross for our sins. I thank God for raising Him from the dead, and I invite Him to be Lord of our lives. Finally, I instruct the congregation to receive the cup by faith, believing that God has cleansed us from all our sins.

I often conclude the Communion service by directing the congregation's attention to the communion trays. Almost always, the trays contain unused emblems. I then remind the worshippers that although we have all received Communion, we have not exhausted God's grace. As hymn writer Ira Stanphill (1946) penned,

> Though millions have come
> There's still room for one;
> Yes, there's room at the cross for you.

15 During a Communion service, should pastors give believers an opportunity to step out in faith for healing?

We should always rejoice that God has given us forgiveness and healing through the Lord's sacrifice. Each time we receive the Lord's Supper, we celebrate all He has done and continues to do for us. Therefore, pastors should lead the people in celebrating Communion often as a regular part of the worship experience. "For whenever you eat this bread and drink this cup, you proclaim the Lord's death until he comes" (1 Corinthians 11:26).

As a pastor, the way in which you handle the ordinances of water baptism and Communion will shape your congregation's view of them. If these ordinances are unimportant to you, they will be unimportant to your congregation. On the other hand, if you see them as sacred rites with a special significance to God's people, so will your congregation.

Therefore, you have a distinct responsibility to help your parishioners understand the spiritual significance of water baptism and Communion and their place in the life of the church. They provide a link to the past as well as insight into the future. "They are permanent, recurrent celebrations, so that in any place or time you would find Christians, you would find them breaking bread and baptizing as visible signs of Christ's presence" (Oden 1983, 111). God is present in a special way in the holy events of water baptism and the Lord's Supper.

Test Yourself

Circle the letter of the *best* answer.

1. A church's guidelines for weddings do NOT need to cover
a) available times.
b) dress code.
c) rental fees.
d) counseling.

2. Details about the wedding ceremony should be listed in the
a) minister's book only.
b) wedding program.
c) wedding checklist.
d) order of service.

3. At a wedding, Communion reminds the couple of
a) fruitfulness.
b) forgiveness.
c) unity.
d) purity.

4. The purpose of baby dedications is to
a) impart salvation to children.
b) cleanse children of their sinful nature.
c) affirm that children belong to God.
d) protect children from evil spirits.

5. Which of these is an act of worship?
a) Baby dedications
b) Weddings
c) Funerals
d) All of the above

6. Often, the most helpful thing a pastor can do for the grieving is to
a) be with them.
b) send them food.
c) tell them not to be sad.
d) pray for the dead person's soul.

7. What ordinances did Jesus give the church?
a) Funerals and weddings
b) Ordination and Communion
c) Water baptism and baby dedications
d) Communion and water baptism

8. Before Christians are baptized, they must
a) confess faith in Jesus.
b) complete a discipleship class.
c) witness to three people.
d) attend a membership class.

9. A pastor should baptize a convert in the name of
a) the Father.
b) Jesus, the Son.
c) the Holy Spirit.
d) the Father, Son, and Holy Spirit.

10. Closed communion means that
a) the service is held in secret.
b) people are silent during the service.
c) only church members may take part.
d) unfaithful believers are denied participation.

Responses to Interactive Questions
Chapter 10

Some of these responses may include information that is supplemental to the IST. These questions are intended to produce reflective thinking beyond the course content and your responses may vary from these examples.

1 What can a church provide to help wedding plans go smoothly?

Written church guidelines (perhaps in manual form) that stipulate cost, procedures, and responsibilities

2 Aside from premarital counseling, what is the pastor's primary task before the wedding?

To help the couple understand that their wedding is an act of worship

3 Who should receive a detailed order of the wedding service?

The wedding coordinator (if there is one), minister, musicians, singers, and the sound technician, as well as any other key people

4 What is the purpose of a baby dedication?

To give the parents an opportunity (1) to acknowledge that their child is a gift from God and (2) to give their child back to Him, committing him or her to the Lord.

5 When dedicating a baby, why should the pastor include a charge to the congregation?

The whole congregation has a role in nurturing the child in a godly manner, according to scriptural principles.

6 Define *obituary* and *eulogy*.

The obituary is a brief biography of the deceased. The eulogy is a speech given at a funeral to honor the deceased.

7 Of what value is a pastor's officiating at the funeral of an unbeliever?

The truths of God can be shared with lives that may be, at that point, more open to the need of the reality and personal comfort of God.

8 Define ordinance, and name the two instituted in the New Testament.

An ordinance is a physical religious ceremony that represents or points to a spiritual truth or reality, such as (1) water baptism and (2) Communion.

9 When do you think a new convert should be baptized?

Answers may vary.

10 During a baptismal service, what truths should a pastor reinforce with all present?

Answer should include profession of faith, purpose of baptism, and the promise of and commitment to a Christian walk.

11 How often do you think a church should receive Communion?

Answers may vary.

12 What is the difference between an open and a closed Communion service?

In a closed service, Communion is served to members only; the open service allows all who are Christians to participate in Communion whether they are members of the local church or not.

13 What encourages believers to examine their spiritual lives before taking Communion?

The pastor's teaching or preaching on the meaning of Communion and the believer's responsibility

14 Summarize the instructions pastors should give at Communion.

(1) Explain who can receive communion; (2) explain what each emblem means, and (3) instruct the people when to collectively partake of the emblems.

15 During a Communion service, should pastors give believers an opportunity to step out in faith for healing?

Answers will vary.

UNIT PROGRESS EVALUATION 3

Now that you have finished Unit 3, review the lessons in preparation for Unit Progress Evaluation 3. You will find it in Essential Course Materials at the back of this IST. Answer all of the questions without referring to your course materials, Bible, or notes. When you have completed the UPE, check your answers with the answer key provided in Essential Course Materials. Review any items you may have answered incorrectly. Then you may proceed with your study of Unit 4. (Although UPE scores do not count as part of your final course grade, they indicate how well you learned the material and how well you may perform on the closed-book final examination.)

The Pastor's Relationships

The final chapters in this course deal with relationships. Pastors' interactions with other spiritual leaders and their commitment to their calling play a huge role in effective, vibrant ministry.

Chapters 11 and 12 give insights about working with lay leaders and staff. Chapters 13–15 are about the relationship of a pastor's work and calling. Many who begin well in pastoral ministry quit after a few years. Some fail because they love their neighbor more than themselves; others develop a root of bitterness that grows into a tree with deadly fruit; and some stumble over their own pride or selfish desires. These chapters present the keys to a long, fruitful, pastoral ministry.

Working with Lay Leaders: Elders, Deacons, and Trustees

What makes a pastor effective? The answers are many and varied—spiritual passion, godly character, vision, leadership ability, a genuine love for people, a heart to serve, administrative ability, and preaching or teaching skills. However, as important as all of these characteristics are, they can be rendered largely ineffective if pastors cannot work with the lay leaders (generally known as elders, deacons, trustees, and so forth) in the congregation.

Tension among leaders can develop from the poor attitude or character of some pastors. They may be insecure and feel threatened by others with strong leadership skills. Or, they may be quarrelsome, taking offense when anyone disagrees with them. Some pastors are overbearing and dictatorial, demanding that everyone do things their way, and some are arrogant, refusing to listen to counsel or advice. The ministry of any such pastors will flounder regardless of their ministry skills.

However, frequently the problem does not originate with the pastor. Many times, pastors inherit a group of lay leaders who are not qualified to serve. They may be carnal, lacking spiritual insight and wisdom. They may be emotionally wounded, rendering it impossible for them to be objective. Or, they may be good people who are simply misguided, misunderstanding their role. Whatever the case, the church's ministry will be hindered until these difficulties can be worked out.

Lesson 11.1   Choose Leaders
Objectives
11.1.1 Summarize how the New Testament church chose elders and deacons.
11.1.2 Contrast the purposes of principles and form.
11.1.3 Identify steps for choosing new deacons or elders.

Lesson 11.2   Define Roles
Objectives
11.2.1 Explain how defining roles can prevent conflict.
11.2.2 Describe the value of sharing vision and ministry with board members.
11.2.3 Evaluate the relationship between pastors and board members.

Lesson 11.3   Build Relationships
Objective
11.3.1 Summarize ways for pastors and board members to build relationships.

11.1.1
OBJECTIVE

Summarize how the New Testament church chose elders and deacons.

1   How can nominating and voting on lay leaders in the same meeting create problems?

11.1.2
OBJECTIVE

Contrast the purposes of principles and form.

Choose Leaders

The New Testament Process

The most effective way to minimize problems with **lay leaders** is to choose qualified people. Unfortunately, in many situations, the way elders or deacons are selected does not lend itself to this end. In many older, more traditional churches, nominations are made from the floor at the annual business meeting and then voted on by the church membership. Yet this process does not allow the leadership to evaluate the nominees' qualifications and often results in election of the most popular candidate, whether or not he or she is the most qualified.

In churches that have experienced explosive growth, many of which are new church plants, the pastor simply appoints **elders and/or deacons**. This is most often an improvement, for the wise pastor prayerfully evaluates each potential leader before appointing him or her. However, the method is not without its risks, especially if the pastor acts independently. Making any decision without wise spiritual counsel is always risky. Proverbs 15:22 says, "Plans fail for lack of counsel, but with many advisers they succeed."

Again, the Scriptures provide guidance in choosing elders and deacons. The New Testament church presents a good model to follow.

For instance, we observe no scriptural record of an election for elders and/or deacons. Acts 14:23 says, "Paul and Barnabas appointed elders for them in each church and, with prayer and fasting, committed them to the Lord, in whom they had put their trust." Also, Paul told Titus, "The reason I left you in Crete was that you might straighten out what was left unfinished and appoint elders in every town, as I directed you" (Titus 1:5).

I see two principles as I read these verses:
1. The appointment of elders was too critical to be entrusted to only one person. In Acts 14, choosing elders was a cooperative effort involving Paul and Barnabas, and in Titus 1:5, Titus worked in consultation with Paul. Thus, cooperation and accountability were important.
2. Appointing elders was a spiritual decision more than an intellectual one; therefore, Paul and Barnabas made prayer and fasting a part of the process.

Yet in Acts 6, we see a different process at work for selecting deacons. This time, the apostles instructed the church body to "choose seven men from among you who are known to be full of the Spirit and wisdom" (Acts 6:3). The people then presented these seven men to the apostles, who "prayed and laid their hands on them" (6:6). Following the laying on of hands and prayer, the seven were released into the ministry of deacons. Thus, in this case, it appears that the church body chose the seven men, subject to the apostles' approval. Exactly how the seven were selected is not mentioned.

From these instances, we can conclude that the New Testament gives us glimpses of the early church's governance, but it does not present a definitive model. Although the principles as outlined above are clear, the form is vague at best.

Yet this is no accident. Principles are universal; that is, they apply to any and every situation. Form, on the other hand, is provincial. Its effectiveness is limited by time and circumstance.

What does this mean for the twenty-first-century church? As long as we do not violate spiritual principles, we are free to choose the form of church government that best suits our situation. In His infinite wisdom, God has given us principles that are absolute and unchanging. At the same time, He has provided a form of church governance that is both flexible and dynamic, enabling the church to respond to a constantly changing society without compromising its core values.

If you serve as the pastor of a more traditional church, you may be tempted to radically change the way your church chooses elders and/or deacons. The temptation will be stronger for those who work with unqualified lay leaders. But be careful. Few things are harder to change than long-held traditions, especially if the lay leadership are not open to the Holy Spirit's leading. Rather than risk dividing the church by forcing the issue, let me suggest that you ask God to bring in new leadership. Once new leaders are in place, you will be in a better position to make needed changes.

2   What is the moral of the piano story?

To illustrate, the story is told of a man who was elected as pastor of a church whose people did not like change. The new pastor noticed that the piano was off in the corner of the platform, too far away to be truly effective in the music and other activities of the service. It really needed to be moved, but he knew that altering its position would upset the congregation. As he prayed about it, he sensed an answer from God that would please everyone: In that first week, the pastor moved the piano one inch toward the place he felt it should be. No one noticed so small a change. In the second week, he moved the instrument another inch. Week after week, inch by inch, the pastor slowly moved the piano across the platform, and after a couple of months, the piano sat where he felt it should be. No one seemed to notice, and better yet, no one complained! With the Lord's leading, the pastor had orchestrated a necessary change one small piece at a time.

Steps for Choosing Leaders

11.1.3
OBJECTIVE
Identify steps for choosing new deacons or elders.

When I became pastor at Christian Chapel, the congregation had a traditional form of church government. The church elected its eight **board members** at the annual business meeting. As a result, our board was a hodgepodge of people. Some board members were deeply spiritual and eminently qualified to serve. Others were spiritually and emotionally immature, making the early years of my tenure there especially challenging.

3   Develop a flowchart to illustrate the six steps for choosing lay leaders.

Midway into my fourth year as pastor, one of the more spiritually mature board **members** met with me to discuss the church's method of electing the official board. He said that while in prayer, the Lord had given him a word of wisdom (1 Corinthians 12:8) regarding the selection process. He then described a very detailed proposal involving several steps:

Step 1: Nominations: Ninety days before the annual business meeting, a thirty-day period is established during which the membership make nominations for board members. Each nomination has to be made in writing and include as much information about the nominee as possible, such as his or her relationship with the church including any ministry involvement, current family life, career path, or place of employment.

4   How should deacons and elders be included in the process of choosing lay leadership?

Step 2: Nominating Review Committee: The pastor and official board appoint a nominating review committee consisting of at least ten church members and chaired by the pastor. No one currently serving on the board is permitted to serve on the nominating review committee. The committee is then divided into two-person teams to conduct a personal interview with each nominee during which they explain the required qualifications (Acts 6:3; 1 Timothy 3:8–13). The teams also describe the responsibilities and time commitment involved in serving on the board. When all the interviews are compete, each team reports in detail to the entire committee. Then, they hold a non-binding vote by secret ballot to determine who the committee feels should be selected. This vote serves only as a recommendation to the pastor and official board.

Step 3: Report to the Official Board: As chair of the review committee, the pastor then makes a detailed report to the board. Afterward, the board votes by secret ballot to determine who they feel should be selected. This vote is non-binding and serves only as a recommendation to the pastor.

Step 4: The Pastor's Selections: After the board votes, the pastor sets aside seven to ten days to pray and seek the Lord before making his or her selections.

Step 5: The Board's Ratification of the Pastor's Selections: The pastor presents his or her selections to the board. The board can then either accept or reject the selections. If they reject a selection, the pastor chooses another person and continues to do so until the board accepts the choices.

Step 6: Presentation of the Nominees to the Membership: Nominees (one per open position) are presented to the membership at the annual business meeting. The church members vote yes or no for each nominee presented. If a nominee is not voted in, the process begins again with Step 4.

5   How should the church body be involved in the process of choosing lay leadership?

6   In the six-step process, when is the pastor's input most strategic and helpful?

As my board member outlined this selection process, I immediately saw its benefits. The membership would have both the first and final say. They would nominate people and elect or reject nominees presented by the pastor and official board. The nominating review committee would do much of the detail work and provide wise counsel. Each nominee would be fully informed of the qualifications and requirements expected of a board member. If the nominee chose to serve, he or she would be committing to meet those requirements. Also, the pastor would have the opportunity to choose the most qualified candidate. If the official board felt the pastor was making an unwise decision, they could refuse to ratify the selection. The process was well thought out, providing the opportunity for both wise counsel and accountability.

When we shared this proposal with our official board, they immediately saw the wisdom of it. They then presented it to the church membership at the annual business meeting in the form of an amendment to the church's constitution and bylaws. The membership was almost unanimous in its vote to accept the amendment.

Although at times during those first four years I was tempted to take matters into my own hands, I am thankful I did not. The Lord's plan was far better than any I could have come up with. And having the plan originate with a board member rather than myself defused much of the inherent opposition. In the ensuing years, the wisdom of our decision was confirmed again and again.

I share what happened in my experience not as a definite model for any other church but only as a testimony of God's faithfulness. The Lord has a plan for every situation, and He will make it known if we seek Him for it. "If any of you lacks wisdom, he should ask God, who gives generously to all without finding fault, and it will be given to him" (James 1:5).

11.2.1
OBJECTIVE
Explain how defining roles can prevent conflict.

Define Roles

In an ideal world, spiritual leaders would never disagree with one another. Since this is unfortunately not the case, a certain amount of conflict is inevitable.

At times, even the most spiritually mature leaders cannot agree. For example, after laboring together for years, Paul and Barnabas had "such a sharp disagreement that they parted company" (Acts 15:39).

If spiritual giants like Paul and Barnabas experienced conflict, we should not be surprised when we have to deal with it. Still, we should do everything we can to minimize conflict within church leadership. One method is to recognize what is causing the conflict and eliminate it if possible.

7   How can pastors and lay leaders be assured of their roles and avoid defensiveness in their relationships?

Conflict often arises because pastors assume that an elder or deacon understands his or her role, or even the pastor's role, the same way they do. One of the most effective ways to eliminate this conflict is to clearly define roles and responsibilities. The people involved should discuss these issues at length until everyone is clearly in agreement. Of course, it is best to resolve these philosophical differences before a person is placed in a leadership position. The six-step selection process at Christian Chapel (see the previous lesson) allowed us to do this in the nominee interviews.

Include Board Members in Vision and Ministry

11.2.2
OBJECTIVE
Describe the value of sharing vision and ministry with board members.

A written task or job description for each lay leader may be helpful, but I believe the situation is deeper than that. Specifically, I think the core issue is how each board member sees his or her relationship to both the pastor and the church. For instance, sometimes board members think their main purpose is to protect the church from the pastor. Although this may not be vocalized, it is clearly an unspoken assumption that underlines the way the board makes decisions. Rather than operating in trust, they operate in skepticism. They do not accept the pastor's actions or proposals at face value. Consciously or unconsciously, they always look for ulterior motives. It takes very little imagination to see the difficulties this presents.

Unfortunately, the responsibility for much of this faulty thinking lies with pastors. In the past, those in ministry have done little or nothing to prepare the laity for leadership. For things to be different in the future, we as ministers must make leadership training a high priority. Using all the resources at our disposal—the pulpit, one-on-one mentoring, lay ministry training, and so on—we can nurture a new generation of leadership.

If we do this, instead of seeing themselves as the people's representatives to the pastor, elders and deacons will see themselves as an extension of the pastor's God-given ministry and vision. They are not "yes" men and women. In fact, they are far from it. When the situation demands it, they take a firm stand. Even then, their purpose is not to oppose the pastor but to counsel and protect him or her. Thus, when both the pastor and the board members understand their roles and responsibilities, much potential conflict is avoided.

8   How do clear guidelines help lay leaders to spiritually guide people when concerns arise?

This new understanding of roles will affect the way complaints against the pastor are handled. Under the old mind-set where board members considered themselves to be the people's representatives, they listened to whoever had a complaint and brought the complaints with them to the next board meeting. Understandably, this resulted in a difficult relationship between the board members and the pastor. However, now that board members see themselves as part of the pastor's God-given ministry, they respond differently. After listening carefully to a complaint, they attempt to diffuse the situation by explaining the pastor's position. If this does not resolve the issue, the lay leaders then suggest that the person speak with the pastor directly (Matthew 18:15). If the person is reluctant, board members may offer to go with the individual to speak with the pastor. If the person is still unwilling to speak with the pastor, the board members dismiss the whole situation without pursuing it further. Imagine what a difference this new approach makes in the relationship between pastor and board.

Encourage Realistic Expectations

11.2.3
OBJECTIVE
Evaluate the relationship between pastors and board members.

Another source of conflict is unrealistic expectations. If the board, consciously or unconsciously, expects the pastor to be perfect, they set themselves up for painful disappointment and anger. And as we know, an angry board member is likely to create conflict.

Wise pastors do themselves and the church a great service by allowing their congregation to see their humanity. Pastors should work to help the congregation understand that, while pastors are far from perfect, they are conscientious and committed. When they do make mistakes, pastors should be quick to acknowledge them and do whatever is necessary to rectify them. Providing the congregation with a more accurate view of the ministry helps them develop more realistic expectations.

9   Why is it sometimes difficult for pastors to balance building friendships and building the Kingdom?

Of course, pastors may have unrealistic expectations of their own. Although mostly unspoken, these are real nonetheless. One common expectation may involve pastors' relationships with individual board members. Pastors may assume that certain church leaders are their best friends. Consequently, pastors can be blindsided and feel betrayed at board meetings when a "friend" chooses the interests of the church over those of the pastor. Or perhaps something pastors share in confidence to a lay leader becomes an item of business at a board meeting. In this case, pastors may feel that the lay leader was disloyal, but the leader may feel the opposite. The lay leader may feel that the information was of a vital interest to the church and superseded any relationship with the pastor.

Does this mean that pastors and board members cannot be friends? No, but it does mean that pastors must recognize the nature of such friendships. That is, pastors must realize that these are working relationships; they can never be "just friends" with members of the board. Board members will most likely consider themselves board members first and then friends of the pastor. Pastors who fail to recognize this and adjust their expectations accordingly risk repeated hurt.

11.3.1
OBJECTIVE
Summarize ways for pastors and board members to build relationships.

Build Relationships

Since it is impossible to avoid all conflict between pastors and church board members, it is important to prepare for it. The pastor–board relationship is much like a marriage. A certain amount of conflict occurs in even the best of marriages, but it does not necessarily destroy the relationship. By working on their marriage, a committed couple makes sure their relationship is greater than their differences.

This principle applies to the pastor–board relationship as well. If a pastor's only interaction with the elders and deacons is the regular (usually monthly) board meeting, they are not likely to develop a strong relationship. Since these meetings center on church business, they do little to build relationships. In this context, the pastor and board discuss issues and make decisions, making differences of opinion inevitable. While these minor disagreements seldom create major problems, they do form the character of the relationship. Should a major conflict arise, the relationship will not likely stand the strain.

10 Compare the pastor–board member relationship with a marriage relationship.

However, by focusing not only on conducting church business but also on building their relationship, the pastor and board members can develop the type of bond that enables them to transcend their differences. The challenge that remains, then, is how should a pastor do this? What can pastors do to form a strong bond with board members?

Fellowship, Prayer, and Ministry

An idea from one pastor is to make the regular board meeting a time not only for business but also for fellowship and ministry. Each meeting begins with a meal for the board members and their wives. Responsibility for planning the meal rotates among the wives. All the meals are potluck, and the wife who is responsible for the evening's meal sets the menu. Following the meal, the group shares a brief time of worship and prayer for one another before the pastor and the board begin their actual board meeting.

Another pastor meets with his board members for an hour every Friday morning before they need to go to work. One week they meet in the pastor's office for prayer. The next week, they meet in a restaurant for breakfast and a time of fellowship. When a book or audiovisual material speaks to the pastor in a special way, he shares it with each board member. During their Friday morning meetings, they then discuss what the Lord is saying to each of them through the book, tape, or DVD. Clearly, these meetings focus on relationship building, not church business.

Retreats

Yet another church sponsors two overnight retreats for their pastor and board each year. One retreat is designed for fun and fellowship, while the second is designed for prayer and planning. Both retreats are designed to help the pastor and board build a strong relationship. The pastor of this church says:

> On the fellowship retreat, we do fun things. We may take a canoe trip down a river or rent a speedboat and go water-skiing. Or we might play volleyball or touch football or just lounge around a bonfire talking and praying. . . . I believe that shared activities create a bond that serves us well when we face the hard issues. Not to mention the fact that a lot of discipleship and mentoring happens in a setting like that.

> The second retreat is far more focused. We spend a considerable amount of time in prayer seeking the mind of God. We talk and plan strategically for the coming year. Something special happens when people spend time together praying and waiting on the Lord. It's probably one of the best investments our church makes. (personal communication)

I am not suggesting that your church needs to do any of these specific things, but it is important that you deliberately plan activities and events that will develop a strong relationship between pastor and board. If you make this a high priority, be assured that it will pay enormous dividends.

Agendas

A final thought concerns the board meetings themselves. You can minimize conflict—or at least the fallout from conflict—simply by preparing a printed agenda before the meeting. To make this work, you will need to require board members to submit any agenda items to you a week in advance. Anything not on the agenda cannot be discussed at the meeting.

11 How does a meeting agenda benefit the pastor–board member relationship?

When you give each board member a copy of the agenda a few days before the meeting, they can prayerfully prepare for the business at hand. If an agenda item is especially volatile, the board members have an opportunity to prayerfully work through their emotions before coming to the meeting. As a result, the ensuing discussion should be less acrimonious. Of course, this also allows you as the pastor to better prepare for the meeting, and it should keep you from being blindsided by an unexpected issue.

Remember, there are no perfect churches and no perfect pastors. When difficulties arise, as they surely will, you have a choice: (1) You can look for someone to blame, or (2) you can turn to God. You can be part of the problem or part of the solution.

If you have been sinned against, forgive. If you have sinned against another, take responsibility for your actions. Seek forgiveness and make restitution. Be bold in following your God-given vision. Walk humbly before God, and trust Him to make you into the person He has called you to be.

As you allow Him to change you, others will follow your example. Bill Hybels writes, "The local church is the hope of the world and its future rests primarily in the hands of its leaders" (2002, 27). Consider Paul's instructions to the young pastor Timothy:

> Set an example for the believers in speech, in life, in love, in faith and in purity. . . . Devote yourself to the public reading of Scripture, to preaching and to teaching. . . . Be diligent in these matters; give yourself wholly to them, . . . Watch your life and doctrine closely. Persevere in them, because if you do, you will save both yourself and your hearers. . . . I charge you, in the sight of God and Christ Jesus and the elect angels, to keep these instructions without partiality, and to do nothing out of favoritism. (1 Timothy 4:12–13, 15–16; 5:21)

Test Yourself

Circle the letter of the *best* answer.

1. The deacons for the Jerusalem church (Acts 6) were chosen by
a) members of the church.
b) Peter and James.
c) Stephen and Philip.
d) Paul and Barnabas.

2. The New Testament teaches that the
a) church should vote for leaders.
b) pastor should choose leaders.
c) church board should choose leaders.
d) process for choosing leaders may vary.

3. In contrast to forms, biblical principles
a) follow cultural patterns.
b) change in meaning over time.
c) are true in every culture.
d) depend on the situation.

4. In the six-step process of choosing lay leaders, the first step is for members to
a) nominate potential leaders.
b) volunteer to serve as leaders.
c) interview possible leaders.
d) vote for new leaders.

5. In the six-step process for choosing church leaders, who has the last word?
a) Board members
b) A review team
c) Church members
d) The pastor

6. The process of defining roles should include
a) explaining.
b) discussing.
c) agreeing.
d) all of the above.

7. Elders or deacons are best seen as
a) pastor police.
b) partners in ministry.
c) protectors of the people.
d) friends of the pastor.

8. When leaders hear complaints against a pastor, they should first
a) try to resolve the problem.
b) gently rebuke the church members.
c) explain the pastor's position.
d) share the complaint with the board.

9. The relationship between pastors and board members should be based on
a) legal commitments.
b) reasonable expectations.
c) professional conduct.
d) impersonal events.

10. A pastor can build relationships with board members at
a) planning meetings.
b) Wednesday night services.
c) board meetings.
d) retreats.

Responses to Interactive Questions
Chapter 11

Some of these responses may include information that is supplemental to the IST. These questions are intended to produce reflective thinking beyond the course content and your responses may vary from these examples.

1 How can nominating and voting on lay leaders in the same meeting create problems?

This is usually a formula for popularity contest and has little to do with prayerful consideration of the best candidate. Nominees may be needlessly embarrassed if it is discovered that they do not fully qualify.

2 What is the moral of the piano story?

Answers may vary. There is a right time and right way to bring about change.

3 Develop a flowchart to illustrate the six steps for choosing lay leaders.

Answers will vary.

4 How should deacons and elders be included in the process of choosing lay leadership?

The deacons and elders assist in appointing a review committee, advising the pastor about candidates, and (along with the membership) approving or disapproving of selections.

5 How should the church body be involved in the process of choosing lay leadership?

The body recommends leader candidates and approves or disapproves of the selections.

6 In the six-step plan, when is the pastor's input most strategic and helpful?

Early in the process, after the deacons present the reviewed list to him or her

7 How can pastors and lay leaders be assured of their roles and avoid defensiveness in their relationships?

Roles need to be defined initially, discussed and reaffirmed as time progresses, and adjusted according to need.

8 How do clear guidelines help lay leaders to spiritually guide people when concerns arise?

The board members use the spiritual principles that the team has learned, making them an extension of the pastor's vision and an effective example and guide on how to handle concerns.

9 Why is it sometimes difficult for pastors to balance building friendships and building the Kingdom?

Answers may vary.

10 Compare the pastor–board member relationship with a marriage relationship.

Both require commitment to work through differences by affirming communication and acceptance for the greater good of the couple or church.

11 How does a meeting agenda benefit the pastor–board member relationship?

An agenda provided a few days before the board meeting prepares both the pastor and the board for exactly what will be discussed. It keeps both from being blindsided by unexpected issues and helps minimize animosity.

Pastor–Staff Relationships

Although committed volunteers will always do much of the ministry, there is a growing need for effective pastoral **staff**. As a congregation increases in its size and scope of ministry, it requires a competent pastoral staff to provide oversight and direction. Staff positions common in larger congregations include these:

- Assistant or Associate Pastor
- Church Administrator or Executive Pastor
- Youth Pastor
- Minister of Christian Education
- Music Pastor
- Minister of Pastoral Care
- Minister of Evangelism
- Children's Pastor
- Senior Adult Pastor
- Young Adults or Singles Pastor
- Fine Arts Pastor
- Media Pastor

The purpose of the pastoral staff is not to relieve the laity of their ministry but to more effectively equip them for it (Ephesians 4:12). The staff accomplishes this through training, pastoral oversight, preaching or teaching, and church administration.

Because few pastors inherit a large church with pastoral staff already in place, the challenge for most is how to build an effective staff. How do pastors know when to add staff to the church? Which positions should they fill first?

Some pastors believe in "staffing for growth," or adding staff before the congregation's actual size mandates it. In their minds, they can facilitate growth by filling key positions. Their challenge is to fund the position while waiting for the expected increase in attendance and giving.

Other pastors add more staff only when the congregation's size makes it necessary. This minimizes the financial burden on the church, but it often means that the current staff is overworked. Consequently, they have little or no time for developing vision or adding new ministries.

Whatever strategy you choose, you will have to decide the first position to fill and the best candidate to fill it. Once the staff is in place, you will need to exercise a leadership style that develops team spirit and facilitates the personal growth and ministry of each individual staff member.

Lesson 12.1   Identifying Needed Staff Positions
Objectives
12.1.1 Explain why team ministry works best.
12.1.2 Describe how pastors should build staff based on vision.

Lesson 12.2   Choosing the Right People
Objective
12.2.1 Explain guidelines for choosing staff members.

Lesson 12.3   Building Team Spirit
Objective
12.3.1 Summarize principles for developing team spirit.

12.1.1
OBJECTIVE

Explain why team ministry works best.

1   Give three biblical examples of team ministry.

2   Identify three benefits of team ministry from Ecclesiastes 4:9–12.

3   How did the apostle Paul benefit from team ministry?

12.1.2
OBJECTIVE

Describe how pastors should build staff based on vision.

4   When do staff positions help the church become all God wants it to be?

Identifying Needed Staff Positions

Value Team Ministry

Scripture contains many examples and principles in regard to team ministry. Both Mark 6:7 and Luke 10:1 state that Jesus sent the disciples out to minister in teams of two. And the New Testament church continued the practice: In Acts 3, God used the team of Peter and John to heal a crippled man, and Acts 8:14–17 states:

When the apostles in Jerusalem heard that Samaria had accepted the word of God, they sent Peter and John to them. When they arrived, they prayed for them that they might receive the Holy Spirit, because the Holy Spirit had not yet come upon any of them; they had simply been baptized into the name of the Lord Jesus. Then Peter and John placed their hands on them, and they received the Holy Spirit.

When Peter visited Cornelius's house, "some of the brothers from Joppa went along" (Acts 10:23). Other New Testament ministry teams included Paul and Barnabas (13:2), Barnabas and John Mark (15:39), Paul and Silas (15:40), and Paul and Timothy (Philippians 2:22).

These and many other Scripture passages make it readily apparent that God's plan for ministry is built on the team concept. Ecclesiastes 4:9–12 declares:

Two are better than one, because they have a good return for their work. If one falls down, his friend can help him up. But pity the man who falls and has no one to help him up! Also, if two lie down together, they will keep warm. But how can one keep warm alone? Though one may be overpowered, two can defend themselves. A cord of three strands is not quickly broken.

The Scriptures also suggest that using the team concept brings increased anointing, effectiveness, and encouragement. The presence of an anointed brother or sister encourages us as few things can. Paul communicated this he wrote, "For when we came into Macedonia, this body of ours had no rest, but we were harassed at every turn—conflicts on the outside, fears within. But God, who comforts the downcast, comforted us by the coming of Titus" (2 Corinthians 7:5–6). If the apostle Paul needed the comfort of his fellow ministers, how much more do we?

Focus on Vision

When the congregation has reached a place where you as pastor can no longer minister effectively without help, you must decide which staff position to fill first. Because you care about your people, you may be tempted to build your staff around their perceived needs. However, if you do so, you will likely discover that you have built a staff more for maintenance than for growth. On the other hand, if you select staff positions based on your God-given vision, you will position yourself and the church to become all God has called you to be. While need-centered thinking usually looks inward, vision generally looks outward.

Some years ago, I faced this very dilemma in a church I pastored. Some parishioners thought we should add a music minister to the pastoral staff to lead the number of professional musicians and singers in our congregation. While I understood their thinking, I had to weigh it against the vision God had given me for our body. I knew we were reaching an increasing number of spiritually wounded people through our radio ministry. And as more and more of them flowed into our fellowship, we were overwhelmed with requests for counseling. To me, then, the need for a minister of pastoral care was far more critical than the need for a minister of music. We had gifted volunteers capable of directing our music ministry but no one to oversee the ministry to the hurting people God was sending to us. To fulfill our God-given vision to be a healing center, we needed someone to direct our counseling center and lead our healing groups.

Thankfully, after much prayer and discussion, the elders came to the same conclusion. With their blessing, I invited a minister of pastoral care to serve with us. Scores of desperately hurting people found healing and deliverance under her leadership. She also trained a number of anointed lay leaders to help with the ministry. Together, they developed healing groups for victims of abuse, sexual addiction, domestic violence, divorce recovery, and post-abortion counseling.

Under the leadership of gifted volunteers, our worship ministry continued to flourish. Undoubtedly, a trained professional could have taken it to another level, and had circumstances been different, that may have been the best option. However, in our situation, it was not to be. God had not called us to be a center for praise and worship—although that was an important part of our ministry—but to be a healing center for hurting people.

The principle, therefore, is this: Build your staff based on your God-given vision, not on your congregation's perceived needs. Add staff to facilitate growth, not simply to maintain the status quo.

12.2.1
OBJECTIVE
Explain guidelines for choosing staff members.

5   Why should pastors not choose friends to serve on staff?

6   When can choosing a strong leader as a staff member be a disadvantage?

Choosing the Right People

Once you have determined which staff position to fill, the next step is to select the right person. As I look back over nearly forty years of pastoral ministry, I realize that some of my best and worst decisions concerned staffing. My only comfort is knowing I am not alone, for when I compare notes with my ministerial colleagues, they readily acknowledge similar experiences. For the most part, our mistakes are painfully clear in retrospect; but at the time, we were convinced that our decisions were good.

Since the success of almost any endeavor depends on the people we work with, let me share five guidelines I have developed over the years for choosing staff. Had I noted these guidelines early in my ministry, I might have avoided some painfully bad staffing decisions:

1. Do not select a friend to serve on your pastoral staff.

Although some people can manage the difficult task of being both friend and boss to an individual, most of us cannot. One of the first people I invited to serve on my staff was a close friend, and while he was enormously talented, it quickly grew into an impossible situation. When I needed to give pastoral direction, I ended up merely making friendly suggestions. When he should have deferred to my decisions as senior pastor, he appealed to our friendship. Finally, I had no choice but to ask him to resign, and in the process, I lost a dear friend.

2. Do not select a primary leader to fill a supporting role.

By temperament and talent, some of us are primary or strong leaders, and others are support personnel. When you try to squeeze primary leaders into support roles, you limit their effectiveness and increase their frustration. The narrow confines of supporting roles can make strong leaders feel constricted, and if you are not careful, they may challenge your role as primary leader. Even if you successfully withstand such a challenge, the resulting fallout will have long-term consequences.

This principle generally applies to mature ministers who have developed their ministerial identity. By the time people reach their early to mid-thirties, it should be obvious whether they have the temperament of primary leaders—senior pastors—or of those better suited to serve as staff pastors. Do not make the mistake of thinking you can make these individuals into something they are not.

By the same token, many young people have the gifts of primary leaders but need experience and mentoring before they are ready to assume such roles. Inviting them to serve on your staff while they develop their gifts can prove enormously beneficial. However, you must remain aware that one day they will move to a situation where they can fulfill their calling as primary leaders.

3. Do not plan to change anyone after you put him or her on staff.

7 What does "What you hire is what you get" mean?

After several frustrating experiences, I have concluded that "what you hire is what you get." You can train people, but you cannot change them. I know because I have tried it more times than I care to remember.

I know of one pastor who tells of hiring a brilliant man:

His resume was impressive. Both his educational achievements and his work experience were exceptional. He was articulate, creative, and possessed outstanding social skills. Yet, too late, I discovered that he was also lazy. If I gave him an assignment, he did it in record time, but that's as far as it went. He had little or no vision, no ideas of his own, and seemed intent on doing as little as possible.

I understand that pastor's difficult dilemma. In such a situation, he had two choices: (1) fire the staff member and deal with the consequences or (2) live with him. Trying to change him would have been an absolute waste of time.

4. Check references for potential staff.

Many staffing mistakes are made in failing to check references. If an individual's resume looks good and the interview goes well, it is tempting to bypass the tedious task of checking references. Nevertheless, even if you know the applicant personally, you cannot afford to ignore this time-consuming task. The way a person interacts socially and the way he or she performs as a pastoral staff member may be totally different. Only someone who has worked with the candidate previously can offer the truth about the person's work ethic and habits.

Of course, an additional word of caution is necessary: Do not accept an individual's references at face value. Consider the references' relationship to the candidate and what they may stand to gain by giving him or her a positive recommendation. Carefully weigh their comments against your own feelings. Be sensitive to anything the Holy Spirit might be trying to impress upon you.

5. Remember that attitude is more important than either talent or experience.

Most pastors agree that nothing poisons staff relationships faster than a bad attitude. One pastor half-jokingly referred to a bad attitude as a "staff infection"—a disease that destroys the entire staff! Business executives face the same problem with their management teams and readily admit that it is the worst part of their jobs. Almost to a person, they will say that no amount of talent or experience compensates for a bad attitude. Yet a great attitude can overcome any lack of experience.

John Maxwell tells of a Princeton seminary professor who studied great preachers in an attempt to discover the secret of their effectiveness. "He noted their tremendous varieties of personalities and gifts. Then he asked the question, 'What do these outstanding pulpiteers all have in common besides their faith?' After several years of searching he found the answer. It was their cheerfulness" (1993, 35). They had a positive attitude.

Bill Hybels, senior pastor of Willow Creek Community Church near Chicago, Illinois, has developed what he refers to as "the three Cs of team selection": (1) character, (2) competence, and (3) chemistry. He says, "After experimenting with different selection criteria through the years, I have landed on these three in the precise order in which they are mentioned" (2002, 69). That is, Hybels makes a point to put character first. He admits that in the past he did not always do this, that occasionally he was seduced by the applicant's competence and his own optimism:

> I used to think that if I discovered a potential team member who was terrifically competent but a little shaky in regard to character, I could go with the competence and address the character defects over time. Ever the optimist, I thought that if that person were in a healthy church environment, surrounded by godly people who would hold him or her accountable, it would eventually work out. But after thirty years of optimism I have had to admit defeat. Face it. Every adult interviewing for a key role has already spent twenty-five, thirty, or thirty-five years in a process of character formation. Not much is going to change after that. (2002, 70)

8   How would you measure an applicant's character?

You can determine much about individuals' character by observing their spiritual walk. Are they committed to spiritual disciplines? Is their commitment to honesty evident? Are they teachable? Do they demonstrate humility, reliability, and a healthy work ethic? If the persons do not manifest these character traits, then beware. No amount of competence makes up for character defects. As Hybels notes, "In church work an occasional lapse in competence can be accepted. But lapses in character create problems with far-reaching implications" (2002, 69).

If applicants pass the character test, Hybels then considers their competence. Have their ministry gifts been developed and refined? Are they capable of doing the ministry required? It is important to match people's abilities with tasks; otherwise, pastors may cause sincere people to fail.

9   Other than godly character, what is essential for successful team ministry?

The final criteria Hybels considers is personal chemistry. That is, he determines whether the applicant relates well to the senior pastor and the other members of the pastoral team. Hybels remarks, "Ken Blanchard, coauthor of The *One Minute Manager*, counseled me never to invite a person onto my team who doesn't have a positive emotional effect on me the minute he or she walks into my office" (2002, 72). That may seem harsh at first glance, but since you will be working so closely with your staff, a positive relationship between you and each staff member is critical.

10   What are two benefits of choosing staff from within the local church?

My experience has shown that good selections for staff can often come from within your own church body. Having observed them in volunteer ministerial roles, you have firsthand knowledge of their character, competence, and chemistry fit, allowing you to make a wiser, more informed decision. No matter how careful you are when selecting a staff member from outside your congregation, your chances of a good selection are still only fifty-fifty. Yet when you choose someone from within, your chance of success increases dramatically.

Years ago, when Christian Chapel needed a minister of pastoral care, we invited a woman from our congregation to join our staff. At the time, she was a schoolteacher and professional counselor who was also working as a volunteer counselor in the ministry. Over a period of months, I witnessed her effectiveness. She was a hard worker, and people related well with her. Her impact on the staff was positive and uplifting. She was loyal and trustworthy. Working with her beforehand showed me that she was the person we needed. In fact, we are still working together, as she and her husband now direct our ministry office. Hiring her was one of the best staff decisions I ever made.

Not only do you have an advantage when choosing someone from your congregation, but so does the person you select. People who work within the ministry as volunteers are familiar with your vision and goals. They understand your leadership style and how you relate to the ministry team. They also have the congregation's respect. When these faithful people join your team, they are ready to work.

Of course, sometimes you will have to go outside your congregation to find a person with the experience and skills your situation requires. Still, I think it is wise to begin your search with your congregation and expand it only when you eliminate the possibility of choosing someone from within.

11 If you want to hire someone from another church, what should you do first?

Usually the kind of person you are looking for—spiritually mature, experienced, and gifted—will already have a position. In advising Pastor Bill Hybels about selecting leaders, management pioneer Peter Drucker said, "The kind of people you are looking for are probably making huge contributions and setting records somewhere. They are probably deliriously happy and much loved by the people they work with. Go after that type. Go after proven competence" (Hybels 2002, 72). People of this caliber seldom send a resume or hunt for a job; rather, jobs come looking for them. Therefore, be prepared to make the initial contact. Keep in mind, however, that if they are already in a ministry position, ministerial ethics require you to contact their senior pastor before approaching them.

To fulfill the vision God has given you, you must surround yourself with the best people that you can. Yet do not get in a hurry to fill a position and thus settle for second best. Take your time, be patient, and give God time to bring you the very best.

12.3.1
OBJECTIVE
Summarize principles for developing team spirit.

12 What is an open-door policy?

Building Team Spirit

When your pastoral team is in place, it is up to you the pastor to develop and maintain team spirit. This is not a one-time event, but an ongoing process. Your attention to this issue demonstrates the importance you place on the staff as a whole as well as each individual member.

From a practical standpoint, things like weekly staff meetings, job descriptions, and an **open-door policy** provide the foundations on which team spirit is built. That is, making time to regularly meet with your staff clearly communicates your priorities. It says they are important to you and to the ministry of the church. By making yourself available to meet with them individually, as the need arises, you demonstrate your commitment to invest in their lives and ministry.

Based on my pastoral experience, I identify five aspects crucial to team spirit: (1) communication, (2) care, (3) loyalty, (4) trust, and (5) respect.

Communication

It is impossible for a team to be on the same agenda without clear communication. Since communication starts at the top, it is your (the pastor's) responsibility to clearly communicate your God-given vision. You should also ensure the each staff member understands the part he or she plays in accomplishing it.

If you want your staff to accompany you on this spiritual visionary journey, you need to help them experience the things you are experiencing. For instance, if God uses a particular book to speak to you personally or about the church, share the book with your staff. After they have read it, discuss it together. Do the same thing with a tape or DVD that speaks to you in a special way.

During your weekly staff meetings, give each staff member the opportunity to report on their ministry accomplishments and plans as well as to share concerns. Place all events on the master church calendar to avoid scheduling conflicts, and communicate any changes to the entire staff.

Nothing undermines team spirit more quickly than a breakdown in communication, and therefore, you should make every attempt to avoid such a breakdown. It is better to risk repeating yourself than to chance leaving someone out of the communication loop. To avoid any possibility of misunderstanding, communicate important information not only in verbal words but also in writing. Of course, all official staff policy should be in writing, and each staff member should have a copy.

Care

13 List some ways that pastors can care for their staff.

The most effective pastors go to great lengths to let their staffs know how much they are appreciated. For example, one pastor takes all of his staff, along with their spouses, to dinner anytime a staff member is ordained or graduates from college or seminary. His rationale for doing this is to "rejoice with those who rejoice" (Romans 12:15). He may act as though this is a simple thing, but when it comes to building team spirit, that kind of caring goes a long way.

Another pastor takes his entire staff to the District Council and other special meetings. This limits the type of accommodations he can afford to stay in, but the fellowship the team enjoys far outweighs this small sacrifice. The team eats together and spends many hours talking about the services and what God is saying to them individually. The camaraderie these special times foster lasts long after the staff returns home, and it fuels their labor together.

14 Why is it important to recognize each staff member?

Another pastor sets aside one Sunday each year as Staff Appreciation Day. He encourages members of the congregation to write notes of love and appreciation to honor each staff member. On that Sunday, he personally recognizes the individual staff members from the pulpit and highlights their contributions to the life and ministry of the church. His inspiration for this service comes from Paul's epistles, specifically Romans 16:1–15, where Paul writes:

> I commend to you our sister Phoebe, a servant of the church in Cenchrea. I ask you to receive her in the Lord in a way worthy of the saints and to give her any help she may need from you, for she has been a great help to many people, including me.

> Greet Priscilla and Aquila, my fellow workers in Christ Jesus. They risked their lives for me. Not only I but all the churches of the Gentiles are grateful to them.

> Greet also the church that meets at their house.

> Greet my dear friend Epenetus, who was the first convert to Christ in the province of Asia.

> Greet Mary, who worked very hard for you.

Greet Andronicus and Junias, my relatives who have been in prison with me. They are outstanding among the apostles, and they were in Christ before I was.

Greet Ampliatus, whom I love in the Lord.

Greet Urbanus, our fellow worker in Christ, and my dear friend Stachys.

Greet Apelles, tested and approved in Christ.

Greet those who belong to the household of Aristobulus.

Greet Herodion, my relative.

Greet those in the household of Narcissus who are in the Lord.

Greet Tryphena and Tryphosa, those women who work hard in the Lord.

Greet my dear friend Persis, another woman who has worked very hard in the Lord.

Greet Rufus, chosen in the Lord, and his mother, who has been a mother to me, too.

Greet Asyncritus, Phlegon, Hermes, Patrobas, Hermas and the brothers with them.

Greet Philologus, Julia, Nereus and his sister, and Olympas and all the saints with them.

If God thought it necessary to include the expression of appreciation in the inspired Scriptures, then it must be important. He gives us a model to follow, an example of how we should relate to our team. Affirm them. Make them feel special, loved, and valued.

15 Suggest ways a pastor could show personal concern for each staff member.

Another critical aspect of caring is providing pastoral care for the staff and their families. In times of crisis, you should be the first to minister to them. When they face a challenging family situation, you should be there to provide prayer and counsel. Loving care in times of crisis cultivates team spirit in a way few other things can. That is not the motive behind your caring, but it is a consequence.

Loyalty

Good communication and care generate loyalty, trust, and respect. Pastoral staff members find it easy to be loyal to you as the pastor when they know you truly care about them and want what is best for them. As you continually invest yourself, your time, and your energy into their lives and ministries, they feel a spiritual bond with you. Even when you may experience differences of opinion, they have no trouble staying loyal to you because they know and trust your heart.

16 How should a pastor handle complaints against staff members?

Yet loyalty goes both ways. You need to demonstrate your loyalty to the team at every opportunity. On occasion, members of the congregation may approach you with complaints about a staff member. The way you handle this will strongly determine the quality of your team spirit. If you side with the church member, your staff will feel betrayed—not just the accused staff member, but the entire team. A better way to handle such a situation is to affirm your confidence in the staff member and not accept the complaint at face value. If the church member continues to express concern, offer to meet with that person and the staff member together to discuss the situation. Under no circumstances should you rebuke the staff member publicly! If the situation requires correction, handle it privately, with love and sensitivity.

If a valid complaint involves a character issue, you must deal with it quickly and firmly. Being a caring person with a pastor's heart, you may be tempted to exercise patience in the hope that things will get better. But I have found that the issue is rarely resolved that way. You must take action—the sooner, the better.

In the event that the staff member must be asked to resign for reasons of character, the pastor and elders should devise a spiritual restoration plan. Your ultimate goal is not to rid yourself of a problem but to see a brother or sister's character healed and restored through the Holy Spirit's work. As difficult as it is, termination is the only way to deal with transgressions involving character or morality. Significant change and healing rarely occur if the person is allowed to remain on staff.

Trust

17 What are the two directions of entry-level trust?

Foundational to team spirit is mutual trust. By inviting someone to join the pastoral team, you are expressing a certain level of trust in that person. When individuals accept your invitation to join the staff, they also demonstrate a level of trust in you. I call this "entry-level" trust. Moving beyond this level requires time and experience. The kind of trust needed to sustain team spirit must be earned; it is built slowly, one experience at a time.

When I became the senior pastor at Christian Chapel, the congregation had severe financial problems. They could not make timely payments toward debts totaling hundreds of thousands of dollars. Yet through a series of divinely orchestrated events, God delivered us from our debt. In twenty-two months, we went from being totally without money and nearly $750,000 in debt to being completely debt free with $500,000 in the bank. As a result, the congregation and elders' trust in me increased significantly. It reminded me of the people's response to Joshua when God stopped the flow of the Jordan River for the Israelites to cross: "That day the Lord exalted Joshua in the sight of all Israel; and they revered him all the days of his life, just as they had revered Moses" (Joshua 4:14).

Respect

Respect is a small word, but it carries a lot of weight. When members of the pastoral team respect one another, it permeates all they do. They never belittle each other's ideas or efforts, either publicly or privately. They never use humor to undermine a fellow team member's self-worth. Instead, they look for every opportunity to acknowledge and affirm one another. This is what Paul had in mind when he wrote, "Respect those who work hard among you, who are over you in the Lord and who admonish you. Hold them in the highest regard in love because of their work. Live in peace with each other" (1 Thessalonians 5:12–13).

18 In what ways can you model respect for your pastoral staff?

The way you relate to your staff will set the tone for the entire team. If you model respect in your interactions with the staff, they will likely be respectful of each other and of you. On the other hand, if you criticize their ideas and contributions, a spirit of disrespect will invade everything the team does. Once respect is gone, it is only a matter of time until the team falls apart.

One pastor speaks of experiencing ongoing dissension on his staff until he finally called in a ministry consultant. After a week of in-depth evaluation, the consultant said, "I have some good news and some bad news. The good news is the entire staff loves you. The bad news is they can't stand each other." When the consultant left, the Lord began to deal with that pastor's heart. In prayer, he came to see that he was reaping what he had sown. The Lord showed him how he had subtly played the staff against each other to further his own agenda. Under deep conviction, he humbled himself and sought the Lord's forgiveness. The Lord forgave him, but it was impossible to undo the damage to the relationships among the staff.

When it comes to team spirit, you as the pastor are the key. The pastoral staff will reflect your attitudes and values. If you communicate openly and model caring, loyalty, trust, and respect, each aspect will return to you in full measure. "So in everything, do to others what you would have them do to you" (Matthew 7:12).

One of my favorite cartoons pictures a boy named Linus watching television. His older sister Lucy walks into the room, looks at the program, and orders Linus to change the channel. Linus looks up and asks, "What makes you think that you can walk into the room and just like that say, 'Change the channel'?"

Lucy replies, "You see this hand? Individually, these five fingers don't amount to much, but rolled together tightly into a fist, they become a formidable weapon."

Linus promptly changes the channel.

After Lucy is comfortable and involved in her own program, Linus looks at his own fingers and says, "Why can't you guys get organized like that?"

I believe that good pastoral leadership can transform the insignificant "fingers" of the pastoral team into a formidable fist to accomplish God's vision for a congregation. Identify needed staff positions based on that God-given vision. Select team members who have character, competence, and the right chemistry. Then work hard to build and maintain team spirit, for together you can accomplish everything through Him who gives us strength (Philippians 4:13).

Test Yourself

Circle the letter of the *best* answer.

1. Team ministry can provide
a) encouragement.
b) spiritual strength.
c) effectiveness.
d) all of the above.

2. A pastor should build a staff based on the church's
a) needs.
b) vision.
c) programs.
d) resources.

3. A pastor should NOT hire a
a) young person.
b) woman.
c) friend.
d) student.

4. The foundation for ministry is
a) competence.
b) chemistry.
c) character.
d) experience.

5. Pastors should first try to hire staff from
a) Bible schools.
b) nearby churches.
c) local businesses.
d) their own churches.

6. When hiring staff, a pastor should assume that a staff member will change
a) not at all.
b) just a little.
c) somewhat.
d) a lot.

7. The communication principle involves
a) sharing vision.
b) showing respect.
c) asking questions.
d) caring for needs.

8. Who should care for the needs of staff members?
a) Board members
b) Church members
c) Ministers of pastoral care
d) Senior pastors

9. The product of communication and care is
a) character.
b) loyalty.
c) growth.
d) security.

10. Pastor–staff relations will fail without
a) conflict.
b) intimacy.
c) trust.
d) fellowship.

Responses to Interactive Questions
Chapter 12

Some of these responses may include information that is supplemental to the IST. These questions are intended to produce reflective thinking beyond the course content and your responses may vary from these examples.

1 Give three biblical examples of team ministry.

Answers may vary. The IST provides several: Peter and the brothers from Jerusalem who visit Cornelius; Paul and Barnabas; Barnabas and John Mark; Paul and Silas; Paul and Timothy.

2 Identify three benefits of team ministry from Ecclesiastes 4:9–12.

Answers will vary, but here are four possible responses: If one falls, the other can help the fallen one rise; if two lie down together, they will keep warm; two can defend themselves better than one can; and a cord of three strands is stronger.

3 How did the apostle Paul benefit from team ministry?

Paul received comfort and assistance in the work from team members.

4 When do staff positions help a church become all God wants it to be?

When they are selected on the basis of the church's God-given vision

5 Why should pastors not choose friends to be on their staff?

Most people cannot handle being both a friend and a boss. One of the two relationships will suffer. Friends see themselves as equals, but the employer/employee relationship is different.

6 When can choosing a strong leader as a staff member be a disadvantage?

When a mature primary leader is in a limited, supporting position, he or she may feel frustrated and tempted to compete with the pastor. The senior pastor must resist the challenge, often at the expense of relationships and staff morale.

7 What does "What you hire is what you get" mean?

People will probably not change after they are hired. What individuals are like as applicants is what they will be like as staff pastors. You can train but not change a person.

8 How would you measure an applicant's character?

Answers will vary but could include using hypothetical ethical situations that the applicant must respond to.

9 Other than godly character, what is essential for successful team ministry?

Answers may vary. The right attitude, competence, and good relationship skills are three possibilities.

10 What are two benefits of choosing staff from within the local church?

(1) They can be observed beforehand, over a period of time, so the pastor can become thoroughly familiar with character and skills. (2) The congregation is familiar with them and confident in their commitment.

11 If you want to hire someone from another church, what should you do first?

Ask permission from his or her present employer before approaching the individual about a job.

12 What is an open-door policy?

A practice that allows staff to have access to the senior pastor whenever they feel a need to communicate

13 List some ways that pastors can care for their staff.

Answers will vary but could include recognizing achievements, spending time together in retreats, attending special meetings together as a team, and encouraging the congregation to express love to the staff.

14 Why is it important to recognize each staff member?

Individuals need to know they are loved and valued. Paul left this example in Romans 16.

15 Suggest ways a pastor could show personal concern for each staff member.

Answers will vary.

16 How should a pastor handle complaints against staff members?

Answers may vary. Do not be quick to believe complaints against staff members; address complaints with the staff member and the congregant present; publicly express trust in the staff member; and never scold staff publicly.

17 What are the two directions of entry-level trust?

(1) A pastor's hiring a staff member shows trust in that person, and (2) a candidate's accepting the position shows trust in the senior pastor.

18 In what ways can pastors model respect for their pastoral staff?

Answers will vary but might include these ideas: Encourage ideas and efforts; be careful not to criticize, but offer suggestions in love; do not belittle anyone or attack them through humor.

The Rhythm of Life in Ministry

Once when a Southern Baptist denominational executive was on the Midwestern Seminary campus in the late 1990s, he asserted that statistics show that for every twenty men who enter the ministry, by the time those men reach age sixty-five, only one will still be in the ministry. Despite all the commitment with which they began the race, despite all the investment of time and money to prepare, despite the years spent in service, despite the cost of retooling and redirecting their lives, nearly all will leave the ministry. Some will opt out for health reasons. Some will wash out in their private lives. Some will bow out, realizing they misread the call of God. Some will bail out because the stress is so great. Some will be forced out by their churches. Some will walk out from sheer frustration and a sense of failure. And if you haven't given serious thought to leaving the ministry, you haven't been in it very long. (Whitney 2000)

One of the leading causes of ministerial dropout is burnout. No one is at greater risk for burnout than conscientious ministers who love their work. With single-minded devotion, they passionately pursue their calling. At first, nothing seems to bother them—not the long hours or the missed family times or the canceled vacations. But over time, everything begins to take its toll. By mid-life, these pastors are often worn out. When such a cycle is well established, they may be tempted to resent the people they serve and dread the ministry they have committed to.

This is the dilemma: The people who consistently find fulfillment in their ministry are those who sincerely love what they do. Yet these same people are at greatest risk of burning out. The challenge, then, is to find a way to enjoy your ministry without allowing it to overtake your life. The key is to balance the rhythm of ministry with the rhythms of rest and worship. Perhaps the first step is learning to live a God-centered life rather than a need-centered one.

Note: Much of the material in this chapter is taken from *Living in Harmony: Moving to a Better Place in Your Life*, by Richard Exley (Green Forest, AR: New Leaf Press, 2003).

Lesson 13.1   Get in Step with the Rhythm of Work
Objective
13.1.1 Identify the danger of an imbalanced ministry and principles for establishing healthy work patterns.

Lesson 13.2   Take Time for the Rhythm of Rest
Objective
13.2.1 Explain the principle of Sabbath rest.

Lesson 13.3   Live in the Rhythm of Worship
Objective
13.3.1 Describe principles related to worship.

13.1.1
OBJECTIVE
Identify the danger of an imbalanced ministry and principles for establishing healthy work patterns.

Get in Step with the Rhythm of Work

I know from experience that the most faithful ministers—the ones who love their ministries the most—are the ones in most danger of **burnout**. In about forty years of pastoral ministry, I have had more than one brush with burnout. When it happens, you can usually read about it in my journal:

I'm tired, Lord.
Bone weary from the inside out.
I'm tired of a constantly cluttered desk and an overcrowded calendar.
I'm tired of broken things,
like marriages with too little love
and families with too much anger.
I'm tired of problems I can't solve and hurts I can't heal.
I'm tired of deadlines and decisions—duties done without pleasure.

I'm tired, Lord. I really am.
My creative juices are at a low ebb.
I have no inspiration,
    no insight,
    no freshness.
It's been a long time since I have felt truly alive.
I can't remember the last time I walked barefoot in the park
or lay on my back in the grass watching the clouds
or sat in my study at night with only a kerosene lamp for light,
thinking of Grandma Miller and the good times we had.

I'm homesick for the mountains,
  for the smell of pines after the rain,
    for the sound of the wind in the aspens.
I'm hungry for home-baked bread and country cream,
  home-canned peaches,
    and fresh tomatoes right off the vine.

I'm tired of books that satiate my mind without touching my soul.
I want to feel.
I want to laugh and cry,
  live life to the fullest,
    love and be loved.

Help me, Lord.
I've gotten so caught up in my work that I'm missing life's best.
Remind me to balance my busyness with rest and worship.

Learn Limits

1 What causes pastors to be need-centered?

Most conscientious ministers tend to be need-centered. They find it hard to rest as long as any task remains unfinished. They continually push themselves to and beyond the point of exhaustion. Every need—world missions, evangelism, church growth, world hunger, human rights, the plight of the homeless, and so on—becomes their personal responsibility. As far as they are concerned, if they don't do it, no one will. Usually such people live lives of frantic busyness, rushing around trying to meet every need imaginable. Although they love Jesus passionately and are deeply committed to His kingdom, they often know little or nothing about the abundant life He promised.

I know of one minister who often said, "The need is the call." Being a man of great vision and nearly endless energy, he accomplished many worthwhile things, yet he seemed to take little pleasure in his achievements. No one who knew him doubted his devotion to God, but he built his relationship with the Lord on work rather than intimacy. Even in prayer, he focused on things that needed to be done rather than fellowship with the Father.

This need-centered lifestyle eventually took its toll, and during mid-life, his health began to fail. Those closest to him advised him to cut back on his work, but he would not listen. Not even his doctor could persuade him to adopt a more moderate lifestyle. Each time he experienced a health problem, he simply plunged back into work with renewed determination. To him, his health issues were just another obstacle to overcome.

Then, one late night while he was praying, the Lord spoke to him. In a voice that was nearly audible, God said, "Go to bed. I will watch the world for the rest of the night." At that moment, this pastor recognized his drivenness, his need-centered living, for what it was—not humble service but a thinly disguised pride. Deep in his heart, he did not think God could manage without him. Of course, he never would have verbalized any such thought, but in light of the Lord's rebuke, this man's true attitude became apparent.

Unfortunately, this kind of need-centered thinking usually comes from ministerial colleagues. In a misguided effort to motivate us to love one another, sincere ministers often make us feel responsible for the whole world—a burden too heavy to bear. The world is God's responsibility, not ours.

I do not mean to suggest that we have no responsibility toward our fellow humans. I only emphasize that our compassion must be tempered with wisdom. Only God is infinite; we are not. Although He never sleeps, our bodies require regular rest. Only as we recognize and live within our limits will we know the joy of co-laboring with Him (1 Corinthians 3:9).

Follow Jesus' Example

Let Jesus be your model. Like us, He was often pressured on all sides. Everywhere He went, needy people mobbed Him. So great were the demands of His ministry that Mark says, "[Jesus] and his disciples were not even able to eat" (Mark 3:20). Yet Jesus knew how to balance the work of ministry with both rest and worship. In fact, He frequently withdrew from public ministry to renew His physical energies and restore His spiritual strength. It was not weakness but wisdom that motivated Him to seek solitude for a season.

2 According to John 5:19, what needs did Jesus respond to?

Although Jesus was moved with compassion by the needs of suffering humanity (Matthew 9:36), He was governed only by the Father's will (John 4:34; 6:38). He responded to human need only when the Father directed Him to do so. Jesus said, "I tell you the truth, the Son can do nothing by himself; he can do only what he sees his Father doing, because whatever the Father does the Son also does" (John 5:19).

On some occasions, Jesus healed every sick person in sight (Matthew 8:16), but at other times, He literally stepped over suffering humanity to minister to only one person (John 5:2–9). The only conclusion I can draw from this is that Jesus was God-centered rather than need-centered. He did only what the Father directed Him to do. Dare we do anything else?

3 Explain the difference between being God-centered and being need-centered.

If Jesus needed to be God-centered instead of need-centered, if He needed to practice the **rhythm** of life to remain effective in ministry and fulfilled as a person, how much more so do we. The pace of contemporary life merely amplifies our necessity for that delicate balance of work, rest, and worship.

13.2.1
OBJECTIVE

Explain the principle of Sabbath rest.

4   What is the principle of Sabbath rest?

Take Time for the Rhythm of Rest

The Sabbath is God's answer to our need-centered drivenness. In His infinite wisdom, God designed the Sabbath to protect us from the dangers of physical exhaustion, psychological stress, and the interpersonal alienation that results from idolizing work, including the work of ministry. God instructs, "Six days do your work, but on the seventh day do not work, so that your ox and your donkey may rest and the slave born in your household, and the alien as well, may be refreshed" (Exodus 23:12).

In the Jewish tradition, the Sabbath began at sundown on Friday. Preparations were to be completed ahead of time so the Sabbath could be free of mundane concerns. Individuals were to put aside the week's tensions and conflicts so the Sabbath could be enjoyed. These traditions continue in Jewish homes:

> Friday evening traditionally is spent at home with family and friends, thus providing a regular opportunity for family members to become reacquainted with one another and their neighbors. . . . The prohibitions against riding, the use of money, and work serve to keep everyone within the boundaries of the neighborhood and to encourage socializing, contemplation, study, dialogue, and those activities that promote refreshment and personal renewal. [The Sabbath's] holiness rests in its emphasis on time—time for interpersonal relationships, for reestablishing contact with the world of nature, for the expression of the emotional dimensions of being, and for the enjoyment of the present. On the Sabbath everyday activities and weekly routines are put aside and time is made for oneself, one's family and one's friends. (Goldberg 1987, 148–149)

For centuries, the Christian church continued to practice the principle of the Sabbath, although they observed it on the first day of the week instead of the seventh in honor of the Lord's resurrection. Like the Jews, the Christians would neither work nor shop on their Sabbath. They considered Sunday a sacred day not to be violated except under the most unusual circumstances.

World War II changed that with the first widespread practice of seven-day-a-week industrial production. By the 1960s and 1970s, retailers began to follow suit, and eventually, the Sabbath principle became largely a thing of the past. Not coincidentally, the decline of the Sabbath principle was accompanied by a significant increase in emotional dysfunction, juvenile delinquency, and divorce. Without the rhythm of rest provided by the Sabbath, life was unraveling.

5   Why is it important for pastors to have a Sabbath?

As a minister, you may be tempted to think you cannot take a day off; your work is too important. Yet do not deceive yourself. Rest is not optional; it cannot wait. "Six days you shall labor, but on the seventh day you shall rest; even during the plowing season and harvest you must rest" (Exodus 34:21). Keep in mind that the plowing season and harvest were absolutely critical to the life cycle of Israel's agrarian culture. A single day could mean the difference between feast and famine. Still, God said, "You must rest."

Under the Law, those who broke the Sabbath were executed: "Whoever does any work on it [the Sabbath] must be put to death" (Exodus 35:2). And those who break the Sabbath today suffer the same consequences—not at the hands of a religious or judicial system but as the inevitable consequence of their transgression. When individuals violate the Sabbath principle of rest, their souls suffer, as do their relationships, their creative energies, and ultimately their physical health.

This truth became real to me several years ago as I served as pastor of Christian Chapel in Tulsa, Oklahoma. For more than a year, I had ignored the Sabbath principle. I had not taken a day off. I knew it was wrong, but one emergency seemed to occur after another, on top of the ever-present demands of a growing congregation. I was preaching five to six times per week, leading a discussion group at a local seminary, continuing a heavy counseling load, and hosting a weekly radio program. The church was just completing a major building program. My father's open-heart surgery and an emergency gall bladder operation within a three-week period simply added to my stress.

Physically and emotionally, I was more drained than I realized. I began to resent my work, particularly the counseling with it constant requirement to be affirming and encouraging. I told my wife I felt like a piece of raw meat in a tank of piranhas, but for a while, I thought I could work through it. I mean, what choice did I have? If I did try to take a few days off, my work just piled up and was always waiting for me when I returned. Besides, I had been away from the church as much as I dared during my father's illness.

For the most part, I managed to minister with surprising proficiency. However, on the inside, I was falling apart. My nerves were rubbed raw. I had no spiritual and emotional reserves left. Many times, my wife and daughter received the brunt of my anger and frustration.

One holiday weekend, things finally came to a breaking point. I lost control and screamed at my wife over nothing. I hated myself for it. My brother, Bob, and his wife were spending the weekend with us, and I found myself sharing my pent-up feelings with him. Once I started to talk, I could not seem to stop. I was tired, but there seemed to be no time to rest. I loved my work, but it was killing me. I felt trapped and hated that feeling too. By then, I was sobbing. All the pain I had kept under control came pouring out. It truly scared me. I had not realized just how close I was to breaking down.

6   When overworked, what is the first step in regaining balance in life?

With Bob's help, I made some important decisions that weekend. First, I had to admit that I could not do it all. Then I had to decide what to keep doing, what to delegate, and what to let go undone. Finally, I had to return to the rhythm of rest. I had to faithfully take my day off.

The emotional release of that time of sharing with Bob proved invaluable. Yet it would have been of little lasting benefit without the subsequent lifestyle change. Now I am learning to live within my emotional limits. Just as I must budget my finances to live within my means, I must also budget my emotional and spiritual resources. If I give out more than I take in, I become overdrawn. By practicing the Sabbath principle of rest and solitude, I make regular deposits in my emotional bank account and return to my public ministry with renewed energy and effectiveness. In addition, taking needed rests allows me to be a much better husband and father and a more satisfied man.

For ministers, Sunday can hardly be considered a day of rest. In fact, it is generally the most demanding day of the week. For instance, while serving as senior pastor of Christian Chapel, I often preached three times on Sunday morning, again on Sunday evening, and hosted a live, weekly radio program. Although I no longer serve as pastor of a local congregation, I still preach three or four times each Sunday. That is a taxing load for anyone, and when my day is done, I need more than a good night's sleep to restore my energies.

Since Sunday is not a Sabbath for ministers and their spouses, they must set aside another day to rest. I have learned that it should be the same day each week for the maximum benefit, as this routine creates a rhythm of rest and renewal.

My wife and I tried different days of the week but settled on Monday for our Sabbath. Nothing is particularly special about Monday, but after Sunday's exhausting schedule, we needed a day to recover. Also, in general, fewer events are scheduled early in the week, making it easier for us to honor our commitment. We often stay at home all day, enjoying our privacy. If we do venture out, it is usually just to share a quiet lunch in a nearby restaurant. We use Monday to catch up on our rest, frequently napping for a few hours in the afternoon. We talk at length, sharing deeply and catching up on the bits of news we have been too busy to share with each other during the rest of the week. Sometimes we read, listen to music, or take a leisurely walk.

Consistently honoring our commitment to the Sabbath renews our energies—physically, emotionally, and spiritually—and helps us maintain a quality family life even as we give ourselves to the work of the ministry. In the process, we have realized that, in reality, merely pausing for rest and renewal once a week is not enough. To live the abundant life Jesus promised, we need to carry the spirit of the Sabbath rest into each day. In other words, everyday should contain something of the Sabbath: a time for rest, a time for relationships, and a time for worship. But this does not happen by itself; you will have to work at it.

7 Explain the twofold miracle of the Sabbath.

The true miracle of the Sabbath is not that it sets us apart from the world but that it returns us to the world clear-eyed and caring, tenderhearted and compassionate. The Sabbath celebrates both solitude and service, both reflection and risk. It gives us permission to focus on our personal needs for a time, to sit at Jesus' feet without feeling a need to do anything, and to enjoy the comforts of home and the love of family without feeling guilty. Yet it also moves us to compassionate concern for those less fortunate than we are.

Without the Sabbath, without rest and renewal, we would never have the inner resources to embrace a hurting world. In our weariness, we would be tempted to resent the needy with their ever-present claims on us. But renewed by a Sabbath rest, we can embrace them with the love of Christ. Rather than isolating us, the Sabbath restores our spiritual and emotional vitality so we can return to our mission with renewed vision.

Live in the Rhythm of Worship

Worship Is a Way of Life

13.3.1
OBJECTIVE
Describe principles related to worship.

To consistently experience the physical, emotional, and spiritual renewal necessary to remain fresh in the ministry, a pastor must add worship to the rhythm of work and rest. As we have already noted, for most ministers, Sunday is not a day of rest; nor is it primarily a time of worship. In fact, what happens in service on Sunday is more work than worship for pastors.

This does not mean that pastors do not worship, for they do. While a part of them worships passionately, singing and praying, on another level, they are conscious of their pastoral responsibilities. Whereas others come to the service to receive, pastors come to give, to minister to their flocks. They are God's representatives. They are responsible to direct the service and preach the Word. On a more mundane level, they are also responsible for the logistics of the service, such as supervising greeters, ushers, musicians, sound technicians, and so on. The average worshipper gives little thought to such things, but they are never far from the conscientious pastor's mind.

Because pastors' responsibilities often prevent them from worshipping fully in a Sunday service, where can they experience worship and the spiritual renewal it provides? Conferences, retreats, and workshops are helpful to a degree, but no pastor can attend more than three or four a year. That is hardly enough to provide the worship their souls crave. So what are they to do?

8   What is worship?

Perhaps we need to rethink our theology of worship. It is not just something that happens in the church sanctuary. In fact, perhaps the truth is that what happens in the church service is really designed to sensitize us to God's presence in our everyday world. Frederick Buechner states, "Church isn't the only place where the holy happens. Sacramental moments can occur at any moment, any place and to anybody. . . . If we weren't blind as bats, we might see that life itself is sacramental" (2000, 201).

I remember experiencing a "sacramental moment" some years ago. It was early evening, and the church office was quiet for the first time since morning. The last office assistant had gone home. Taking a deep breath, I admitted to myself just how tired I was. The midweek service was scheduled to begin in ninety minutes, and I could not imagine where I would get the energy to preach.

Wearily, I went through the motions of brewing a cup of coffee. When it was finished, I walked back into my office, but instead of returning to my desk, I turned toward the window, which opened on an eleven-acre field. It was dusk, and the last rays of the setting sun were glistening on the rain-wet grass. As I sipped my coffee, I watched a man romping with two of the prettiest hunting dogs I had ever seen.

Standing there enjoying the beauty of God's creation, I felt the day's tension drain out of me. A holy quietness settled over me, and all at once, I sensed God's presence. I found myself quoting Jacob: "Surely the Lord is in this place, and I was not aware of it" (Genesis 28:16). Like Moses standing barefoot before the burning bush or Elijah hearing that "still small voice," I knew I was standing on holy ground. I cannot explain it; I can only describe what happened. For a moment, God met me in the midst of my busyness. And when He did, it seemed He made all things new.

My coffee had chilled, but my heart was strangely warmed. Returning to my desk, I found myself refreshed in both spirit and body. Just moments before, I had no energy to minister, and now, my heart was full to overflowing. Having been renewed by my worship encounter, I could not wait to minister to the hungry souls who would soon gather in the sanctuary.

Worship Is a Discipline

Sometimes worship is like that—unexpected, without any effort on our part— but not often. Generally, we must prepare ourselves for it by deliberately turning our attention toward the eternal. For me, that often means quieting my noisy soul. Amidst my frantic faithfulness, I frequently hear God say, "Be still, and know that I am God" (Psalm 46:10).

Even then, it is not easy to still my noisy heart or quiet my anxious thoughts. But with determined deliberateness, I do the things that have worked in the past. For instance, I brew a cup of coffee, light the oil lamp in my study, and force myself to sit and be still. At first, numerous thoughts wrestle for my attention: people I need to call, things I need to do the next day, chores I should be doing around the house. Yet God reminds me again, "Be still."

9 What elements lead pastors to an inner stillness?

Bit by bit, I feel the tensions slip away. The noise of the world is pushed back for a little while. Even the discordant voices within grow quiet. Out of the silence, God speaks in a still small voice (1 Kings 19:12) and renews my soul. I know who I am: a child of God. I know who He is: my heavenly Father. Within the warmth of His embrace, within the comfort of His presence, my concerns and even my fears become so inconsequential. The circumstances that caused them are still present, but they are no longer of any real concern.

It is such an incredible worship experience, unspeakable in its profoundness. Why then do I go to this holy place only as a last resort? Could it be that I fear the solitude? Am I afraid that nothing will be there, that when the noise stops I will not hear His still small voice? All these things play a role, I'm sure, as does the knowledge that parting is inevitably painful, even for a short time. Yet as Anne Morrow Lindbergh states, "Once it is done, I find there is a quality to being alone [with God] that is incredibly precious. Life rushes back into the void, richer, more vivid, fuller than before" (1981, 79).

If this is what your heart hungers for—a richer, more vivid, fuller life—let me urge you to make the rhythm of worship a part of your daily routine. It will not necessarily be easy, but it will be worth whatever effort it takes. You will not only be renewed as a person but will also return to the work of ministry with a fresh anointing from the Spirit.

10 What three things must you maintain for strong ministry?

After almost forty years of pastoral ministry, I am convinced that finishing well is no accident. To finish strong in the ministry, you will have to maintain your spiritual vitality, emotional wholeness, and physical strength. The spiritual disciplines that make this happen are well documented. Although they are relatively simple, they are not easy. They include, but are not limited to, daily prayer, the study of Scripture, regular fasting, solitude, and corporate worship.

An equally important but less recognized discipline is the rhythm of life— that delicate balance between work, rest, and worship. Without it, life's richness hangs by a slender thread, and even the hardiest minister risks burnout.

Life's fullness flows out of its rhythm. All of God's creation is designed to experience total fruition only by observing the rhythm of life. Common sense tells us it is foolish to try to plant in the heart of winter or reap a harvest during planting time. The fruitfulness of farmers' work depends on their willingness to work within the seasons of nature, within the rhythm of the land. Likewise, our lives are self-defeating if we ignore the God-ordained rhythm of work, rest, and worship. To truly become all God has called you to be as an individual and a minister, you must live in rhythm with Him. To finish well in the ministry, you will need to practice the rhythm of life, especially in times of increased stress and busyness.

Test Yourself

Circle the letter of the **best** answer.

1. Most pastors burn out because they do not
a) take care of themselves.
b) have ministry callings.
c) care about people.
d) have social support.

2. Often, pastors burn out because they are
a) work-centered.
b) preaching-centered.
c) people-centered.
d) need-centered.

3. One key for avoiding burnout is to
a) preach less often.
b) understand your limits.
c) take every seventh year off.
d) do only what you enjoy.

4. We can honor the Sabbath rest principle by
a) spending time with family.
b) resting from work.
c) caring for personal needs.
d) doing all of the above.

5. A pastor should have one day off
a) every week.
b) every other week.
c) every month.
d) every six weeks.

6. A person must learn the rhythm of work, rest, and
a) laughter.
b) fellowship.
c) worship.
d) study.

7. When ministering, Jesus
a) always pressed to do more.
b) met whatever needs He encountered.
c) worried about having enough time.
d) was faithful to His Father's will.

8. The key to a healthy ministry is
a) simplicity.
b) balance.
c) efficiency.
d) quality preaching.

9. Which word best describes worship?
a) Activity
b) Moment
c) Event
d) Lifestyle

10. In preparing to worship, pastors should
a) read devotional books.
b) go to the church.
c) still their thoughts.
d) turn down the lights.

Responses to Interactive Questions
Chapter 13

Some of these responses may include information that is supplemental to the IST. These questions are intended to produce reflective thinking beyond the course content and your responses may vary from these examples.

1 What causes pastors to be need-centered?

They base their ministry on the extent of need that surrounds them and are compelled to meet all the needs personally.

2 According to John 5:19, what needs did Jesus respond to?

Only those His Father directed Him to meet

3 Explain the difference between being God-centered and being need-centered.

It is the conflict of doing whatever presents itself as need versus doing what God directs you to do.

4 What is the principle of Sabbath rest?

The Sabbath rest is to labor six days and stop for one day to get renewed by the things that refresh you and your personal relationships with God and family.

5 Why is it important for pastors to have a Sabbath?

Answer may vary.

6 When overworked, what is the first step in regaining balance in life?

Admitting that you cannot keep up with your schedule of things to do

7 Explain the twofold miracle of the Sabbath.

The Sabbath (1) meets our needs and (2) enables us to care about others.

8 What is worship?

The ability to enter into God's presence and abide there throughout each day

9 What elements lead pastors to an inner stillness?

A restful place, a relaxing atmosphere, and an open attitude

10 What three things must you maintain for strong ministry?

(1) spiritual vitality, (2) emotional wholeness, and (3) physical strength

Keeping Your Passion for Ministry

As I leaf through my prayer journal, I notice that, not surprisingly, several entries focus on the physical and emotional toll of ministry. In one entry from 1988, I described my weariness—not just physically and emotionally, but a deep tiredness from the inside out. The cumulative weight of twenty-two years of ministry was wearing me down. At that point, had I been able to think of a way to support my family, I might have considered leaving the ministry. I felt unsatisfied, restless, and unfulfilled. I questioned whether the Lord was through with me or whether He was preparing me for significant changes.

Yet, in this journal entry, I also recorded the reassurance God spoke to my heart. He explained that my exhaustion caused normal tasks and situations to seem difficult and relationships to seem overwhelming. He said, "Like Elijah the prophet, you need some real rest and a safe place with a special friend. You need to focus on your relationship with Me rather than your ministry. How long has it been since you simply enjoyed My presence, simply rested in My love?" He admonished me not to seek perfection or to strive to meet others' expectations. He wanted my fulfillment to come from Him and Him alone. He was changing me, He said, but slowly. He reminded me to be still and know that He is God, to simply live one day at a time without rushing ahead. His words refreshed my soul and began to renew my strength. They gave me a fresh challenge and a new vision.

My experience is not unique. Everywhere I turn, I find ministers who are worn out and at times looking for a way out. Sometimes, they are reeling from a major catastrophe, but usually they are simply spiritually and emotionally exhausted. Ministry is high-risk; there is no way to escape the toll it takes. Most ministers continue the course, but more and more are dropping short of the finish line.

To keep running the race and staying the course of ministry takes effort, but it can be done. Jude 20 says, "Build yourselves up in your most holy faith and pray in the Spirit." Paul says, "I pray that out of his glorious riches he may strengthen you with power through his Spirit in your inner being" (Ephesians 3:16). As long as your internal spiritual support is stronger than the external pressures, you can overcome. To press on in ministry, then, you must guard your relationship with Christ, your heart, and your spirit.

Lesson 14.1   Guard Your Faith

Objective

14.1.1 Summarize the roles of prayer, journal keeping, and Bible study in relation to faith.

Lesson 14.2   Guard Your Heart

Objective

14.2.1 Discuss how to overcome the dangers of success, comparison, and wealth.

Lesson 14.3   Guard Your Spirit

Objective

14.3.1 Evaluate keys for guarding your spirit.

14.1.1
OBJECTIVE

Summarize the roles of prayer, journal keeping, and Bible study in relation to faith.

1 What three areas must you guard to maintain your inner strength?

2 How is a relationship with Jesus like any other relationship?

3 Explain the value of silence during times of prayer.

Guard Your Faith

Guarding your faith, that is, your relationship with Jesus, means never letting the ministry rob you of your time with Him. As improbable as it may sound, the ministry can crowd Jesus out of your life so that you no longer enjoy intimate fellowship with Him. Instead of sitting at His feet with Mary, you will be busy in the kitchen, helping Martha with the demands of ministry (Luke 10:38–42). And if you spend too much time in the "kitchen" and too little time at Jesus' feet, you will likely begin to resent the ministry.

I identify with Ken Gire when he writes,

I don't want to live in the kitchen of religious activity, distracted with all my preparations. I don't want to live slumped over some steamed-up stove, worried and upset about so many things. I want to live at the Savior's feet, gazing into His eyes, listening to His words. . . . At His feet is where we learn to pause. . . . It starts by loving Him and longing to hear His voice. When we're slaving away in some kitchen where the pots and pans are clanging, it's hard to hear that voice. But when we're at His feet and our heart is still, we can hear Him even when He whispers. (1996, 36)

Pray and Listen

As with any other relationship, your relationship with Jesus requires time and attention. It is not complicated, but it is demanding. You do not need to master any trick techniques, to adhere to any religious rituals, or carefully keep rules. But a relationship with Jesus does require devotion and discipline.

Communication is the key to any relationship, including your relationship with Jesus. To truly commune with Him, you need to spend time together, both in prayer and in God's Word. While it is important that you share your deepest feelings and concerns with Him, you must be careful not to let your devotional prayers degenerate into endless babbling (Matthew 6:7).

I have found that devotional praying is most effective when I spend the majority of my prayer time listening. Usually, the Holy Spirit speaks through silence. However, for many of us, silence is uncomfortable or even frightening, and we succumb to the temptation to fill our lives and relationships with noisy busyness. Conversation becomes our primary communication method, and we exchange information without really relating to one another. After a while, this may seem normal, but it is not fulfilling.

The same thing occurs in our relationship with Jesus. Worship and prayer, designed to still us before the Lord, are turned into things we do rather than opportunities to "be still and know." As a result, silence is lost and, by virtue of its absence, becomes foreign. Without that holy stillness, our spiritual life is diminished, for silence has always characterized a truly intimate relationship with the Lord.

To recover the renewing power of holy silence, we must first come to terms with it. Silence is not an enemy to avoid but a friend to embrace. It is the language of the soul, the language of intimacy. Through silence, the heart speaks to God and God speaks to the heart. In silence, God teaches us the deep mysteries of the Spirit, the things that can never be communicated with mere words.

As we wait at Jesus' feet in holy quietness, something happens. We experience a growing awareness that we are not alone, even though no other person is in the room. An awakening, a stirring, occurs deep within; in the words of the psalmist, "Deep calls to deep" (Psalm 42:7). An old mystic described it as

God's putting His face against the windowpane of our lives, or as Jacob said, "I saw God face to face" (Genesis 32:30). In prayer, God can become that real to us. It is this kind of intimate praying that sustains our relationship with Jesus, no matter how hectic the demands of ministry become.

Keep a Journal

4 How can journaling benefit a person's relationship with the Lord?

Because my relationship with Jesus centers on matters of the heart, I find it effective to use a prayer journal during my devotional time. By disciplining myself to listen prayerfully and then write my thoughts and feelings in detail, I am better able to understand what the Lord is speaking to me.

According to Elizabeth O'Connor, we grow when we take time to reflect on, examine, and question ourselves. Journaling "is one of the most helpful ways" to do this (1982, 100). In his practical little volume on journaling, author Robert Wood adds: "Keeping a journal helps us process the spiritual meaning of each day's events" (1978, 9). (See Lesson 2.1 for additional discussion about keeping a prayer journal.)

Study the Bible

We must balance the subjective discipline of devotional prayer and journaling with the objective discipline of devotional study, especially the study of God's Word. The Bible is the food for our souls: "Man does not live on bread alone, but on every word that comes from the mouth of God" (Matthew 4:4). According to Psalm 119, the Word of God makes us wise (v. 98) and is a lamp to our feet and a light to our path (v. 105). Its statutes are our delight (v. 24). Hiding them in our hearts helps to keep us from sin (v. 11). When our souls are weary, God's Word strengthens us (v. 28); when our souls faint, His Word is our hope (v. 81). It is eternal, standing firm in the heavens (v. 89) and is more precious than much gold and silver (v. 72).

5 What is the key to enjoying God's presence daily?

Pastors who are faithful in their devotional life will know a spiritual richness unimagined by the casual believer. Prayer gives pastors' lives a holy center, a sacred place. The Word of God renews their minds. They know God and have an inner stability enabling them to continue from strength to strength no matter how heavy the weight of ministry. By guarding their relationships with Jesus, pastors can maintain vitality in their ministries throughout their lives.

14.2.1
OBJECTIVE

Discuss how to overcome the dangers of success, comparison, and wealth.

6 Give the biblical meaning of heart.

Guard Your Heart

Ministers need to guard not only their faith but also their own hearts. They need to keep their lives and their motives pure. Proverbs 4:23 declares, "Above all else, guard your heart, for it is the wellspring of life."

When Scripture speaks of the heart, it does not refer to the physical organ that circulates blood throughout the body. Rather, it refers to the core of a person, to whom he or she really is. In the language of Scripture, the heart is the source of emotions, the fountainhead of thoughts and desires, the motivating force of life.

Everything a person does, whether good or evil, originates in the heart. Jesus said, "Out of the overflow of the heart the mouth speaks. The good man brings good things out of the good stored up in him, and the evil man brings evil things out of the evil stored up in him" (Matthew 12:34–35).

The Danger of Success

As a minister, you will have to guard your heart not only against feelings of discouragement but also against the dangers of success. Adversity will test your character and perseverance. Success, on the other hand, tests integrity—your ability to stay true to yourself, to remain morally and ethically pure.

Successful pastors are often treated preferentially. They may be invited to serve on prestigious boards and committees. Important people may seek their advice. Powerful people may court them and confide in them. If such ministers do not guard their hearts, pride and ambition will soon take root.

7 Do you use your power to serve or to be served?

While it is not wrong for pastors to want success, they need to manage that desire lest it ruin their ministries. That is, to guard their hearts, ministers must recognize personal ambition for what it is and deal with it honestly. The real trouble begins when they interpret success as divine approval of all their motives. When this happens, little or nothing can restrain a pastor's ambitious ego. Unrestrained, ambition will eventually shipwreck a pastor's ministry.

When Jesus came, He introduced us to a new kind of power—a selfless power that grows out of obedience rather than ambition. He voluntarily gave up His divine rights to show us how to use power redemptively. In His incarnation and ministry, He gave up every advantage of His divine nature and renounced His rights to accept the higher calling of a servant-minister (Philippians 2:3–8). He said of himself, "The Son of Man did not come to be served, but to serve" (Matthew 20:28). Notice that Jesus did not give up His responsibility or role as a leader but only His rights and privileges.

Based on Jesus' example, therefore, we must conclude that practicing discipline and self-denial is the only way to guard our hearts against vain ambition. Ministers must voluntarily limit their lifestyles to keep human nature in check. Indulge the old nature a little, and it will demand more and more. According to Richard Foster, "Inordinate passions are like spoiled children and need to be disciplined, and not indulged" (1985, 223).

The Danger of Comparison

Pastors must also guard their hearts against unhealthy comparisons (2 Corinthians 10:12). Many a pastor has become depressed, developed a critical spirit, or been overtaken with envy as a result of comparing himself/herself to other more successful ministers.

In the first fourteen years of my ministry, I served small churches (fewer than one hundred members) in remote rural areas. In my mind, nothing I accomplished could compare with the success of pastors in larger cities. As long as I kept to myself in my own pastorate, I managed to deal with my relative insignificance. However, I became troubled when I attended district meetings or national conferences where the speakers were always "successful" pastors. In their presence, I felt like a nobody. I often found their achievements more intimidating than inspiring.

When the accomplishments of one of my peers exceeded my own, jealousy overtook me. One national conference I attended featured a peer as one of the speakers. I had to admit that he was committed, gifted, and articulate. Still, I mentally picked his message apart while fourteen thousand worshippers listened with rapt attention. Inwardly, I seethed. The better he preached, the more jealous I became.

For weeks afterward, I alternated between anger and depression. Envy was eating a hole in my soul. Jealousy was making me sick. Finally, I confessed my sinful feelings to God and admitted that I was powerless to subdue them. I also confessed my feelings of failure and inadequacy, and the Lord gently dealt with me.

8   How do you determine your value?

Slowly, I learned a new way to determine my self-worth. I did not have to measure myself against others' achievements. I no longer relied on numbers to measure success. Instead, I learned to base my success on my relationship with Jesus. With God's help, I set new goals for building my character. I determined to measure my success only by my obedicnce to Jesus Christ and my willingness to allow the Holy Spirit to conform me to God's image.

For the first time in my life, I felt liberated. The work of the ministry was no less important to me, but for a different reason. It was now the by-product of my relationship with Jesus instead of an attempt to prove my worth. I felt content rather then competitive, and for the first time, I genuinely rejoiced in my peers' achievements.

A few years later, while serving as senior pastor at Christian Chapel, I finally experienced the kind of "success" I had always dreamed of. The church was growing significantly, and I had a number of books published. I hosted a national radio broadcast and was invited to preach both nationally and internationally. As a result, I began to feel smug and even a little proud. Again, the Lord dealt with me gently but firmly. He seemed to say, "Richard, if you couldn't build your self-esteem on your ministry accomplishments when your church numbered less than a hundred people, you can't do it now."

Resisting the temptation to compare yourself with others who are more successful will spare you from the pitfalls of depression and envy. Likewise, resisting the temptation to compare yourself with others who are less successful will spare you from the perils of pride.

The Danger of Greed

Pastors must also guard their hearts against the love of money. Although no one enters the ministry hoping to get rich, money soon becomes a critical issue for almost every minister. If pastors do not make enough money to meet their family's needs, they may be tempted to doubt God's goodness or to blame tightfistedness of the congregation. In either case, lack of funds can pollute the spirit.

If pastors serve churches that are willing and able to bless them financially, they may come to believe the ministry owes it to them. After years of observation, I have identified a subtle but dangerous progression: Financially blessed pastors start by accepting the congregation's provision with thanksgiving. Yet after a time, they may begin to expect it, and if the funds stop coming, they may become resentful. Once pastors begin to expect the same standard of compensation, it is but a short step for them to start demanding it. The fourth and final step is then abusing finances.

Instead, wise ministers carefully consider Paul's warnings to Timothy about the danger of riches:

People who want to get rich fall into temptation and a trap and into many foolish and harmful desires that plunge men into ruin and destruction. For the love of money is a root of all kinds of evil. Some people, eager for money, have wandered from the faith and pierced themselves with many griefs. But you, man of God, flee from all this, and pursue righteousness, godliness, faith, love, endurance and gentleness. . . . Command those who are rich in this present world not to be arrogant nor to put their hope in wealth, which is so uncertain, but to put their hope in God, who richly provides us with everything for our enjoyment. Command them to do good, to be rich in good deeds, and to be generous and willing to share. In this way they will lay up treasure for themselves as a firm foundation for the coming age, so that they may take hold of the life that is truly life. (1 Timothy 6:9–19)

After many years in the ministry, I have discovered that the only effective way to deal with the love of money is to deliberately live below my means so I can give more. God measures the size of our gifts not by how much we give but by how much we keep (Luke 21:1–4).

14.3.1
OBJECTIVE

Evaluate keys for guarding your spirit.

Guard Your Spirit

To maintain vitality in your ministry, you will need to guard not only your faith and your heart but also your spirit. People will inevitably disappoint you and let you down. Some may even betray you, wounding your spirit. If you are not careful, you may become bitter.

Learning Principles

Over the years, I have learned some principles to help me protect my spirit. Older, wiser ministers imparted some of these principles to me, and some I received directly from the Lord:

1. Determine that you will never let anyone make you into something you are not.
2. Never blame God for the things His children do.
3. Always remember God loves the people who hurt you as much as He loves you.
4. Be aware that unforgiveness hurts only yourself.
5. Remember that in any situation, you always have a choice in the way you respond.

Be Yourself

The first principle was modeled for me when a dear friend experienced some devastating disappointment in the ministry and was forced to resign. Considering his age and poor health, his prospects for future ministry were limited. In addition, he faced some significant financial challenges. If ever a person had a right to be bitter, he did, but I never heard him speak badly of those who had mistreated him. Finally, I asked him how he maintained such a positive attitude. Without a moment's hesitation, he replied, "I have never been a bitter and vindictive person, and I am not going to let anyone make me into something I am not."

Do Not Misrepresent God's Role

Another friend was forced to resign as a senior pastor and later was asked to leave his position as president of a Bible college. In both instances, he was the victim of a power play orchestrated by unscrupulous people. Of course, he felt betrayed by those who had at one time been his strongest supporters. In the painful aftermath, when many questioned his competence for ministry, he was tempted to give himself over to anger, bitterness, and self-pity. For a time, he was also tempted to blame God, to conclude that the Lord had let him down.

In the midst of the spiritual crisis, this minister began to understand that he blamed God for the actions of a few sinful individuals. When he realized what was happening, he was able to realign his thinking. What could have been an embittering ordeal became a learning and growing experience. It also became a source of wisdom and insight that he passed on to many other ministers. Repeatedly, I have heard him counsel those who have been wounded by the church body, "Don't blame God for what His children do."

Remember God's Immeasurable Love

Early in my ministry, I was victimized in a slanderous attack designed to force me to resign my pastoral position. Like David, I prayed, "Tell me what to do, O Lord, and make it plain because I am surrounded by waiting enemies. Don't let them get me, Lord! Don't let me fall into their hands! For they accuse me of things I never did, and all the while are plotting cruelty" (Psalm 27:11–12, TLB). Yet, for all my desperate prayers, nothing changed. I only grew angrier and was tempted with an all-consuming desire to retaliate. Try as I might, I could not feel anything but contempt for those who had orchestrated the whole sordid thing. I could not understand why God allowed such evil people to wreak havoc in His church. I wanted God to punish them, and if He would not, I was ready to do it for Him.

9 How should pastors respond to those who oppose them?

Gently but firmly, the Lord reminded me that He loved the people behind the lies as much as He loved me. That realization totally changed my thinking. I no longer thought of them as enemies to destroy but as misguided brothers and sisters to be restored. With God's help, I could separate their sinful actions from who they were as individuals. Like Job, I was finally able to pray for my "friends" (Job 42:10), and as a result, God delivered me from bitterness and restored me to effective ministry.

Choose Forgiveness

10 Who is hurt the most when a person does not forgive?

Two other principles have served me well when facing the hurtful actions of people I trusted. First, when I am tempted not to forgive people, I remind myself that unforgiveness hurts me more than it hurts anyone else. Allowing myself to become bitter and unforgiving is like drinking poison and expecting the other person to die. Second, no matter how painful a situation may be, I always have a choice in my response. I can be part of the problem or part of the solution. Human nature encourages us to be part of the problem—to behave as antagonists. However, the Spirit guides us to respond with love and wisdom—to be protagonists.

Handling Criticism

11 Explain the difference between the two types of criticism.

Let me conclude this chapter by addressing the issue of criticism. While some criticism is undoubtedly motivated from a desire to wound, constructive criticism is designed to provide needed correction. The ability to discern between the two is absolutely crucial to your well-being and effectiveness in ministry.

Constructive criticism is motivated by love. It is carefully thought out and has your best interest at heart (Proverbs 15:31–32). On the other hand, hurtful criticism—what the Bible calls "reckless words" (Proverbs 12:18)—is designed to destroy you. The Scriptures clearly teach that constructive criticism, painful though it may be, is essential for correction. Proverbs 15:32 says, "He who ignores discipline despises himself, but whoever heeds correction [constructive criticism] gains understanding."

Yet most of us find criticism—even constructive criticism—to be painful. Perhaps that is why we have so much difficulty dealing with it. When criticism is sincere but ungrounded, we feel misunderstood and unfairly judged. If it is legitimate, we are grieved because we have not measured up to our own expectations, let alone the expectations of others. Following are four ways to best respond to criticism:

12 What are four steps in handling criticism?

1. *Make the criticism a matter of prayer.* No matter how hurtful criticism may be, let me urge you to pray about it. An element of truth often resides in the most outlandish criticism. In prayer, ask God if He is trying to tell you something through this criticism. Ask Him to purify your spirit and remind you that He loves the one who unfairly criticized you just as much as He loves you.

2. *Consider the source.* Although God can use anyone to correct us, He generally speaks through trustworthy people. Therefore, I give considerable more weight to criticism when it comes from a peer or a mature believer.

3. *Carefully weigh the criticism, separating what is valid from what is not.* Even the most sincere person is capable of injecting his or her personal feelings into a situation. For that reason, I am careful not to accept everything at face value. On occasion, I have found it beneficial to discuss the criticism with a third person to get a more objective view.

4. *With God's help, make any needed corrections.* It is rarely easy to admit we are wrong, especially if it means reversing a decision or changing a policy. However, it is absolutely mandatory. "He who heeds discipline shows the way to life, but whoever ignores correction leads others astray" (Proverbs 10:17).

More than half of those who enter the ministry will quit their calling. And having dropped out, they will live the rest of their lives with a haunting sense of failure. Although the risks are high, you do not need to be a casualty. Determine now that you will "watch your life and doctrine closely. Persevere in them, because if you do, you will save both yourself and your hearers" (1 Timothy 4:16).

Peter writes:

Be shepherds of God's flock that is under your care, serving as overseers—not because you must, but because you are willing, as God wants you to be; not greedy for money, but eager to serve; not lording it over those entrusted to you, but being examples to the flock. And when the Chief Shepherd appears, you will receive the crown of glory that will never fade away. (1 Peter 5:2–4)

13 What will God give you if you remain faithful to Him and your calling?

If you faithfully guard your relationship with Jesus, your heart, and your spirit, the last years of your ministry will be your best. Years of experience will give you wisdom; age and maturity will give your ministry depth; and a lifetime of selfless service will conform you to the image of Jesus. When you come to the end of your life, may you say with Paul, "I have fought the good fight, I have finished the race, I have kept the faith. Now there is in store for me the crown of righteousness, which the Lord, the righteous Judge, will award to me on that day—and not only to me, but also to all who have longed for his appearing" (2 Timothy 4:7–8).

Test Yourself

Circle the letter of the ***best*** answer.

1. To balance time in the "kitchen," a pastor must spend time in
a) fellowship with others.
b) nature.
c) study.
d) silence.

2. Keeping a journal can help a pastor
a) reflect on daily events.
b) work through problems.
c) respond to God's voice.
d) do all of the above.

3. As stated in this chapter, food for our souls comes from
a) fasting.
b) Bible study.
c) Communion.
d) Sabbath rest.

4. Hard times test perseverance, but success tests
a) character.
b) patience.
c) vision.
d) commitment.

5. Pastors should measure their success by
a) personal goals.
b) the success of others.
c) their relationship with Jesus.
d) past experience.

6. Pastors must guard their hearts against success, comparison, and
a) greed.
b) education.
c) laziness.
d) loneliness.

7. If pastors do not guard their hearts, disappointments may lead to
a) discipline.
b) bitterness.
c) rejection.
d) selfishness.

8. An important way for us to guard our spirits is to
a) separate ourselves from the world.
b) attend weekly church services.
c) take Communion.
d) forgive offenses.

9. When a friend needs correction, we should
a) not criticize at all.
b) speak in love.
c) do it in a group.
d) boldly speak whatever is true.

10. We should respond to criticism by
a) acting as though we never heard it.
b) assuming that it is true and repenting.
c) humbly responding to whatever is true.
d) rebuking the person who criticizes us.

Responses to Interactive Questions
Chapter 14

Some of these responses may include information that is supplemental to the IST. These questions are intended to produce reflective thinking beyond the course content and your responses may vary from these examples.

1   What three areas must you guard to maintain your inner strength?

(1) Your faith, or your relationship with Jesus, (2) your heart, and (3) your spirit

2   How is a relationship with Jesus like any other relationship?

It requires communication, time, and attention.

3   Explain the value of silence during times of prayer.

It allows listening, the opportunity to hear the Lord communicate, and indicates closeness and strength.

4   How can journaling benefit a person's relationship with the Lord?

Journaling—putting thoughts on paper—forces people to reflect, deepening their understanding and allowing what is on the inside to be produced on the outside.

5   What is the key to enjoying God's presence daily?

Discipline to regularly spend time in the Word and in prayer

6   Give the biblical meaning of *heart*.

The Scriptures describe the heart as who a person really is; it is the source of emotions, thoughts, and desires and motivates life.

7   Do you use your power to serve or to be served?

Answers may vary.

8   How do you determine your value?

Answers may vary.

9   How should pastors respond to those who oppose them?

Go to God in prayer, and let Him change your reactions and thoughts first.

10 Who is hurt the most when a person does not forgive?

The one who holds on to unforgiveness

11 Explain the difference between the two types of criticism.

Motivated by love, constructive criticism heals and promotes change. Motivated by selfish desires, hurtful criticism wounds and leads to destruction.

12 What are four steps in handling criticism?

(1) Pray about it; (2) consider the source; (3) carefully weigh the criticism; and (4) make needed corrections.

13 What will God give you if you remain faithful to Him and your calling?

You will see depth in your ministry as you mature and the good fruit of your years of service.

Lessons from the Pastorate

It is said that experience is the best teacher. Unfortunately, acquiring wisdom usually means making mistakes that can be both costly and painful in the ministry. Is there a better way to glean the benefits of experience without the high cost of our own errors?

This is possible only if we have a teachable spirit and are willing to learn from those who have gone before us. Even then, it will not be easy, for without the pain of a difficult situation, the full impact of an experience may be lost to us. Still, the principles gleaned from others' experiences may lodge in our minds, available whenever needed.

With this in mind, let me invite you to reminisce with me and learn from the many life-shaping experiences of my years in pastoral ministry. Each experience taught me principles that have served me well through the years. Perhaps the three most important principles I can convey to you are to (1) ask God for wisdom, (2) take responsibility for your mistakes, and (3) seek to serve. I share these in the hope that you too may profit from the lessons God has taught me.

Lesson 15.1   Ask God for Wisdom

Objective

15.1.1 Apply the wisdom principle.

Lesson 15.2   Take Responsibility for Your Mistakes

Objective

15.2.1 Summarize and apply four principles related to mistakes in ministry.

Lesson 15.3   Seek to Serve

Objective

15.3.1 Describe the pastor's purpose as a servant.

15.1.1
OBJECTIVE
Apply the wisdom principle.

1 What things offend church members today?

2 Name three ways the author was tempted to respond to complaints.

3 In your own words, summarize the prayer in 1 Kings 3:7, 9.

4 A pastor's ignorance is God's opportunity to do what?

5 How does Proverbs 3:5–6 relate to wisdom?

Ask God for Wisdom

God's Wisdom Brings Humility and Restoration

I was only twenty years old when the Assembly of God church in Holly, Colorado, called me to be their pastor. I was young and inexperienced, mostly ignorant of what it took to be a pastor. The congregation was small—with fewer than twenty members—and troubled. They had gone through five pastors and suffered two painful splits in the three years immediately preceding my appointment. Nevertheless, I entered this pastorate with high expectations.

Unfortunately, nothing in my experience had prepared me for the task at hand. In less than six months, I managed to offend almost every member of our small congregation. A wiser, more experienced pastor may have seen the pitfalls ahead; but I was neither wise nor experienced, so I was blindsided. How was I to know that serving coffee and doughnuts to the adult class meeting in the fellowship hall would offend the congregation? Or how could I have known that allowing visitors to transgress the unspoken dress code would create a firestorm or that my mustache would create division in the church? Soon an ugly undercurrent of resentment permeated the congregation, making every service a struggle.

Most of the complaints seemed petty to me, and I was tempted to ignore them. At other times, I wanted to defend myself and rally support for my position. Still, something restrained me, and I held my peace.

When the problems persisted, I knew something had to be done, but what? I considered resigning but could not get a release in my spirit to do so. In desperation, I turned to the Lord. Day after day, I lay flat on my face before Him and prayed the prayer of Solomon: "O Lord my God, . . . I am only a little child and do not know how to carry out my duties. . . . So give your servant a discerning heart to govern your people and to distinguish between right and wrong" (1 Kings 3:7, 9).

During those prayer times, I came to realize two things: (1) I had no wisdom to draw on apart from God's. Left to my own devices, I would find a way to mess things up. (2) My ignorance was God's opportunity. If I would but ask, God would grant me wisdom for the situation. James 1:5 became my anchor: "If any of you lacks wisdom, he should ask God, who gives generously to all without finding fault, and it will be given to him."

Slowly, a plan of action began to form in my mind. At first, it was just an impression, hardly more than a thought. But as I prayed and waited before the Lord, it continued to grow to fruition. God wanted me to have a service for men only on a Sunday evening—a service of healing and restoration.

I wish I could tell you that I immediately surrendered to the Lord's direction, but I cannot. The truth is, I argued with Him. Sure, I had made some mistakes, but so had the church members. Why should I be the one to apologize? Considering my youth and inexperience, should they not have been more understanding and supportive? My wife and I were hurting too, so why did the responsibility for rectifying the situation fall only on my shoulders?

Gently, the Holy Spirit turned my thoughts inward, and I found myself praying with David, "Search me, O God, and know my heart; test me and know my anxious thoughts. See if there is any offensive way in me, and lead me in the way everlasting" (Psalm 139:23–24). Now, my pastoral failings came into clear focus. With painful clarity, I saw how my actions had contributed to the alienation within the body. It seemed God allowed me to see myself as others saw me: impatient, brash, and insensitive. In God's presence, I was overwhelmed with remorse, with a desire to make things right. I would apologize to each of the men publicly, and I would seek their forgiveness. I would wash each man's feet as a demonstration of my sincere desire to serve him and his family.

Thus, one Sunday evening before the service, I removed the altar bench from the front of the sanctuary and replaced it with two rows of metal folding chairs, facing each other. I placed the Communion table at right angles to the chairs, creating a U-shaped arrangement. Then I stood behind the table, head bowed in prayer, waiting.

After a time, seven or eight men filed in and walked to the front. Once they were seated, I offered a prayer and then instructed the men to remove their shoes and socks and roll up their pant legs. Although they muttered under their breath, in time they all complied.

6   What did the author confess and pledge?

Reaching under the Communion table, I pulled out a basin of water and a towel. Making my way to the first man, I knelt before him, saying, "I know that I have not been a good pastor to you or to your family. I have let you down. I have disappointed you. I hope you can find it in your heart to believe me when I tell you that I failed you out of ignorance and inexperience, never maliciously. With God as my judge, I never intended to hurt you or your family. That does not excuse my shortcomings, but I hope it does put them into perspective. I have already asked God to forgive me, and now I would like to ask for your forgiveness as well." Without waiting for the man to reply, I continued, "With your permission, I would like to wash your feet as a demonstration of my sincere desire to serve you and your family in all ways, great or small." I then moved from man to man until I had confessed my pastoral failings to each one. I washed their feet, pledging to serve them and their families selflessly.

A miracle took place in that room. While I washed feet, Jesus cleansed hearts, removing all the hurt and bitterness. Although these men rarely showed emotions, their throats grew tight and their eyes glistened with unshed tears. One by one, they extended their forgiveness and agreed to give me another chance.

My obedience to God's direction facilitated a service in which healing and reconciliation occurred. In the weeks and months that followed, the Lord did a marvelous work: A number of people were saved and added to the church. Weekly attendance grew to more than eighty worshippers. Best of all, the petty complaints and squabbles all but disappeared. Each year, when the congregation held their annual pastoral election, my wife and I were reelected by a unanimous vote—something unheard of until then.

God's Wisdom Gives Clear Direction

To be honest, I approached my first annual business meeting at the Holly, Colorado, church with more than a little trepidation. In reviewing the minutes of past meetings, I learned that a thinly veiled spirit of animosity had been at work. In addition, I had heard rumors of heated arguments in past meetings—and some sources suggested that people had even come to blows. Since that sort of trouble was the last thing I wanted to see happen at this business meeting, I sought the Lord's guidance. Once more, He gave me wisdom for the situation.

Two things proved key in creating the right spirit at the annual business meeting. First, we opened the meeting with Communion. This gave each participant the opportunity to prepare his or her life and heart to receive the emblems (1 Corinthians 11:27–29) and to prepare for the business to come. I reasoned that only the most hardhearted could leave the Lord's Supper with animosity in his or her heart.

7 How could rules of order benefit your church's business meetings?

Second, I placed a speaker's podium at the front of the church. Following Communion, I outlined the rules of order and informed the church members that they would need to be recognized by the chairperson (me as pastor) before speaking. I also instructed them to come to the podium before addressing the body.

The Communion service prepared the church body spiritually, while the rules of order provided the kind of structure that facilitates business in an orderly manner. Together, the Communion and rules or order quelled the outbursts of hostility that had characterized past meetings.

8 What is the wisdom principle?

Obviously, I am not suggesting that every church problem can be solved with a foot-washing service. Nor am I proposing that you conduct your church business meetings exactly the way I did as a young pastor. Rather, both incidents are examples of a far more important principle—the wisdom principle. If we seek God's direction before we act, He will grant us wisdom. He will show us what to do in any and every situation.

15.2.1
OBJECTIVE
Summarize and apply four principles related to mistakes in ministry.

Take Responsibility for Your Mistakes

Through the foot-washing service described in Lesson 15.1, I learned not only to ask God for wisdom but also to take responsibility for my mistakes. Washing the men's feet would have had little effect had I not been willing to identify and own my pastoral failures. Had I tried to excuse my behavior or somehow justify my mistakes, I would have only further alienated the people I was trying to reach.

Admit Mistakes and Accept the Consequences

You might assume that from my experiences in Holly, Colorado, I learned once and for all to seek God's wisdom and direction before making a major decision. Yet that was not the case.

For example, at Christian Chapel, in Oklahoma, my pride again led me astray. I relied on my own understanding rather than godly counsel. Disregarding my wife's concerns and the church board's advice, I invited a close friend to serve on my pastoral staff. I should have known better—a number of warning signals indicated danger—but I had my heart set on it.

In retrospect, I can see that the working relationship was doomed from the start. This was my first experience with a staff pastor, and I was poorly prepared. The fact that my associate pastor was a close friend only made things more difficult. When I should have been giving clear pastoral direction, I instead made friendly suggestions. To further complicate matters, this pastor friend saw himself as a primary leader—more of a co-pastor than an associate. In addition, unresolved issues loomed over his marriage and personal life. I knew much of this from the beginning, but I was sure I could handle it.

9 Why was the author's hiring his friend a mistake?

Although we both tried to make things work, it soon proved to be an unworkable arrangement. After ten months, I knew I had made a mistake and something had to change. Reluctantly, I decided to ask for his resignation. It was perhaps the most difficult decision of my life.

Soon afterward, I invited him into my office, and with a sense of despair, I informed him of my decision. I tried to make it as painless as possible—the church board had agreed to a generous severance package, including four months' pay, a love offering from the congregation, and a reception in his honor. But such a hurtful thing cannot be done painlessly. All he heard was my rejection, and for the next twenty minutes, he vented his hurt and frustration.

I just listened, saying nothing, without attempting to defend myself or justify my decision. I had already explained my reasons, and there was nothing more I could do. No matter what I might say, he would still misunderstand and blame me.

When he left my office, I sat at my desk a long time and wept silently. To fully understand my failure and pain, you must remember that this man was a close friend. I was not simply terminating a staff member; I was asking a dear friend to resign. It felt similar to a divorce. We had been friends for ten years, and I knew this might well mean the end of our friendship. I did not want our friendship to end; I just recognized that painful possibility.

The days that followed resembled those experienced by a grieving family when a loved one dies. I did my duties by rote, fulfilled my obligations, and completed my tasks, but it felt like I was sleepwalking. And the hurt never went away.

Focus on the Future, Not the Past

I blamed myself for the mistake of hiring my friend in the first place. *If only* I had heeded the reservations of the church board. *If only* I had sought the counsel of my spiritual mentor. *If only* I had listened to my wife's concerns. But no, I had to do it my way, and now look what I had done: I had not only lost a friend but had also shamed him, wounding his spirit and causing my congregation much pain. The unspeakable grief deep inside me was terrible, more real than any sorrow I had ever experienced.

The congregation was hurt and confused. They loved us both, yet as a natural consequence of the situation, they were forced to choose sides. They observed our public politeness to each other but could not help but compare it to the comfortable camaraderie we had initially exhibited. Our pain and brokenness became theirs, and a somberness settled over our fellowship.

Because my friend's resignation was not effective for three weeks, he continued to come into the office almost daily, although he had little reason to do so. After the first day, there were no more outbursts but just an unnatural politeness. We spoke to each other carefully lest we inflict more hurt, and our guardedness was more painful than anything we might have said. He felt betrayed and ashamed. I felt guilty. We made small talk and tried to pretend everything was all right, but we could not forget the terrible thing that had happened, something from which our friendship might never recover.

Those three weeks were the longest of my life; it seemed they would never end. Finally, the reception was over, and he moved out of the office. Still, my grief remained. Depression made me lethargic, fed my self-doubt, and haunted me with painful questions. Had my friend been right in his criticism? That first morning, he had called me insecure, two-faced, jealous, and incapable of an honest relationship. Could all of that be true? Perhaps I was not capable of serving as the senior pastor of a church with multiple staff. Maybe it was all my fault. *If only* I could go back and do it all again.

10 Contrast *if only* with *next time*.

My painful thoughts triggered a memory of something I had heard long before. I recalled hearing a noted psychologist say that the two saddest words in the human vocabulary are *if only*. He explained that many people are trapped in their failures and spend a lifetime saying, "If only." *If only* I had tried harder. *If only* I had been a better parent. *If only* I hadn't been unfaithful. To avoid this kind of bondage, he suggested replacing the phrase *if only* with the phrase *next time*. *Next time* I will use better judgment. *Next time* I will be a better parent, a better spouse. *Next time* I will try harder.

If only focuses on past failures and sentences us to a lifetime of regret. *Next time* turns our attention to the future and inspires us to try again.

With determination, I decided to face the future. I decided that I would not live the rest of my life imprisoned by my failure. Certainly, I would learn from it, and I would do my best never to make the same mistakes again. But nothing could be gained by continually berating myself.

Learn from Failure

11   How can failure be a friend instead of an enemy?

Focusing on the future reminded me of the advice T. J. Watson, the founder of IBM, once gave a struggling writer:

> You're making a common mistake. You're thinking of failure as the enemy of success. But it isn't that at all. Failure is a teacher—a harsh one, perhaps, but the best. You say you have a desk full of rejected manuscripts? That's great! Every one of those manuscripts was rejected for a reason. Have you pulled them to pieces looking for that reason? That's what I have to do when an idea backfires or a sales program fails. You've got to put failure to work for you. (Gordon 1974, 73)

Watson said that failure is not an enemy but a teacher. What a thought! I could learn from my failure; I did not need to let it destroy me. The awful, unrelenting pain could become an ally, a friend to teach me. Yes, failure was a harsh teacher, but the harshness sensitized me to lessons I might have never learned otherwise.

12   What must we do to learn from failure?

With this in mind, I embraced and made peace with my pain. It did not go away immediately, or even for a long time afterward. Yet now it had a purpose, making it somehow more bearable. I resolved that I would not waste that failure. It had cost me dearly, and I was determined to learn everything I could from it.

Carefully, I examined the entire episode. Step-by-step, I reviewed it, beginning with the initial idea and working toward its tragic end. I cataloged my mistakes, searching for faulty logic, improper motives, inaccurate conclusions, and even relational failures. And I found them where I never thought they would be. This too was painful, for I saw myself more clearly than ever before. Yet I was strengthened in knowing that God was redeeming my mistakes. He would use each painful lesson to make me a more effective pastor and a more compassionate person.

Confess Mistakes Publicly and Ask for Forgiveness

One final thing remained, and I had to choose what to do about it. My congregation was still troubled, unanswered questions lingered, and my credibility was suspect. After much prayer, I decided to confess my failures publicly to the congregation. I would take responsibility for my mistakes and seek the forgiveness of those I had wronged.

13   How should pastors apologize to their congregations?

I stood before our congregation with fear and trembling. A host of questions flooded my mind: Would the people understand what I was trying to do, or would they see my confession as self-serving? Would they see my deep regret as genuine repentance or simply personal weakness? Would they ever be able to trust my judgment again? Would they follow my leadership in the future?

Pushing those thoughts aside, I addressed my church family. After acknowledging their grief and confusion, I apologized for having placed them in this position. I then took full responsibility for the entire situation and detailed my mistakes:

1. I disregarded my wife's counsel.
2. I ignored the official board's reservations.
3. I refused to consult with my spiritual mentor because I knew he would advise me against moving forward with my plans.
4. I abdicated my pastoral responsibility by giving friendly suggestions rather than providing clear pastoral leadership to the staff.
5. I blatantly ignored the fact that my friend was also a primary leader rather than a staff pastor.

I concluded by saying,

I acknowledge my sinful mistakes, and I humbly ask for your forgiveness. It was not a mistake to ask my friend to resign, but it was a mistake to have called him to serve on our staff in the first place. By doing so, I caused him and his family deep distress and no little harm. My irresponsible action has also caused this congregation to suffer deeply, not to mention the sorrow I have brought upon my own family. Regrettably, I cannot change the past. But with God's help, I can pledge to you that I will never make the same mistakes again.

God used that service to restore my credibility and to heal our wounded congregation. Thankfully, we did not lose a single family as a result of my irresponsible actions. In my ten more years as their senior pastor, God blessed the church in every way. We purchased property and built a large facility. Attendance grew significantly, and our missions giving increased.

14 Why do people lose confidence in leaders who do not recognize their mistakes?

As I think about the whole situation now, more than twenty-five years later, I realize that as painful as it was, it was an invaluable learning experience. God did not cause that failure, nor did He will it—that was completely my own doing. But He did use it. Undoubtedly, the most valuable lesson He taught me from the experience was the importance of taking responsibility for my mistakes. People will forgive us of almost any mistake, as long as they know we understand where we erred and are willing to take responsibility for our actions. What they cannot forgive is our denial and self-justifying explanations or excuses. To them, if we do not know where we have gone wrong, it will be only a matter of time until we make the same type of mistake again.

15.3.1
OBJECTIVE
Describe the pastor's purpose as a servant.

Seek to Serve

The foot-washing service in Holly, Colorado, has one final lesson to teach. In fact, it may be the most important lesson of all—at least it was for me. It completely changed my understanding of ministry and my identity as a minister.

When I took a basin of water and a towel and humbled myself, something changed inside me. Until then, I thought of ministers, myself included, as "sanctified executives." That is, we were the "big shots," the ones directing the action. In my misguided thinking, the church existed to help pastors achieve their goals.

Such an idea had not come from my childhood pastor, for he was one of the humblest people I knew. Nor had it come from Jesus, for His entire life and ministry modeled selfless service. Certainly my view had not arisen from the

Scriptures, for they teach us to be "not greedy for money, but eager to serve; not lording it over those entrusted to [us], but being examples to the flock" (1 Peter 5:2–3).

15 In Mark 10:35–40, where do you think James and John's idea of thrones originated?

Most likely my model for ministry was my own creation, a patchwork quilt sewn together out of my insecurities, pride, and selfish ambition. Little wonder that I had failed my flock. I was not thinking about *them*; I was thinking about *me*. I was not concerned with their needs; I was concerned only with my own. In Jesus' words, I was not a shepherd but a hired hand (John 10:12–13).

I realized the painful truth that Sunday evening as I washed the callused feet of the men in my congregation. I had begun the evening service thinking they were the problem, only to discover that I was wrong: I was the problem. God was changing my heart.

After the last man left, I sat for a long time in the empty sanctuary, reflecting on the incredible transformation the Lord had done. I felt so different. The "sanctified executive" was gone, and in his place was a servant. The spiritual dictator making demands and giving directions was gone; in his place was a shepherd who truly cared for the sheep. I opened my journal and wrote,

> *Lord,*
> *Forgive me for all the times I act like a big shot administrator;*
> *like some kind of spiritual foreman,*
> *like a divinely appointed dictator.*
> *Every time I do, people get turned off—big time!*
> *My aggressive, domineering nature threatens them*
> *and they become defensive.*
> *Communication channels get clogged*
> *and Your message gets lost in the ego battles that ensue.*
> *Help me to trade my big stick for a basin of water and a towel.*
> *Free me from my need to be boss.*
> *Make me content to be a servant in Your name. Amen.*

Leaving the church, I turned toward home invigorated. I was realistic enough to expect challenges ahead, but I was confident that God's grace would see me through. In the weeks and months that followed, two Scripture passages proved especially helpful to me in maintaining the right attitude toward ministry:

16 What lesson does John 13:12–17 teach?

When he had finished washing their feet, he put on his clothes and returned to his place. "Do you understand what I have done for you?" he asked them. "You call me 'Teacher' and 'Lord,' and rightly so, for that is what I am. Now that I, your Lord and Teacher, have washed your feet, you also should wash one another's feet. I have set you an example that you should do as I have done for you. I tell you the truth, no servant is greater than his master, nor is a messenger greater than the one who sent him. Now that you know these things, you will be blessed if you do them." (John 13:12–17)

17 Summarize the lesson of Philippians 2:3–8.

Do nothing out of selfish ambition or vain conceit, but in humility consider others better than yourselves. Each of you should look not only to your own interests, but also to the interests of others. Your attitude should be the same as that of Christ Jesus: Who, being in very nature God, did not consider equality with God something to be grasped, but made himself nothing, taking the very nature of a servant, being made in human likeness. And being found in appearance as a man, he humbled himself and became obedient to death—even death on a cross! (Philippians 2:3–8)

Since I now see myself as a servant, no task is too low for me. I find joy in serving whatever the task—whether preaching or washing someone's feet. I know that whatever I do and for whomever I do it, I do it for Christ (Matthew 25:40).

Experience is truly the best teacher. I pray that you can learn from the experiences God has given not only to me but also to others who have gone before you. In particular, I hope you can grasp the three essential lessons we studied in this chapter:

1. *Ask God for wisdom.* We are all ignorant apart from the wisdom the Lord gives. However, our ignorance is God's opportunity. To everyone who asks, God promises to give a generous portion of His wisdom (James 1:5).

2. *Take responsibility for your mistakes.* People will forgive almost any of our mistakes if they are assured that we understand the error and take responsibility for our actions. Then, once you have dealt with your mistakes, move on. Forget your errors, but remember the lessons they taught you.

3. *Seek to serve.* People become great in God's eyes only through humble service. Those who serve faithfully will one day hear Him say, "Well done, good and faithful servant! You have been faithful with a few things; I will put you in charge of many things. Come and share your master's happiness!" (Matthew 25:21).

Test Yourself

Circle the letter of the *best* answer.

1. The key to handling complaints is
a) listening to people.
b) asking people to be positive.
c) focusing on the future.
d) teaching people not to complain.

2. Which book tells us to ask God for wisdom?
a) Mark
b) John
c) Romans
d) James

3. Pastors can best prepare people for business meetings by
a) fellowshipping with them at meals.
b) leading them into God's presence.
c) preaching sermons about submission.
d) telling them what they should vote for.

4. To keep a business meeting orderly,
a) allow only elders to speak.
b) assume that people will be polite.
c) print a schedule for the meeting.
d) establish some rules of order.

5. When pastors make mistakes, they should first
a) forgive the people they have hurt.
b) explain their reasons for the offense.
c) admit that they are at fault.
d) verbally review their actions.

6. When you consider your mistakes, what phrase should replace *if only?*
a) I'm sorry.
b) Next time
c) Already
d) I wish.

7. Failure is a harsh but excellent
a) teacher.
b) enemy.
c) police officer.
d) student.

8. If pastors admit mistakes in front of their congregations, their members will most likely
a) see them as weak leaders.
b) lose confidence in them.
c) ask them to resign.
d) forgive and accept them.

9. Pastors are best compared with
a) owners.
b) managers.
c) servants.
d) customers.

10. Christian leaders should follow the humble example of
a) Abraham.
b) Jesus.
c) Peter.
d) Paul.

Responses to Interactive Questions
Chapter 15

Some of these responses may include information that is supplemental to the IST. These questions are intended to produce reflective thinking beyond the course content and your responses may vary from these examples.

1 What things offend church members today?

Answers will vary.

2 Name three ways the author was tempted to respond to complaints.

He was tempted to (1) ignore the complaints, (2) defend himself and look for support, or (3) resign.

3 In your own words, summarize the prayer in 1 Kings 3:7, 9.

Answers will vary.

4 A pastor's ignorance is God's opportunity to do what?

To give wisdom

5 How does Proverbs 3:5–6 relate to wisdom?

It teaches us to depend on the Lord rather than our own ability to reason and control. Then God will guide our lives.

6 What did the author confess and pledge?

He confessed to failing as a pastor and pledged to serve the families of the church.

7 How could rules of order benefit your church's business meetings?

Answers will vary but should mention control, organization, and order.

8 What is the wisdom principle?

If we seek God's direction before we act, He will give us wisdom.

9 Why was the author's hiring his friend a mistake?

He ignored godly counsel, choosing to satisfy his own pride. He ignored warning signs such as these: (1) Their friendship caused the author to be less of an authority figure. (2) His friend was a primary leader, not suited to be a staff pastor. (3) His friend had personal problems that affected his ministry.

10 Contrast *if only* with *next time*.

If only concentrates on the past; *next time* focuses on the future. *If only* emphasizes our failures and regrets; *next time* anticipates our successes and inspirations.

11 How can failure be a friend instead of an enemy?

Failure can teach us many lessons that will prepare us for future challenges.

12 What must we do to learn from failure?

We must accept it as a teacher, make peace with our pain, review our mistakes, and recognize that failure has a purpose.

13 How should pastors apologize to their congregations?

Answers will vary but should include references to honesty, directness, humility, and sincerity.

14 Why do people lose confidence in leaders who do not recognize their mistakes?

They have less reason to believe the leader will behave differently or make better decisions in the future.

15 In Mark 10:35–40, where do you think James and John's idea of thrones originated?

From their worldly awareness and experiences, not from Jesus

16 What lesson does John 13:12–17 teach?

Answers will vary.

17 Summarize the lesson of Philippians 2:3–8.

Answers will vary.

UNIT PROGRESS EVALUATION 4 AND FINAL EXAMINATION

You have now concluded all of the work in this independent-study textbook. Review the lessons in this unit carefully, and then answer the questions in the last unit progress evaluation (UPE). When you have completed the UPE, check your answers with the answer key provided in Essential Course Materials at the back of this IST. Review any items you may have answered incorrectly. Review for the final examination by studying the course objectives, lesson objectives, self-tests, and UPEs. Review any lesson content necessary to refresh your memory. If you review carefully and are able to fulfill the objectives, you should have no difficulty passing the closed-book final examination.

Taking the Final Examination

1. **All final exams must be taken closed book.** You are not allowed to use any materials or outside help while taking a final exam. You will take the final examination online at www.globaluniversity.edu. If the online option is not available to you, you may request a printed final exam. If you did not request a printed final exam when you ordered your course, you must submit this request a few weeks before you are ready to take the exam. The Request for a Printed Final Examination is in the Forms section of Essential Course Materials at the back of this IST.

2. Review for the final examination in the same manner in which you prepared for the UPEs. Refer to the form Checklist of Study Methods in the front part of the IST for further helpful review hints.

3. After you complete and submit the online final examination, the results will be immediately available to you. Your final course grade report will be e-mailed to your Global University student e-mail account after your Service Learning Requirement (SLR) report has been processed.

4. If you complete the exam in printed form, you will send your final examination, your answer sheets, and your SLR report to Berean School of the Bible for grading. Your final course grade report will be sent to your GU student e-mail account. If you do not have access to the Internet, your grade will be sent to your mailing address.

 Glossary

		Chapter
board members	— lay leaders, including elders and deacons, who work with the pastor to make policies and decisions that govern and guide the church	11
burnout	— lack of energy, emotional strength, or motivation as a result of working too hard or too much	13
closed Communion	— celebration of the Lord's Supper in which only members of a certain church are welcome to participate	10
Communion	— the celebration and proclamation of the Lord's death through partaking of bread and grape juice, usually as a group of believers; sometimes call the Lord's Supper	10
elders and/or deacons	— lay leaders who work with the pastor to serve a local church	11
historical context	— the background, setting, and circumstances related to a biblical passage, including information about the author, date, first readers, and purpose for writing	2
lay leaders	— generally called board members, elders, deacons, or trustees. Some churches may use other terms such as advisory board, church council, and so forth.	11
literary context	— the written setting that surrounds a biblical passage, including the subdivision, section of a book, the book itself, and the entire Bible	2
open Communion	— celebration of the Lord's Supper in which all believers are welcome to participate	10
open-door policy	— a pastor's practice of welcoming the staff to walk into the office and talk with him or her anytime a need arises; a principle of allowing the staff to have access to the senior pastor at any time	12
ordinance	— a religious rite or ceremony; a sacred practice of the church	10
prayer journal	— a written account of requests and answers to prayer	2
presumption	— a foolish or proud action or attitude not based on facts, truth, sound counsel, Scripture, or hearing from God	7
rhythm	— pace, cadence; a balance of work, rest, and worship that enables a person to live a fruitful, joyful life	13
spiritual disciplines	— practices, such as prayer, fasting, Bible study, and meditation, that become habits and a way of life for believers	2
staff	— the group of people in a church, whether paid or volunteer, who work with the pastor	12

		Chapter
vision	— the ability, whether natural or supernatural, to see things in the future and make provision for them	7
water baptism	— an ordinance of the church in which a believer publicly and outwardly shows an inward change; a rite symbolizing that a believer buries the old life with Christ when submerged and rises out of the water to live a new life united with Christ	10

 # Reference List

"A/G Ministers Report, 2003: Credentials, Marital, and Ministry Status by Gender." Revised 04/20/04. Office of the Statistician, General Council of the Assemblies of God. http://womeninministry.ag.org/resources/stats_agmin.pdf.

Annual Church Ministries Report (ACMR). Office of the General Secretary, General Council of the Assemblies of God. Springfield, MO: 2003.

Bergren, Wendy. 1982. *Mom Is Very Sick: Here's How to Help.* N.p.: privately printed. Distributed by Focus on the Family.

Bergstrom, Richard L. 1987. "Stunned by an Inside Job." *Leadership* 8, no. 1 (Winter).

Bicket, Zenas J. 1997. "Dealing with Questions on the Role of Women in Ministry." *Enrichment* (Spring): 80–84.

Britton, Janet. 1985. "Well, Janet Told Me . . ." *Moody* (January): 82–83.

Buechner, Frederick. 1977. *Telling the Truth: The Gospel as Tragedy, Comedy, and Fairy Tale.* San Francisco: Harper and Row Publishers.

———. 2000. "Wishful Thinking." In *Disciplines for The Inner Life*, Bob Benson and Michael W. Benson, 201. Deeper Life Press.

Exley, Richard. 2003. *Living in Harmony: Moving to a Better Place in Your Life.* Green Forest, AR: New Leaf Press.

"Female Ministers, 1977–2003." Revised 04/20/04. Office of the Statistician, General Council of the Assemblies of God. http://womeninministry.ag.org/resources/stats_femmin.pdf.

"Forum: Private Sins of Public Ministry." 1988. *Leadership* (Winter): 20.

Foster, Richard J. 1978. *The Celebration of Discipline.* San Francisco: Harper and Row.

———. 1985. *Money, Sex & Power.* San Francisco: Harper and Row Publishers.

Gill, Deborah M. 1997. "Called by God: What's a Woman to Do, and What Can We Do to Help Her?" *Enrichment* (Spring): 32–35.

———. 1995. "The Contemporary State of Women in Ministry in the Assemblies of God." *PNEUMA: The Journal of the Society for Pentecostal Studies* 17, no. 1 (Spring): 33–36.

Gill, Deborah M., and Barbara L. Cavaness. 2004. *God's Women: Then and Now.* Springfield, MO: Grace & Truth.

Gire, Ken. 1996. *Windows of the Soul.* Grand Rapids, MI: Zondervan Publishing House.

Goldberg, Alan D. 1987. "The Sabbath: Implications for Mental Health." *Counseling and Values* 31, no. 2 (April): 148–149.

Gordon, Arthur. 1974. *A Touch of Wonder.* Old Tappan, NJ: Fleming H. Revell Company.

Harris, Ralph W., ed. 1989. *Romans–Corinthians.* Vol. 6, *The Complete Biblical Library: The New Testament Study Bible.* Springfield, MO: World Library Press, Inc.

Horton, Stanley M. 2001. *Acts: A Logion Press Commentary.* Springfield, MO: Logion Press.

Hughes, R. Kent. 1991. *Disciplines of a Godly Man.* Wheaton, IL: Crossway Books.

Hybels, Bill. 2002. *Courageous Leadership*. Grand Rapids, MI: Zondervan Publishing House.

Hybels, Bill, and Lynne Hybels. 1995. *Rediscovering Church*. Grand Rapids, MI: Zondervan Publishing House.

Klein, William W., Craig L. Blomberg, and Robert L. Hubbard Jr. 1993. *Introduction to Biblical Interpretation*. Dallas: Word Publishing.

Kübler-Ross, Elisabeth. 1997. *On Death and Dying*. New York: Touchstone.

L'Engle, Madeleine. 1980. *Walking on Water*. Wheaton, IL: Harold Shaw Publishers.

Larsen, David L. 1992. *The Evangelism Mandate: Recovering the Centrality of Gospel Preaching*. Wheaton, IL: Crossway Books.

Larson, Bruce, and Keith Miller. 1977. *Living the Adventure*. Waco, TX: Word Book Publishers.

Lindbergh, Anne Morrow. 1981. "Praise Ye the Lord!" In *Dawnings: Finding God's Light in the Darkness*, ed. Phyllis Hobe. Waco, TX: Word Books Publisher.

Mace, David R. 1973. *Marriage as Vocation*. Quoted in Dorothy T. Samuel, *Fun and Games in Marriage*. Waco, TX: Word Book Publishers.

Maxwell, John C. 1993. *The Winning Attitude*. Nashville: Thomas Nelson Publishers.

McDill, Wayne V. 1999. *The Moment of Truth: A Guide to Effective Sermon Delivery*. Nashville: Broadman and Holman Publishers.

McGhee, Quentin, and G.D. Claunch. 2004. *Preach the Word*. Springfield, MO: Global University.

McKenna, David L. 1977. *The Jesus Model*. Waco, TX: Word Book Publishers.

Melville, Herman. 1998. *Moby Dick*. New York: Penguin Group.

Menzies, William W., and Stanley M. Horton. 1993. *Bible Doctrines*. Springfield, MO: Gospel Publishing House.

Menzies, William W., and Robert P. Menzies. 2000. *Spirit and Power*. Grand Rapids, MI: Zondervan Publishing House.

Merrill, Dean. 1985. *Clergy Couples in Crisis*. Waco, TX: Word, Inc.; Carol Stream, IL: Christianity Today, Inc.

Minutes of the 51st Session of the General Council of the Assemblies of God with Revised Constitution and Bylaws. Springfield, MO: Gospel Publishing House, 2005.

Nouwen, Henri. 1979. *The Wounded Healer*. New York: Random House, Inc.

O'Connor, Elizabeth. 1982. *Letters to Scattered Pilgrims*. New York: HarperCollins.

Oden, Thomas C. 1983. *Pastoral Theology*. New York: Harper and Row Publishers, Inc.

Pearlman, Myer. 1950. *The Minister's Service Book*. Springfield, MO: Gospel Publishing House.

Pettry, Ernest. 1984. *Preaching and Teaching*. Springfield, MO: Global University.

Robbins, Paul D. 1984. "Must Men Be Friendless?" *Leadership* (Fall): 27.

"The Role of Women in Ministry." Official Assemblies of God Position Paper. http://ag.org/top/Beliefs/Position_Papers/pp_4191_women_ministry.cfm.

Spurgeon, Charles H. 1963. *The Soul Winner*. Grand Rapids, MI: Wm. B. Eerdmans Publishing Co.

Stanphill, Ira F. 1946. "Room at the Cross." Singspiration Music/ASCAP.

Wallis, Arthur. 1971. *God's Chosen Fast*. Fort Washington, PA: Christian Literature Crusade.

Whitney, Donald S. 2000. "The Almost Inevitable Ruin of Every Minister . . . and How to Avoid It." The Center for Biblical Spirituality. http://www.spiritualdisciplines.org/ruin.html.

Wilkerson, David. 1967. *I'm Not Mad at God*. Minneapolis: Bethany Fellowship, Inc.

Willard, Dallas. 1988. *The Spirit of the Disciplines*. San Francisco: Harper and Row.

Wood, Robert. 1978. *A Thirty-Day Experiment in Prayer*. Nashville: The Upper Room.

Essential Course Materials

CONTENTS

CHECKLIST OF MATERIALS TO BE SUBMITTED TO BEREAN SCHOOL OF THE BIBLE

at Global University; 1211 South Glenstone Avenue; Springfield, Missouri, 65804; USA:

- ❑ Service Learning Requirement Report (required)
- ❑ Round-Tripper Forms (as needed)
- ❑ Request for a Printed Final Examination (if needed)

Service Learning Requirement Assignment

BEREAN SCHOOL OF THE BIBLE

SLR INSTRUCTIONS

This Service Learning Requirement (SLR) assignment requires you to apply something you have learned from this course in a ministry activity. Although this assignment does not receive a grade, it is required. You will not receive credit for this course until you submit the satisfactorily completed SLR Report Form. This form will not be returned to you.

Seriously consider how you can design and complete a meaningful ministry* activity as an investment in preparing to fulfill God's calling on your life. If you are already involved in active ministry, plan how you can incorporate and apply something from this course in your ongoing ministry activity. Whether or not full-time ministry is your goal, this assignment is required and designed to bring personal enrichment to all students. Ask the Holy Spirit to guide your planning and completion of this ministry exercise.

> * Meaningful ministry is defined as an act whereby you give of yourself in such a way as to meet the needs of another or to enhance the well-being of another (or others) in a way that exalts Christ and His kingdom.

You will complete the SLR by following these instructions:

1. Complete a ministry activity of your choice that you develop according to the following criteria:

    a. Your ministry activity must occur during your enrollment in this course. Do not report on activities or experiences in which you were involved prior to enrolling in this course.

    b. Your ministry activity must apply something you learned in this course, or it must incorporate something from this course's content in some way. Provide chapter, lesson, or page number(s) from the independent-study textbook on which the activity is based.

    c. Your ministry activity must include interacting with at least one other person. You may choose to interact with an individual or a group.

    d. The activity you complete must represent meaningful ministry*. You may develop your own ministry activity or choose from the list of suggestions provided in these instructions.

    e. Consider a ministry activity outside your comfort zone such as sharing the message of salvation with unbelievers or offering loving assistance to someone you do not know well.

2. Then fill out the SLR Report Form following these instructions OR online by accessing the online course. Students who will take the final exam online are encouraged to complete the online report form.

3. Sincere reflection is a key ingredient in valid ministry and especially in the growth and development of your ministry knowledge and effectiveness.

4. Global University faculty will evaluate your report. Although the SLR does not receive a grade, it must be completed to the faculty's satisfaction before a final grade for the course is released. The faculty may require you to resubmit an SLR Report Form for several reasons, including an incomplete form, apparent insincerity, failing to interact with others, and failure to incorporate course content.

Do NOT submit your SLR notes, essays, or other documents; only submit your completed SLR Report Form. No prior approval is needed as long as the activity fulfills the criteria from number one above.

Suggested SLR Ministry Activities

You may choose to engage in any valid and meaningful ministry experience that incorporates this specific course's content and interacts with other people. The following list of suggestions is provided to help you understand the possible activities that will fulfill this requirement. Choose an idea that will connect well with your course material. You may also develop a ministry activity that is not on this list or incorporate content from this course in ministry activity in which you are actively involved at this time:

- Teach a class or small group of any size.

- Preach a sermon to any size group.

- Share the gospel with non-believers; be prepared to develop new relationships to open doors to this ministry. We strongly encourage you to engage in ministry that may be outside your comfort zone.

- Lead a prayer group experience or pray with individual(s) in need, perhaps over an extended period.

- Disciple new believers in their walk with Jesus.

- Interview pastors, missionaries, or other leaders on a topic related to something in your course (do not post or publish interview content).

- Intervene to help resolve personal conflicts.

- Personally share encouragement and resources with those in need.

- Organize and/or administer a church program such as youth ministry, feeding homeless people, transporting people, visiting hospitals or shut-ins, nursing home services, etc.

- Assist with starting a new church.

- Publish an online blog or an article in a church newsletter (include a link in your report to the content of your article or blog).

- For MIN327 only: present a summary of risk management to a church board or other leadership group; interview community business people regarding their opinion of church business practices.

To review sample SLR Reports and to access an online report form, go to this Web address: library. globaluniversity.edu. Navigate to the Berean School of the Bible Students link under "Resources for You." Another helpful resource is our GlobalReach Web site: www.globalreach.org. From that site you can download materials free of charge from Global University's School for Evangelism and Discipleship. These proven evangelism tools are available in many languages.

BSB SERVICE LEARNING REQUIREMENT (SLR) REPORT

Please print or type your responses on this form, and submit the form to Berean School of the Bible.
Do not submit other documents. This report will not be returned to you.

MIN381 Pastoral Ministry: Third Edition

Your Name.. **Student Number** .... **Date** ....

1. Ministry activity date .... **Description of ministry activity and its content:** Briefly describe your ministry activity in the space provided. (You are encouraged to engage in ministry such as sharing your faith with unbelievers, or other activities that may be outside your comfort zone.)

....

....

....

Identify related course content by chapter, lesson, or page number. ....

....

2. Results: What resulted from your own participation in this activity? Include descriptions of people's reactions, decisions to accept Christ, confirmed miracles, Spirit and water baptisms, life changes, etc. Describe the individuals or group who benefited from or participated in your ministry activity. Use numbers to describe results when appropriate (approximate when unsure).

....

....

....

....

Record numbers here: Unbelievers witnessed to?...................... New decisions for Jesus?......................

Holy Spirit baptisms?...................... Other?..

3. Reflection: Answer the following questions based on your experience in completing this assignment:

Did this activity satisfy an evident need in others? How so? ....

....

Were you adequately prepared to engage in this activity? Why or why not? ....

....

What positive or negative feelings were you aware of while you were completing this activity? ....

....

In what ways were you aware of the Holy Spirit's help during your ministry activity? ....

....

What would you change if you did this ministry activity again? ....

....

What strengths or weaknesses within yourself did this assignment reveal to you?......................................

....

....

Did you receive feedback about this activity? If so, describe: ....

....

....

Unit Progress Evaluations

The unit progress evaluations (UPEs) are designed to indicate how well you learned the material in each unit. This may indicate how well prepared you are to take the closed-book final examination.

Taking Your Unit Progress Evaluations

1. Review the lessons of each unit before you take its unit progress evaluation (UPE). Refer to the form Checklist of Study Methods in the How to Use Berean Courses section at the front of the IST.

2. Answer the questions in each UPE without referring to your course materials, Bible, or notes.

3. Look over your answers carefully to avoid errors.

4. Check your answers with the answer keys provided in this section. Review lesson sections pertaining to questions you may have missed. Please note that the UPE scores do not count toward your course grade. They may indicate how well you are prepared to take the closed-book final examination.

5. Enter the date you completed each UPE on the Student Planner and Record form, located in the How to Use Berean Courses section in the front of this IST.

6. Request a printed final examination **if** you cannot take the final examination online. You should do this a few weeks before you take the last unit progress evaluation so that you will be able to take the final examination without delay when you complete the course.

UNIT PROGRESS EVALUATION 1
MIN381 Pastoral Ministry, Third Edition
(Unit 1—Chapter 1–3)

MULTIPLE CHOICE QUESTIONS

Select the best answer to each question.

1. The call of God is like an anchor in that it
   a) shows the minister which direction to go.
   b) shows whom God wants the minister to be.
   c) helps the minister stand firm during hard times.
   d) keeps the minister from teaching false doctrine.

2. According to our study, a ministerial call is tested by time and
   a) persecution.
   b) education.
   c) popularity.
   d) open doors.

3. The time test usually proves that a minister's
   a) call is genuine.
   b) education is adequate.
   c) age is sufficient.
   d) life is sanctified.

4. A person who feels called into the ministry should
   a) marry and attend Bible school.
   b) start preaching at large churches.
   c) choose twelve disciples.
   d) begin serving in small ways.

5. A genuine call to the ministry will
   a) continue as time goes by.
   b) continually satisfy the minister.
   c) cause any other occupation to be unsuccessful.
   d) result in personal sanctification.

6. The most important element of ministry is
   a) skills.
   b) character.
   c) talents.
   d) knowledge.

7. Good character is best built by
   a) studying theology.
   b) listening to sermons.
   c) thinking and acting right.
   d) praying for a person.

8. Ministry is built on a call, plus
   a) skills and abilities.
   b) talent and choices.
   c) character and gifts.
   d) gifts and talent.

9. The Scriptures show that Jesus
   a) prayed privately, but not publicly.
   b) made prayer a way of life.
   c) prayed only during significant events.
   d) did not need to pray since He was divine.

10. The historical context includes
    a) author.
    b) outline.
    c) theme.
    d) grammar.

11. Reading books by wise authors is like
    a) thinking about a harvest instead of reaping it.
    b) sitting at the feet of people with insights.
    c) adding too much sugar to tea.
    d) reading books in the New Testament.

12. An alternative to personal Bible study is
    a) listening to recorded sermons.
    b) listening to the Bible on tape or CD.
    c) reading expository sermons of proven quality.
    d) not to be found.

13. A "Daniel fast" is another name for a
    a) normal fast.
    b) partial fast.
    c) complete fast.
    d) supernatural fast.

14. Ministers should demonstrate love for their spouse by
    a) understanding and meeting the spouse's needs.
    b) working hard to provide for the family.
    c) encouraging the spouse to be involved in ministry.
    d) enjoying the spouse's fellowship more than their time with the Lord.

15. What statement best describes the church's perspective on singleness in ministry?
    a) Elders must be the husband of one wife.
    b) It is usually assumed that unmarried ministers have sexual identifications problems.
    c) Evangelical churches in the U.S. are mainly marriage-and-family focused.
    d) There are no differences as to the way single and married ministers are perceived.

16. A godly Old Testament individual who experienced a broken marriage is
   a) Jeremiah.
   b) Ezekiel.
   c) Joseph.
   d) Hosea.

17. What is the best biblical justification for singleness in ministry?
   a) Jesus was single.
   b) Paul was single and recommended singleness for others.
   c) Jesus treated singleness, like marriage, as a special gift.
   d) One should not take on the responsibilities of marriage if the times are especially difficult.

18. The early church's use of women in leadership is attributed to
   a) prominent women leaders in Jerusalem.
   b) the fact that men were unwilling to serve in ministry.
   c) the influence of Mary, the mother of Jesus.
   d) Jesus' teaching and example.

19. What is the best theological basis for ordaining women?
   a) Jesus commanded that women be ordained to the ministry.
   b) Paul specifically taught that women should be ordained.
   c) The Holy Spirit equips all people, male and female, for God's work.
   d) Both men and women are created in God's image.

20. To encourage women in ministry, some Assemblies of God districts have
   a) provided special training in ministry for minorities.
   b) shown preferential treatment in appointing women as senior pastors.
   c) instructed churches to appoint at least one woman to the ministerial staff.
   d) begun Credentialed Women's Fellowships and special sessions at Schools of Ministry.

21. David failed as a father by
   a) not spending time with his children.
   b) setting an example of ungodliness.
   c) disciplining his children too harshly.
   d) not loving his children.

22. Children should primarily learn about God from
   a) pastors.
   b) parents.
   c) teachers.
   d) friends.

23. A pastor needs friends so that he or she can
   a) discuss ministry problems.
   b) receive support and strength.
   c) balance work and study.
   d) disciple them for ministry.

24. Concerning the relationship between a pastor and church members, the effective pastor
   a) must be pastor first and personal friend second.
   b) cannot have personal friends within the congregation.
   c) does not have time for personal friendships.
   d) knows that the call to ministry sets him or her apart from other Christians.

25. The Bible teaches us to
   a) be a friend to everyone.
   b) have only a few friends.
   c) build friendships slowly.
   d) avoid friendships in ministry.

After answering all of the questions in this UPE, check your answers with the answer key. Review material related to questions you may have missed, and then proceed to the next unit.

UNIT PROGRESS EVALUATION 2
MIN381 Pastoral Ministry, Third Edition
(Unit 2—Chapter 4–6)

MULTIPLE CHOICE QUESTIONS

Select the best answer to each question.

1. To *delegate* means to
   a) empower others to do tasks.
   b) do important work oneself.
   c) assign boring tasks to others.
   d) put first things first.

2. When setting priorities, one should first ask,
   a) Where is there a need?
   b) What things have deadlines?
   c) What do I do best?
   d) What has God called me to do?

3. The first step in preparing a message is
   a) selecting a topic.
   b) choosing a text.
   c) preparing your heart.
   d) writing an introduction.

4. A pastor must listen with both ears to hear
   a) two wise leaders.
   b) the Spirit and the people's needs.
   c) two people at the same time.
   d) both sides of an issue.

5. The minor story in a Bible passage is about
   a) people.
   b) Israel.
   c) children.
   d) God.

6. Preachers should
   a) not practice their sermons lest they lessen the anointing.
   b) not practice sermons because preaching is not a performance.
   c) practice sermons to improve their messages.
   d) practice sermons so they seem well educated.

7. When preaching, a person should act
   a) natural.
   b) simple.
   c) spiritual.
   d) dignified.

8. Preachers are more effective when they are
   a) passionate.
   b) articulate.
   c) loud.
   d) all of the above.

9. To help listeners connect to your stories, you should
   a) use the names of your members.
   b) share about common struggles.
   c) use stories that everyone has heard.
   d) tell stories in the present tense.

10. When preaching openly, ministers should emphasize
    a) God's grace.
    b) temptation's power.
    c) their faults.
    d) others' faults.

11. Yielding control of the service to the Holy Spirit makes
    a) our ministry more effective.
    b) our personalities change.
    c) people listen to our sermons.
    d) people pay their tithes.

12. As a worship leader, the pastor is responsible for
    a) guiding the service.
    b) planning the songs.
    c) causing people to respond.
    d) staying on schedule.

13. By creating a model for using spiritual gifts, a pastor
    a) maintains the service schedule.
    b) keeps order in the service.
    c) limits the freedom of the Spirit.
    d) reduces the spiritual to the natural.

14. After showing people how to use spiritual gifts, you should
    a) explain what spiritual gifts are.
    b) show them how to prophesy.
    c) teach about spiritual fruit.
    d) allow them to use their gifts.

15. Always preach to cause
    a) decision.
    b) church growth.
    c) excitement.
    d) guilt.

16. Pastors should give an invitation
   a) when they see new people at church.
   b) only after preaching about salvation.
   c) at the close of each sermon.
   d) on the first Sunday of each month.

17. A successful altar service requires
   a) leading people to a private room.
   b) subsequent house calls from the minister.
   c) the guidance of the Holy Spirit.
   d) a vision from heaven.

18. The altar time is important because it
   a) gives the pastor time to greet visitors.
   b) helps people make spiritual decisions.
   c) allows people to fellowship with others.
   d) shows whether the sermon was anointed.

19. A pastor should pray with people in crisis, but not too
   a) soon.
   b) often.
   c) loudly.
   d) boldly.

20. When ministering to people in crisis, many pastors err in
   a) avoiding the subject of the hurt.
   b) visiting them in the hospital.
   c) reading the Bible to them.
   d) making them feel useless.

21. Sharing another person's feelings is called
   a) grief-bearing.
   b) empathy.
   c) association.
   d) role-play.

22. A grieving person questions God especially during which stage?
   a) Bargaining
   b) Depression
   c) Denial
   d) Anger

23. We should show care to people in crisis first by
   a) giving advice.
   b) crying.
   c) teaching.
   d) listening.

24. The key to ministering to people in crisis is to
   a) relate to them.
   b) show pity to them.
   c) talk to them.
   d) do things for them.

25. If a grieving person expresses anger, you should
   a) absorb the anger.
   b) make excuses for the anger.
   c) give a gentle rebuke.
   d) reflect the anger back.

After answering all of the questions in this UPE, check your answers with the answer key. Review material related to questions you may have missed, and then proceed to the next unit.

UNIT PROGRESS EVALUATION 3
MIN381 Pastoral Ministry, Third Edition
(Unit 3—Chapter 7–10)

MULTIPLE CHOICE QUESTIONS

Select the best answer to each question.

1. One of the main ways God speaks to us is through
   a) angels.
   b) prophets.
   c) situations.
   d) fleeces.

2. Pastors should first seek guidance from
   a) other pastors.
   b) the Scriptures.
   c) their spouses.
   d) counselors.

3. As a pastor, you should not
   a) expect God to speak to you.
   b) tell the church you heard from God.
   c) ask others to confirm your ideas.
   d) try overly hard to hear God's voice.

4. God's vision for a congregation is developed by the pastor
   a) and all members.
   b) and leaders.
   c) and other pastors.
   d) alone.

5. After discerning God's direction, a pastor must next
   a) share the vision.
   b) develop the team.
   c) defend his or her position.
   d) inspire the church.

6. Moses erred in that he did not
   a) seek God for guidance.
   b) allow people to ask questions.
   c) obey the wise counsel of others.
   d) wait for people to accept the vision.

7. Like King David, pastors must lead by
   a) listening.
   b) example.
   c) force.
   d) charisma.

8. When the Israelites crossed the Jordan, who stepped in first?
   a) Priests
   b) An angel
   c) Moses
   d) Warriors

9. Which word describes *presumption*?
   a) Faith
   b) Obedience
   c) Overconfidence
   d) Ignorance

10. The proper order of importance when choosing disciples is
    a) spiritual maturity, character, gifts.
    b) character, gifts, spiritual maturity.
    c) character, spiritual maturity, gifts.
    d) gifts, character, spiritual maturity.

11. What should disciples learn first?
    a) Life lessons
    b) Ministry training
    c) Counseling skills
    d) Bible study

12. An example of a life lesson is how to
    a) know you are a Christian.
    b) manage your money.
    c) disciple others.
    d) pray for the sick.

13. The ministry track is designed
    a) for more immature believers.
    b) specifically to promote bureaucracy.
    c) for retired pastors.
    d) to equip people for specific ministry tasks.

14. Starting a church training ministry compares to the question, How do you
    a) eat an elephant?
    b) train a tiger?
    c) talk to a turtle?
    d) catch a monkey?

15. In the author's congregation, students in Lay Ministry 2 studied
    a) leadership strategies.
    b) principles of preaching.
    c) the Great Commission.
    d) the gifts of the Spirit.

16. In Lay Ministry 1, students learned the basics of
   a) spiritual gifts.
   b) pastoral care.
   c) church business.
   d) music ministry.

17. Many churches focus mostly on
   a) fellowship.
   b) small groups.
   c) worship.
   d) evangelism.

18. Relationships in a small group result in
   a) new churches.
   b) new problems.
   c) pastoral duties.
   d) pastoral care.

19. Small group leaders create a setting for sharing by
   a) playing soft music.
   b) sitting on the floor.
   c) telling a Bible story.
   d) sharing their struggles.

20. Small group leaders may share personal struggles that
   a) they overcame in the past.
   b) they have not yet overcome.
   c) reveal the sins of family members.
   d) are with people in the group.

21. The most important quality in a small group leader is
   a) spiritual maturity.
   b) experience.
   c) talent.
   d) availability.

22. A church's guidelines for weddings need to cover
   a) a schedule of church services.
   b) counseling for the bride and groom.
   c) visiting the grandparents.
   d) a selection of appropriate music.

23. A written order of service for a wedding includes
   a) the vows the couple will repeat.
   b) a diagram of where the wedding party will stand.
   c) the pastor's message to the guests.
   d) a copy of the marriage license.

24. Before a person is baptized, he or she must
   a) complete a written testimony.
   b) become a church member.
   c) understand the meaning of baptism.
   d) witness to three people.

25. Closed communion means that
   a) the service is held in secret.
   b) people are silent during the service.
   c) only church members may participate.
   d) unfaithful believers are denied participation.

After answering all of the questions in this UPE, check your answers with the answer key. Review material related to questions you may have missed, and then proceed to the next unit.

UNIT PROGRESS EVALUATION 4
MIN381 Pastoral Ministry, Third Edition
(Unit 4—Chapter 11–15)

MULTIPLE CHOICE QUESTIONS

Select the best answer to each question.

1. The New Testament teaches that the
   a) church should vote for leaders.
   b) pastor should choose leaders.
   c) church board should choose leaders.
   d) process for choosing leaders may vary.

2. The first step in the author's process of choosing lay leaders involves
   a) nominations from church members.
   b) members' volunteering to serve as leaders.
   c) interviews of potential leaders.
   d) a vote on possible leaders.

3. Conflict can be minimized by
   a) assuming that people understand their roles.
   b) using pastoral authority to quell disagreements.
   c) clearly defining roles.
   d) ignoring philosophical differences.

4. It is important for the pastor and board members to
   a) develop a strong relationship.
   b) focus solely on church business.
   c) ignore differences of opinion.
   d) not become personal friends.

5. Pastors should build staff based on the church's
   a) perceived needs.
   b) programs.
   c) resources.
   d) vision.

6. When hiring staff, a pastor should assume that a staff member will change
   a) not at all.
   b) just a little.
   c) somewhat.
   d) a lot.

7. Pastors should first try to hire staff from
   a) Bible schools.
   b) nearby churches.
   c) local businesses.
   d) their own churches.

8. The communication principle involves
   a) sharing vision.
   b) showing respect.
   c) asking questions.
   d) caring for needs.

9. The product of communication and care is
   a) character.
   b) loyalty.
   c) growth.
   d) security.

10. Most pastors burn out because they do not
    a) have ministry callings.
    b) take care of themselves.
    c) care about people.
    d) have social support.

11. Observing a Sabbath rest results in our
    a) isolation from the world.
    b) disregard for our own personal needs.
    c) missing a needed day of work.
    d) embracing the needy with love.

12. A person must learn the rhythm of work, rest, and
    a) laughter.
    b) fellowship.
    c) worship.
    d) study.

13. The key to a healthy ministry is
    a) simplicity.
    b) balance.
    c) efficiency.
    d) quality.

14. Worship can best be described as
    a) a moment that each of us must seize.
    b) music that points our attention to God.
    c) an event on Sundays at church.
    d) a sensitivity and response to God's presence.

15. To balance time in the "kitchen," a pastor must spend time in
   a) nature.
   b) fellowship.
   c) study.
   d) silence.

16. Pastors should guard against the love of money by
   a) living modestly.
   b) giving most of their money to others.
   c) earning more money than they need.
   d) refusing to accept gifts.

17. Hard times test perseverance, but success tests
   a) vision.
   b) character.
   c) patience.
   d) commitment.

18. We should respond to criticism by
   a) rebuking the critic.
   b) responding humbly to whatever is true.
   c) assuming it is true and repenting.
   d) acting as though we never heard it.

19. One important way to guard your spirit is to
   a) attend church every Sunday.
   b) forgive offenses quickly.
   c) take Communion.
   d) preach under the anointing.

20. A pastor can prepare people for a business meeting by
   a) leading them into God's presence.
   b) preaching a sermon about submission.
   c) telling them what to vote for.
   d) fellowshipping with them at a meal.

21. Which book tells us to ask God for wisdom?
   a) Mark
   b) John
   c) Romans
   d) James

22. The key to handling complaints is to
   a) ask people to be positive.
   b) teach people not to complain.
   c) listen to people.
   d) focus on the future.

23. When pastors make mistakes, they should first
   a) forgive the people they have hurt.
   b) explain their reasons for the offense.
   c) admit that they are at fault.
   d) make excuses for their actions.

24. After making a mistake, a person should replace "if only" with
   a) "I'm sorry."
   b) "next time."
   c) "already."
   d) "I wish."

25. A pastor is like
   a) a president.
   b) a manager.
   c) a servant.
   d) an owner.

After answering all of the questions in this UPE, check your answers with the answer key. Review material related to questions you may have missed. Review all materials in preparation for the closed-book final exam. Complete and submit your SLR assignment and take the final examination.

Taking the Final Examination

1. **All final exams must be taken closed book**. You are not allowed to use any materials or outside help while taking a final exam. You will take the final examination online at www.globaluniversity.edu. If the online option is not available to you, you may request a printed final exam. If you did not request a printed final exam when you ordered your course, you must submit this request a few weeks before you are ready to take the exam. The Request for a Printed Final Examination is in the Forms section of Essential Course Materials at the back of this IST.

2. Review for the final examination in the same manner in which you prepared for the UPEs. Refer to the form Checklist of Study Methods in the front part of the IST for further helpful review hints.

3. After you complete and submit the online final examination, the results will be immediately available to you. Your final course grade report will be e-mailed to your Global University student e-mail account after your Service Learning Requirement (SLR) report has been processed.

4. If you complete the exam in printed form, you will send your final examination, your answer sheets, and your SLR report to Berean School of the Bible for grading. Your final course grade report will be sent to your GU student e-mail account. If you do not have access to the Internet, your grade will be sent to your mailing address.

Answer Keys

- Compare your answers to the Test Yourself quizzes against those given in this section.

- Compare your answers to the UPE questions against the answer keys located in this section.

- Review the course content identified by your incorrect answers.

ANSWERS TO TEST YOURSELF

MIN381 Pastoral Ministry, Third Edition

Answers below are followed by the number of the objective being tested. For any questions you answered incorrectly, review the lesson content in preparation for your final exam.

Chapter 1
1. C 1.1.1
2. D 1.1.2
3. A 1.1.2
4. D 1.1.2
5. B 1.2.1
6. A 1.2.1
7. C 1.2.1
8. A 1.3.1
9. C 1.3.1
10. C 1.3.1

Chapter 2
1. B 2.1.1
2. C 2.1.1
3. A 2.2.1
4. B 2.2.1
5. A 2.2.1
6. D 2.2.2
7. D 2.2.2
8. D 2.3.1
9. B 2.3.1
10. D 2.3.1

Chapter 3
1. D 3.1.1
2. A 3.2.2
3. B 3.2.2
4. C 3.2.3
5. A 3.3.1
6. C 3.3.2
7. D 3.3.3
8. B 3.4.1
9. C 3.4.2
10. A 3.5.2

Chapter 4
1. B 4.1.1
2. C 4.1.1
3. D 4.2.1
4. A 4.2.1
5. A 4.2.2
6. A 4.3.1
7. C 4.3.2
8. D 4.3.3
9. A 4.3.4
10. B 4.3.4

Chapter 5
1. A 5.1.1
2. C 5.1.1
3. B 5.2.1
4. D 5.2.2
5. A 5.2.2
6. A 5.2.2
7. D 5.3.1
8. B 5.3.1
9. A 5.3.2
10. C 5.3.2

Chapter 6
1. C 6.1.1
2. A 6.1.2
3. D 6.1.2
4. B 6.2.1
5. D 6.2.1
6. B 6.2.2
7. C 6.2.2
8. D 6.3.1
9. C 6.3.2
10. A 6.3.2

Chapter 7
1. C 7.1.1
2. B 7.1.1
3. D 7.1.1
4. D 7.1.1
5. B 7.2.1
6. A 7.2.1
7. D 7.2.1
8. A 7.3.1
9. B 7.3.1
10. C 7.3.2

Chapter 8
1. D 8.1.1
2. A 8.1.1
3. B 8.1.1
4. C 8.1.1
5. C 8.2.1
6. D 8.2.1
7. B 8.2.1
8. A 8.3.1
9. D 8.3.1
10. A 8.3.1

Chapter 9
1. D 9.1.1
2. D 9.1.2
3. C 9.1.2
4. A 9.2.1
5. C 9.2.1
6. B 9.2.1
7. D 9.2.1
8. B 9.2.1
9. A 9.3.1
10. C 9.3.1

Chapter 10
1. B 10.1.1
2. D 10.1.2
3. B 10.1.1
4. C 10.1.3
5. D 10.1.4
6. A 10.1.4
7. D 10.2.1
8. A 10.2.1
9. D 10.2.2
10. C 10.2.3

Chapter 11
1. A 11.1.1
2. D 11.1.2
3. C 11.1.2
4. A 11.1.3
5. C 11.1.3
6. D 11.2.1
7. B 11.2.2
8. C 11.2.2
9. B 11.2.3
10. D 11.3.1

Chapter 12
1. D 12.1.1
2. B 12.1.2
3. C 12.2.1
4. C 12.2.1
5. D 12.2.1
6. A 12.2.1
7. A 12.3.1
8. D 12.3.1
9. B 12.3.1
10. C 12.3.1

Chapter 13
1. A 13.1.1
2. D 13.1.1
3. B 13.1.1
4. D 13.2.1
5. A 13.2.1
6. C 13.3.1
7. D 13.3.1
8. B 13.3.1
9. D 13.3.1
10. C 13.3.1

Chapter 14
1. D 14.1.1
2. D 14.1.1
3. B 14.1.1
4. A 14.2.1
5. C 14.2.1
6. A 14.2.1
7. B 14.3.1
8. D 14.3.1
9. B 14.3.1
10. C 14.3.1

Chapter 15
1. A 15.1.1
2. D 15.1.1
3. B 15.1.1
4. D 15.1.1
5. C 15.2.1
6. B 15.2.1
7. A 15.2.1
8. D 15.2.1
9. C 15.3.1
10. B 15.3.1

UNIT PROGRESS EVALUATION ANSWER KEYS
MIN381 Pastoral Ministry, Third Edition

Answers below are followed by the number of the objective being tested. For any questions you answered incorrectly, review the lesson content in preparation for your final exam.

UNIT PROGRESS EVALUATION 1

1.	C	1.1.1	14. A	3.1.1
2.	D	1.1.1	15. C	3.2.2
3.	A	1.1.2	16. D	3.2.3
4.	D	1.1.2	17. C	3.2.3
5.	A	1.1.2	18. D	3.3.1
6.	B	1.2.1	19. C	3.3.3
7.	C	1.2.1	20. D	3.3.3
8.	C	1.3.1	21. B	3.4.1
9.	B	2.1.1	22. B	3.4.2
10.	A	2.2.1	23. B	3.5.1
11.	B	2.2.2	24. A	3.5.1
12.	D	2.2.2	25. C	3.5.2
13.	B	2.3.1		

UNIT PROGRESS EVALUATION 2

1.	A	4.1.1	14. D	5.2.2
2.	D	4.1.1	15. A	5.3.1
3.	C	4.2.1	16. C	5.3.1
4.	B	4.2.1	17. C	5.3.2
5.	A	4.2.2	18. B	5.3.2
6.	C	4.3.1	19. A	6.1.2
7.	A	4.3.2	20. A	6.1.2
8.	A	4.3.3	21. B	6.2.1
9.	B	4.3.4	22. D	6.2.2
10.	A	4.3.4	23. D	6.3.1
11.	A	5.1.1	24. A	6.3.2
12.	A	5.1.1	25. A	6.3.2
13.	B	5.2.2		

UNIT PROGRESS EVALUATION 3

1.	C	7.1.1	14. A	8.3.1
2.	B	7.1.1	15. D	8.3.1
3.	D	7.1.1	16. B	8.3.1
4.	B	7.2.1	17. C	9.1.2
5.	A	7.2.1	18. D	9.2.1
6.	D	7.2.1	19. D	9.2.1
7.	B	7.3.1	20. A	9.2.1
8.	A	7.3.2	21. A	9.3.1
9.	C	7.3.2	22. B	10.1.1
10.	A	8.1.1	23. B	10.1.2
11.	D	8.2.1	24. C	10.2.1
12.	B	8.2.1	25. C	10.2.3
13.	D	8.2.1		

UNIT PROGRESS EVALUATION 4

1.	D	11.1.2	14. D	13.3.1
2.	A	11.1.3	15. D	14.1.1
3.	C	11.2.1	16. A	14.2.1
4.	A	11.3.1	17. B	14.2.1
5.	D	12.1.2	18. B	14.3.1
6.	A	12.2.1	19. B	14.3.1
7.	D	12.2.1	20. A	15.1.1
8.	A	12.3.1	21. D	15.1.1
9.	B	12.3.1	22. C	15.1.1
10.	B	13.1.1	23. C	15.2.1
11.	D	13.2.1	24. B	15.2.1
12.	C	13.3.1	25. C	15.3.1
13.	B	13.3.1		

Forms

The following pages contain two course forms: the Round-Tripper and the Request for a Printed Final Examination.

1. For students who do not have access to e-mail, we are including one **Round-Tripper** for your use if you have a question or comment related to your studies. If you do not have access to the Internet, you will want to make several photocopies of the Round-Tripper before you write on it. Retain the copies for submitting additional questions as needed. Students who have access to e-mail can submit questions at any time to bsbcontent@globaluniversity.edu.

2. Students who do not have access to the Internet-based tests may request a printed final examination. For faster service, please call Enrollment Services at 1-800-443-1083 or fax your **Request for a Printed Final Examination** to 417-862-0863.

ROUND-TRIPPER

MIN381 Pastoral Ministry, Third Edition   Date ....

Your Name .... Your Student Number ....

Send questions and comments by e-mail to bsbcontent@globaluniversity.edu. If you do not have access to e-mail, use this form to write to Berean School of the Bible with questions or comments related to your studies. Write your question in the space provided. Send this form to Berean School of the Bible. The form will make its return, or round-trip, as Berean School of the Bible responds.

YOUR QUESTION:

FOR BEREAN SCHOOL OF THE BIBLE'S RESPONSE:

GLOBAL
UNIVERSITY

1211 South Glenstone Springfield, MO 65804
1-800-443-1083 * Fax 1-417-862-0863
www.globaluniversity.edu

BEREAN SCHOOL OF THE BIBLE
REQUEST FOR A PRINTED FINAL
EXAMINATION
NOTE: All final exams are to be taken closed-book.

Final examinations are available online at www.globaluniversity.edu.

Taking the test online gives immediate results and feedback. You will know your test grade and which learning objectives you may have missed.

Students who do not have access to the Internet-based tests may request a printed final examination. For faster service, please call Enrollment Services at **1-800-443-1083** or fax this form to **417-862-0863**.

If preferred, mail this form to:
    Berean School of the Bible, Global University
    Attn: Enrollment Services
    1211 South Glenstone
    Springfield, MO 65804

Please allow 7–10 business days for delivery of your final examination. **You may only request an exam for the course or courses in which you are currently enrolled.**

_____
Student Number

_____
Name

_____
Address

_____

_____
City, State, Zip Code

_____
Phone

_____
E-mail

Certified Minister	Licensed Minister	Ordained Minister
☐ BIB114 Christ in the Synoptic Gospels	☐ BIB212 New Testament Survey	☐ BIB313 Corinthian Correspondence
☐ BIB115 Acts: The Holy Spirit at Work in Believers	☐ BIB214 Old Testament Survey	☐ BIB318 Pentateuch
☐ BIB117 Prison Epistles: Colossians, Philemon, Ephesians, and Philippians	☐ BIB215 Romans: Justification by Faith	☐ BIB322 Poetic Books
☐ BIB121 Introduction to Hermeneutics: How to Interpret the Bible	☐ THE211 Introduction to Theology: A Pentecostal Perspective	☐ THE311 Prayer and Worship
☐ THE114 Introduction to Pentecostal Doctrine	☐ THE245 Eschatology: A Study of Things to Come	☐ MIN325 Preaching in the Contemporary World
☐ THE142 Assemblies of God History, Missions, and Governance	☐ MIN223 Introduction to Homiletics	☐ MIN327 Church Administration, Finance, and Law
☐ MIN123 The Local Church in Evangelism	☐ MIN251 Effective Leadership	☐ MIN381 Pastoral Ministry
☐ MIN181 Relationships and Ethics in Ministry	☐ MIN261 Introduction to Assemblies of God Missions	☐ MIN391 Advanced Ministerial Internship
☐ MIN191 Beginning Ministerial Internship	☐ MIN281 Conflict Management for Church Leaders	
	☐ MIN291 Intermediate Ministerial Internship	

Signature _____   Date_____